SELECTED CRITICAL WRITINGS
OF GEORGE SANTAYANA

VOLUME II

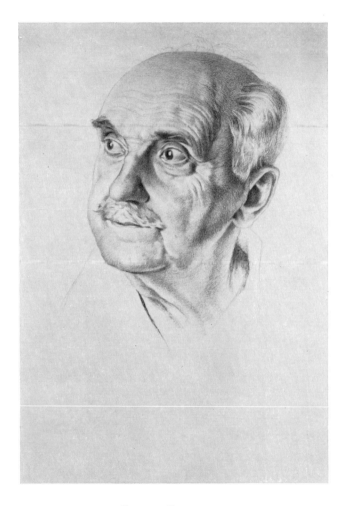

George Santayana

By Lino Lipinsky, 1950

From My Host the World by George Santayana (Charles Scribner's Sons, 1953)
Reproduced by kind permission of the artist

SELECTED
CRITICAL WRITINGS
OF
GEORGE SANTAYANA

Volume II

EDITED BY
NORMAN HENFREY

Assistant Professor of English
Laval University

CAMBRIDGE
AT THE UNIVERSITY PRESS
1968

Published by the Syndics of the Cambridge University Press
Bentley House, 200 Euston Road, London N.W. 1
American Branch: 32 East 57th Street, New York, N.Y. 10022

Introduction by N. Henfrey © Cambridge University Press 1968

Printed in Great Britain
at the University Printing House, Cambridge
(Brooke Crutchley, University Printer)

CONTENTS

Contents

ACKNOWLEDGMENTS

The editor and publishers are grateful to Mr Daniel Cory, the literary executor of the Santayana estate, and the following publishers for permission to reprint copyright material by George Santayana:

Constable and Company Limited for selections from *Soliloquies in England and Later Soliloquies, Character and Opinion in the United States, Obiter Scripta,* and *The Life of Reason* (volumes I, II and III).

J. M. Dent and Sons Limited for selections from *Winds of Doctrine* and *Egotism in German Philosophy.*

There can be no goods antecedent to the natures they benefit, no ideals prior to the wills they define.

GEORGE SANTAYANA,
Reason in Religion, 1905

PREFACE

I have sought to bring together as much as possible of Santayana's best work in literary criticism, moral philosophy, and social and cultural history; to this end, most of the writings drawn upon fall between his thirty-second and fifty-seventh years, when he was at the height of his powers. A notable omission is *Three Philosophical Poets*; it is his best-known work and is in paperback; other criticism has accordingly been preferred, though his general position in that book is set out in the excerpts that have been taken from his Introduction and Conclusion to it.

Essays, and selections from books, are given whole wherever possible, but some curtailment was necessary if the choice was not to be unduly restricted; Santayana was a discursive writer. Where elisions have been made it is on the grounds that the material omitted is not vital, or that it has to do with a subject adequately treated elsewhere in the Selection. In some cases, to avoid breaking up the flow of an argument, I have conflated into one paragraph parts of two which were originally removed from each other by some pages. In three places passages from different chapters of a book have been incorporated into the one excerpt so as to represent Santayana's position satisfactorily: in volume I, the initial excerpt from *The Sense of Beauty* is an amalgam of a section from the first part of that book and three sections from the third, and I supply the title; in volume II, 'The Protestant Heritage' is rounded out with extracts from two later chapters in *Egotism in German Philosophy*, and 'The Belief in a Future Life' with an extract from the ensuing chapter in *Reason in Religion*. Four essays have been cut: 'The Elements and Function of Poetry' and 'Penitent Art' (volume I); 'The Intellectual Temper of the Age' and 'The Philosophy of Mr. Bertrand Russell' (volume II).

Santayana made three collections of his essays: *Interpreta-*

ix

Preface

tions of Poetry and Religion, 1900; *Winds of Doctrine, Studies in Contemporary Opinion,* 1913; *Soliloquies in England and Later Soliloquies,* 1922.

Justus Buchler and Benjamin Schwartz brought out a further collection, with Santayana's approval: *Obiter Scripta*; Lectures, Essays and Reviews, 1936.

The essays in this Selection are drawn from the following sources:

VOLUME I

Platonic Love in Some Italian Poets: written for the Contemporary Club and read at the meeting of 5 February 1896, under the title 'Platonism in the Italian Poets'. Printed by Paul's Press, Buffalo, 1896, 31 pp. Reprinted with modifications in *Interpretations of Poetry and Religion,* 1900.

The Absence of Religion in Shakespeare: *New World,* December 1896, v, pp. 681–91. Reprinted in *Interpretations of Poetry and Religion,* 1900.

The Elements and Function of Poetry: *Interpretations of Poetry and Religion,* 1900.

The Poetry of Barbarism: *Interpretations of Poetry and Religion,* 1900.

Emerson: *Interpretations of Poetry and Religion,* 1900.

Hamlet: in *The University Press Edition of Shakespeare's Works,* Cambridge, U.S.A., 1908, xxx, pp. ix–xxxiii, under the title 'Introduction to *Hamlet'*. Reprinted with slight modifications in *Life and Letters,* June 1928, I, pp. 17–38, and in *Obiter Scripta,* 1936.

Shelley: or the Poetic Value of Revolutionary Principles: *Winds of Doctrine,* 1913.

Hints of Egotism in Goethe: *New Republic,* 2 January 1915, I, pp. 15–16, under the title 'Goethe and German Egotism'. Reprinted in *Egotism in German Philosophy,* 1916.

Dickens: *Dial,* November 1921, LXXI, pp. 537–49. Reprinted in *Soliloquies in England,* 1922.

A Contrast with Spanish Drama: *Athenaeum,* 11 February

Preface

1921, pp. 146–7. Reprinted in *Soliloquies in England*, 1922.

Tragic Philosophy: *Scrutiny*, March 1936, IV, pp. 365–76.

What is Aesthetics?: *Philosophical Review*, May 1904, VIII, pp. 320–7. Reprinted in *Obiter Scripta*, 1936.

Penitent Art: *Dial*, July 1922, LXXIII, pp. 25–31. Reprinted in *Obiter Scripta*, 1936.

VOLUME II

The Intellectual Temper of the Age: *Winds of Doctrine*, 1913.

Classic Liberty: *New Republic*, 21 August 1915, IV, pp. 65–6. Reprinted in *Soliloquies in England*, 1922.

Liberalism and Culture: *New Republic*, 4 September 1915, IV, pp. 123–5. Reprinted in *Soliloquies in England*, 1922.

The Human Scale: *New Republic*, 29 January 1916, V, pp. 326–8. Reprinted in *Soliloquies in England*, 1922.

The Genteel Tradition in American Philosophy: *University of California Chronicle*, October 1911, XIII, pp. 357–80. Reprinted in *Winds of Doctrine*, 1913.

Plotinus and the Nature of Evil: *Journal of Philosophy*, 23 October 1913, X, pp. 589–99, under the title 'Dr Fuller, Plotinus, and the Nature of Evil'. (Review of B. A. G. Fuller, *The Problem of Evil in Plotinus*.) Reprinted with modifications in *Obiter Scripta*, 1936.

The Philosophy of M. Henri Bergson: *Winds of Doctrine*, 1913.

The Philosophy of Mr Bertrand Russell: *Journal of Philosophy*, 3 February 1911, VIII, pp. 57–63; 2 March 1911, VIII, pp. 113–24; 3 August 1911, VIII, pp. 421–32; under the title 'Russell's *Philosophical Essays*'. Reprinted with modifications in *Winds of Doctrine*, 1913: 'Hypostatic Ethics', reprinted in the present Selection, is the fourth and concluding section of the essay.

Where Santayana made or approved modifications in an essay before republication, this later version has been used. Modifications in a title have been similarly retained.

Preface

The Selected Portraits in the first volume come from the following books: the portrait of William James is from *Character and Opinion in the United States*, 1920, and the others are from Santayana's autobiography, *Persons and Places*: the first two from *Background of my Life*, 1944; the next four from *The Middle Span*, 1945; and the two last from *My Host the World*, 1953. The three volumes of the autobiography were written between 1940 and 1944, though Santayana's account of his father and mother may have been drafted as early as 1924: see Santayana's letter to George Sturgis of 29 July 1924 (*The Letters of George Santayana*, ed. Daniel Cory (1955), p. 216).

The selections from *Reason in Common Sense*, *Reason in Society*, *Reason in Religion* and *Reason in Art* are drawn from the first, second, third and fourth volumes of Santayana's five-volume work, *The Life of Reason* (1905–6).

Santayana's footnotes are indicated by asterisks; mine by numerals. In the table of contents, book-titles are in italics to distinguish them from the essays.

Unless otherwise stated, references to essays by Santayana are to the present Selection.

I should like to express my indebtedness to Dr F. R. Leavis, whose incisive discussions of Santayana's essay on Dickens introduced me to his work. I should also like to thank Dr John Newton for his generous aid in setting this edition on foot, and Mr Daniel Cory, Mr Richard Gooder, Mr Pierre Lefranc and Mr Geoffrey Strickland for help they have given me.

Quebec, Canada   N.H.

Liberty and Society

THE INTELLECTUAL TEMPER
OF THE AGE

The present age is a critical one and interesting to live in. The civilization characteristic of Christendom has not disappeared, yet another civilization has begun to take its place. We still understand the value of religious faith; we still appreciate the pompous arts of our forefathers; we are brought up on academic architecture, sculpture, painting, poetry, and music. We still love monarchy and aristocracy, together with that picturesque and dutiful order which rested on local institutions, class privileges, and the authority of the family. We may even feel an organic need for all these things, cling to them tenaciously, and dream of rejuvenating them. On the other hand the shell of Christendom is broken. The unconquerable mind of the East, the pagan past, the industrial socialistic future confront it with their equal authority. Our whole life and mind is saturated with the slow upward filtration of a new spirit—that of an emancipated, atheistic, international democracy.

These epithets may make us shudder; but what they describe is something positive and self-justified, something deeply rooted in our animal nature and inspiring to our hearts, something which, like every vital impulse, is pregnant with a morality of its own. In vain do we deprecate it; it has possession of us already through our propensities, fashions, and language. Our very plutocrats and monarchs are at ease only when they are vulgar. Even prelates and missionaries are hardly sincere or conscious of an honest function, save as they devote themselves to social work; for willy-nilly the new spirit has hold of our consciences as well. This spirit is amiable as well as disquieting, liberating as well as barbaric; and a philosopher in our day, conscious both of the old life and of the new, might repeat what Goethe said of his successive love affairs—that it is sweet to see the moon rise while the sun is still mildly shining.

Meantime our bodies in this generation are generally safe, and often comfortable; and for those who can suspend their irrational labours long enough to look about them, the spectacle of the world, if not particularly beautiful or touching, presents a rapid and crowded drama and (what here concerns me most) one unusually intelligible. The nations, parties, and movements that divide the scene have a known history. We are not condemned, as most generations have been, to fight and believe without an inkling of the cause. The past lies before us; the history of everything is published. Everyone records his opinion, and loudly proclaims what he wants. In this Babel of ideals few demands are ever literally satisfied; but many evaporate, merge together, and reach an unintended issue, with which they are content. The whole drift of things presents a huge, good-natured comedy to the observer. It stirs not unpleasantly a certain sturdy animality and hearty self-trust, which lie at the base of human nature.

A chief characteristic of the situation is that moral confusion is not limited to the world at large, always the scene of profound conflicts, but that it has penetrated to the mind and heart of the average individual. Never perhaps were men so like one another and so divided within themselves. In other ages, even more than at present, different classes of men have stood at different levels of culture, with a magnificient readiness to persecute and to be martyred for their respective principles. These militant believers have been keenly conscious that they had enemies; but their enemies were strangers to them, whom they could think of merely as such, regarding them as blank negative forces, hateful black devils, whose existence might make life difficult but could not confuse the ideal of life. No one sought to understand these enemies of his, nor even to conciliate them, unless under compulsion or out of insidious policy, to convert them against their will; he merely pelted them with blind refutations and clumsy blows. Everyone sincerely felt that the right was entirely on his side, a proof that such intelligence as he had moved freely and exclusively within the lines of his faith. The result of this was that his faith was intelligent, I mean, that he understood it, and had a clear, almost instinctive perception of what was compatible with it. He defended his walls and he cultivated his garden. His position and his possessions were unmistakable.

When men and minds were so distinct it was possible to describe and to count them. During the Reformation, when external confusion was at its height, you might have ascertained almost statistically what persons and what regions each side snatched from the other; it was not doubtful which was which. The history of their respective victories and defeats could consequently be written. So in the eighteenth century it was easy to perceive how many people Voltaire and Rousseau might be alienating from Bossuet and Fénelon. But how shall we satisfy ourselves now whether, for instance, Christianity is holding its own? Who can tell what vagary or what compromise may not be calling itself Christianity? A bishop may be a modernist, a chemist may be a mystical theologian, a psychologist may be a believer in ghosts. For science, too, which had promised to supply a new and solid foundation for philosophy, has allowed philosophy rather to undermine its foundation, and is seen eating its own words, through the mouths of some of its accredited spokesmen, and reducing itself to something utterly conventional and insecure. It is characteristic of human nature to be as impatient of ignorance regarding what is not known as lazy in acquiring such knowledge as is at hand; and even those who have not been lazy sometimes take it into their heads to disparage their science and to outdo the professional philosophers in psychological scepticism, in order to plunge with them into the most vapid speculation. Nor is this insecurity about first principles limited to abstract subjects. It reigns in politics as well. Liberalism had been supposed to advocate liberty; but what the advanced parties that still call themselves liberal now advocate is control, control over property, trade, wages, hours of work, meat and drink, amusements, and in a truly advanced country like France control over education and religion; and it is only on the subject of marriage (if we ignore eugenics) that

5

liberalism is growing more and more liberal. Those who speak most of progress measure it by quantity and not by quality; how many people read and write, or how many people there are, or what is the annual value of their trade; whereas true progress would rather lie in reading or writing fewer and better things, and being fewer and better men, and enjoying life more. But the philanthropists are now preparing an absolute subjection of the individual, in soul and body, to the instincts of the majority—the most cruel and unprogressive of masters; and I am not sure that the liberal maxim, 'the greatest happiness of the greatest number', has not lost whatever was just or generous in its intent and come to mean the greatest idleness of the largest possible population.

Nationality offers another occasion for strange moral confusion. It had seemed that an age that was levelling and connecting all nations, an age whose real achievements were of international application, was destined to establish the solidarity of mankind as a sort of axiom. The idea of solidarity is indeed often invoked in speeches, and there is an extreme socialistic party that—when a wave of national passion does not carry it the other way—believes in international brotherhood. But even here, black men and yellow men are generally excluded; and in higher circles, where history, literature, and political ambition dominate men's minds, nationalism has become of late an omnivorous all-permeating passion. Local parliaments must be everywhere established, extinct or provincial dialects must be galvanized into national languages, philosophy must be made racial, religion must be fostered where it emphasizes nationality and denounced where it transcends it. Man is certainly an animal that, when he lives at all, lives for ideals. Something must be found to occupy his imagination, to raise pleasure and pain into love and hatred, and change the prosaic alternative between comfort and discomfort into the tragic one between happiness and sorrow. Now that the hue of daily adventure is so dull, when religion for the most part is so vague and accommodating, when even war is a vast impersonal business, nationality seems to have slipped into the place of honour. It has become the one eloquent, public, intrepid illusion. Illusion, I mean, when it is taken for an ultimate good or a mystical essence, for of course nationality is a fact. People speak some particular language and are very uncomfortable where another is spoken or where their own is spoken differently. They have habits, judgments, assumptions to which they are wedded, and a society where all this is unheard of shocks them and puts them at a galling disadvantage. To ignorant people the foreigner as such is ridiculous, unless he is superior to them in numbers or prestige, when he becomes hateful. It is natural for a man to like to live at home, and to live long elsewhere without a sense of exile is not good for his moral integrity. It is right to feel a greater kinship and affection for what lies nearest to oneself. But this necessary fact and even duty of nationality is accidental; like age or sex it is a physical fatality which can be made the basis of specific and comely virtues; but it is not an end to pursue or a flag to flaunt or a privilege not balanced by a thousand incapacities. Yet of this distinction our contemporaries tend to make an idol, perhaps because it is the only distinction they feel they have left.

Anomalies of this sort will never be properly understood until people accustom themselves to a theory to which they have always turned a deaf ear, because, though simple and true, it is materialistic: namely, that mind is not the cause of our actions but an effect, collateral with our actions, of bodily growth and organization. It may therefore easily come about that the thoughts of men, tested by the principles that seem to rule their conduct, may be belated, or irrelevant, or premonitory; for the living organism has many strata, on any of which, at a given moment, activities may exist perfect enough to involve consciousness, yet too weak and isolated to control the organs of outer expression; so that (to speak geologically) our practice may be historic, our manners glacial, and our religion palaeozoic. The ideals of the nineteenth century may be said to have been all belated; the age still yearned with Rousseau or speculated with Kant, while it moved with

Darwin, Bismarck, and Nietzsche: and to-day, in the half-educated classes, among the religious or revolutionary sects, we may observe quite modern methods of work allied with a somewhat antiquated mentality. The whole nineteenth century might well cry with Faust: 'Two souls, alas, dwell in my bosom!' The revolutions it witnessed filled it with horror and made it fall in love romantically with the past and dote on ruins, because they were ruins; and the best learning and fiction of the time were historical, inspired by an unprecedented effort to understand remote forms of life and feeling, to appreciate exotic arts and religions, and to rethink the blameless thoughts of savages and criminals. This sympathetic labour and retrospect, however, was far from being merely sentimental; for the other half of this divided soul was looking ahead. Those same revolutions, often so destructive, stupid, and bloody, filled it with pride, and prompted it to invent several incompatible theories concerning a steady and inevitable progress in the world. In the study of the past, side by side with romantic sympathy, there was a sort of realistic, scholarly intelligence and an adventurous love of truth; kindness too was often mingled with dramatic curiosity. The pathologists were usually healers, the philosophers of evolution were inventors or humanitarians or at least idealists: the historians of art (though optimism was impossible here) were also guides to taste, quickeners of moral sensibility, like Ruskin, or enthusiasts for the irresponsibly beautiful, like Pater and Oscar Wilde. Everywhere in the nineteenth century we find a double preoccupation with the past and with the future, a longing to know what all experience might have been hitherto, and on the other hand to hasten to some wholly different experience, to be contrived immediately with a beating heart and with flying banners. The imagination of the age was intent on history; its conscience was intent on reform.

Reform! This magic word itself covers a great equivocation. To reform means to shatter one form and to create another; but the two sides of the act are not always equally intended nor equally successful. Usually the movement starts from the mere sense of oppression, and people break down some established form, without any qualms about the capacity of their freed instincts to generate the new forms that may be needed. So the Reformation, in destroying the traditional order, intended to secure truth, spontaneity, and profuseness of religious forms; the danger of course being that each form might become meagre and the sum of them chaotic. If the accent, however, could only be laid on the second phase of the transformation, reform might mean the creation of order where it did not sufficiently appear, so that diffuse life should be concentrated into a congenial form that should render it strong and self-conscious. In this sense, if we may trust Mr Gilbert Murray, it was a great wave of reform that created Greece, or at least all that was characteristic and admirable in it— an effort to organize, train, simplify, purify, and make beautiful the chaos of barbaric customs and passions that had preceded. The danger here, a danger to which Greece actually succumbed, is that so refined an organism may be too fragile, not inclusive enough within, and not buttressed strongly enough without against the flux of the uncivilized world. Christianity also, in the first formative centuries of its existence, was an integrating reform of the same sort, on a different scale and in a different sphere; but here too an enslaved rabble within the soul claiming the suffrage, and better equipped intellectual empires rising round about, seem to prove that the harmony which the Christian system made for a moment out of nature and life was partial and insecure. It is a terrible dilemma in the life of reason whether it will sacrifice natural abundance to moral order, or moral order to natural abundance. Whatever compromise we choose proves unstable, and forces us to a new experiment...

Trustful faith in evolution and a longing for intense life are characteristic of contemporary sentiment; but they do not appear to be consistent with that contempt for the intellect which is no less characteristic of it. Human intelligence is certainly a product, and a late and highly organized product of evolution; it ought apparently to be as much admired as the eyes of molluscs or the antennae of ants. And if life is better the more intense and concentrated it is, intelligence would seem to be the best form of life. But the degree of intelligence which this age possesses makes it so very uncomfortable that, in this instance, it asks for something less vital, and sighs for what evolution has left behind. In the presence of such cruelly distinct things as astronomy or such cruelly confused things as theology it feels *la nostalgie de la boue*. It was only, M. Bergson tells us, where dead matter oppressed life that life was forced to become intelligence; for this reason intelligence kills whatever it touches; it is the tribute that life pays to death. Life would find it sweet to throw off that painful subjection to circumstance and bloom in some more congenial direction. M. Bergson's own philosophy is an effort to realize this revulsion, to disintegrate intelligence and stimulate sympathetic experience. Its charm lies in the relief which it brings to a stale imagination, an imagination from which religion has vanished and which is kept stretched on the machinery of business and society, or on small half-borrowed passions which we clothe in a mean rhetoric and dot with vulgar pleasures. Finding their intelligence enslaved, our contemporaries suppose that intelligence is essentially servile; instead of freeing it, they try to elude it. Not free enough themselves morally, but bound to the world partly by piety and partly by industrialism, they cannot think of rising to a detached contemplation of earthly things, and of life itself and evolution; they revert rather to sensibility, and seek some by-path of instinct or dramatic sympathy in which to wander. Having no stomach for the ultimate, they burrow downwards towards the primitive. But the longing to be primitive is a disease of culture; it is archaism in morals. To be so preoccupied with vitality is a symptom of anaemia. When life was really vigorous and young, in Homeric times for instance, no one seemed to fear that it might be squeezed out of existence either by the incubus of matter or by the petrifying blight of intelligence. Life was like the light of day, something to use, or to waste, or to enjoy. It was not a thing to worship; and often the chief luxury of living consisted in dealing death about vigorously. Life indeed was loved, and the beauty and pathos of it were felt exquisitely; but its beauty and pathos lay in the divineness of its model and in its own fragility. No one paid it the equivocal compliment of thinking it a substance or a material force. Nobility was not then impossible in sentiment, because there were ideals in life higher and more indestructible than life itself, which life might illustrate and to which it might fitly be sacrificed. Nothing can be meaner than the anxiety to live on, to live on anyhow and in any shape; a spirit with any honour is not willing to live except in its own way, and a spirit with any wisdom is not over-eager to live at all. In those days men recognized immortal gods and resigned themselves to being mortal. Yet those were the truly vital and instinctive days of the human spirit. Only when vitality is low do people find material things oppressive and ideal things unsubstantial. Now there is more motion than life, and more haste than force; we are driven to distraction by the ticking of the tiresome clocks, material and social, by which we are obliged to regulate our existence. We need ministering angels to fly to us from somewhere, even if it be from the depths of protoplasm. We must bathe in the currents of some non-human vital flood, like consumptives in their last extremity who must bask in the sunshine and breathe the mountain air; and our disease is not without its sophistry to convince us that we were never so well before, or so mightily conscious of being alive.

When chaos has penetrated so far into the moral being of nations, they can hardly be expected to produce great men. A great man need not be virtuous, nor his opinions right, but he must have a firm mind, a distinctive, luminous character; if he is to dominate things, something must be dominant in him. We feel him to be great in that he clarifies and brings to expression something which was potential in the rest of us, but which with our burden of flesh and circumstance we were too torpid to utter. The great man is a spontaneous variation in humanity; but not in any direction. A spontaneous variation

11

might be a mere madness or mutilation or monstrosity; in finding the variation admirable we evidently invoke some principle of order to which it conforms. Perhaps it makes explicit what was preformed in us also; as when a poet finds the absolutely right phrase for a feeling, or when nature suddenly astonishes us with a form of absolute beauty. Or perhaps it makes an unprecedented harmony out of things existing before, but jangled and detached. The first man was a great man for this latter reason; having been an ape perplexed and corrupted by his multiplying instincts, he suddenly found a new way of being decent, by harnessing all those instincts together, through memory and imagination, and giving each in turn a measure of its due; which is what we call being rational. It is a new road to happiness, if you have strength enough to castigate a little the various impulses that sway you in turn. Why then is the martyr, who sacrifices everything to one attraction, distinguished from the criminal or the fool, who do the same thing? Evidently because the spirit that in the martyr destroys the body is the very spirit which the body is stifling in the rest of us; and although his private inspiration may be irrational, the tendency of it is not, but reduces the public conscience to act before anyone else has had the courage to do so. Greatness is spontaneous; simplicity, trust in some one clear instinct, are essential to it; but the spontaneous variation must be in the direction of some possible sort of order; it must exclude and leave behind what is incapable of being moralized. How, then, should there be any great heroes, saints, artists, philosophers, or legislators in an age when nobody trusts himself, or feels any confidence in reason, in an age when the word *dogmatic* is a term of reproach? Greatness has character and severity, it is deep and sane, it is distinct and perfect. For this reason there is none of it today.

There is indeed another kind of greatness, or rather largeness of mind, which consists in being a synthesis of humanity in its current phases, even if without prophetic emphasis or direction: the breadth of a Goethe, rather than the fineness of a Shelley or a Leopardi. But such largeness of mind, not to be vulgar, must be impartial, comprehensive, Olympian; it would not be greatness if its miscellany were not dominated by a clear genius and if before the confusion of things the poet or philosopher were not himself delighted, exalted, and by no means confused. Nor does this presume omniscience on his part. It is not necessary to fathom the ground or the structure of everything in order to know what to make of it. Stones do not disconcert a builder because he may not happen to know what they are chemically; and so the unsolved problems of life and nature, and the Babel of society, need not disturb the genial observer, though he may be incapable of unravelling them. He may set these dark spots down in their places, like so many caves or wells in a landscape, without feeling bound to scrutinize their depths simply because their depths are obscure. Unexplored they may have a sort of lustre, explored they might merely make him blind, and it may be a sufficient understanding of them to know that they are not worth investigating. In this way the most chaotic age and the most motley horrors might be mirrored limpidly in a great mind, as the Renaissance was mirrored in the works of Raphael and Shakespeare; but the master's eye itself must be single, his style unmistakable, his visionary interest in what he depicts frank and supreme. Hence this comprehensive sort of greatness too is impossible in an age when moral confusion is pervasive, when characters are complex, undecided, troubled by the mere existence of what is not congenial to them, eager to be not themselves; when, in a word, thought is weak and the flux of things overwhelms it.

Without great men and without clear convictions this age is nevertheless very active intellectually; it is studious, empirical, inventive, sympathetic. Its wisdom consists in a certain contrite openness of mind; it flounders, but at least in floundering it has gained a sense of possible depths in all directions. Under these circumstances, some triviality and great confusion in its positive achievements are not unpromising things nor even unamiable. These are the *Wanderjahre* of faith; it

13

looks smilingly at every new face, which might perhaps be that of a predestined friend; it chases after any engaging stranger; it even turns up again from time to time at home, full of a new tenderness for all it had abandoned there...

These are but gusts of doctrine; yet they prove that the spirit is not dead in the lull between its seasons of steady blowing. Who knows which of them may not gather force presently and carry the mind of the coming age steadily before it?

CLASSIC LIBERTY

When ancient peoples defended what they called their liberty, the word stood for a plain and urgent interest of theirs: that their cities should not be destroyed, their territory pillaged, and they themselves sold into slavery. For the Greeks in particular liberty meant even more than this. Perhaps the deepest assumption of classic philosophy is that nature and the gods on the one hand and man on the other, both have a fixed character, that there is consequently a necessary piety, a true philosophy, a standard happiness, a normal art. The Greeks believed, not without reason, that they had grasped these permanent principles better than other peoples. They had largely dispelled superstition, experimented in government, and turned life into a rational art. Therefore when they defended their liberty what they defended was not merely freedom to live. It was freedom to live well, to live as other nations did not, in the public experimental study of the world and of human nature. This liberty to discover and pursue a natural happiness, this liberty to grow wise and to live in friendship with the gods and with one another, was the liberty vindicated at Thermopylae by martyrdom and at Salamis by victory.

As Greek cities stood for liberty in the world, so philosophers stood for liberty in the Greek cities. In both cases it was the same kind of liberty, not freedom to wander at hazard or to let things slip, but on the contrary freedom to legislate more precisely, at least for oneself, and to discover and codify the means to true happiness. Many of these pioneers in wisdom were audacious radicals and recoiled from no paradox. Some condemned what was most Greek: mythology, athletics, even multiplicity and physical motion. In the heart of those thriving, loquacious, festive little ant-hills, they preached impassibility and abstraction, the unanswerable scepticism of silence. Others practised a musical and priestly refinement of life, filled with metaphysical mysteries, and formed secret societies, not without a tendency to political domination. The cynics railed at the conventions, making themselves as comfortable as possible in the role of beggars and mocking parasites. The conservatives themselves were radical, so intelligent were they, and Plato wrote the charter of the most extreme militarism and communism, for the sake of preserving the free state. It was the swan-song of liberty, a prescription to a diseased old man to become young again and try a second life of superhuman virtue. The old man preferred simply to die.

Many laughed then, as we may be tempted to do, at all those absolute physicians of the soul, each with his panacea. Yet beneath their quarrels the wranglers had a common faith. They all believed there was a single solid natural wisdom to be found, that reason could find it, and that mankind, sobered by reason, could put it in practice. Mankind has continued to run wild and, like barbarians, to place freedom in their very wildness, till we can hardly conceive the classic assumption of Greek philosophers and cities, that true liberty is bound up with an institution, a corporate scientific discipline, necessary to set free the perfect man, or the god, within us.

Upon the dissolution of paganism the Christian Church adopted the classic conception of liberty. Of course, the field in which the higher politics had to operate was now conceived differently, and there was a new experience of the sort of happiness appropriate and possible to man; but the assumption remained unchallenged that Providence, as well as the human soul, had a fixed discoverable scope, and that the business of education, law, and religion was to bring them to operate in harmony. The aim of life, salvation, was involved in the nature of the soul itself, and the means of salvation had been ascertained by a positive science which the Church was possessed of, partly revealed and partly experimental. Salvation was simply what, on a broad view, we should see to be health, and religion was nothing but a sort of universal hygiene.

The Church, therefore, little as it tolerated heretical liberty,

the liberty of moral and intellectual dispersion, felt that it had
come into the world to set men free, and constantly demanded
liberty for itself, that it might fulfil this mission. It was
divinely commissioned to teach, guide, and console all nations
and all ages by the self-same means, and to promote at all
costs what it conceived to be human perfection. There should
be saints and as many saints as possible. The Church never
admitted, any more than did any sect of ancient philosophers,
that its teaching might represent only an eccentric view of the
world, or that its guidance and consolations might be suitable
only at one stage of human development. To waver in the
pursuit of the orthodox ideal could only betray frivolity and
want of self-knowledge. The truth of things and the happiness
of each man could not lie elsewhere than where the Church,
summing up all human experience and all divine revelation,
had placed it once for all and for everybody. The liberty of the
Church to fulfil its mission was accordingly hostile to any
liberty of dispersion, to any radical consecutive independence,
in the life of individuals or of nations.

When it came to full fruition this orthodox freedom was
far from gay; it was called sanctity. The freedom of pagan
philosophers too had turned out to be rather a stiff and severe
pose; but in the Christian dispensation this austerity of true
happiness was less to be wondered at, since life on earth was
reputed to be abnormal from the beginning, and infected with
hereditary disease. The full beauty and joy of restored liberty
could hardly become evident in this life. Nevertheless a certain
beauty and joy did radiate visibly from the saints; and while
we may well think their renunciations and penances misguided
or excessive, it is certain that, like the Spartans and the
philosophers, they got something for their pains. Their bodies
and souls were transfigured, as none now found upon earth.
If we admire without imitating them we shall perhaps have
done their philosophy exact justice. Classic liberty was a sort
of forced and artificial liberty, a poor perfection reserved for
an ascetic aristocracy in whom heroism and refinement were
touched with perversity and slowly starved themselves to death.

Since those days we have discovered how much larger the universe is, and we have lost our way in it. Any day it may come over us again that our modern liberty to drift in the dark is the most terrible negation of freedom. Nothing happens to us as we would. We want peace and make war. We need science and obey the will to believe, we love art and flounder among whimsicalities, we believe in general comfort and equality and we strain every nerve to become millionaires. After all, antiquity must have been right in thinking that reasonable self-direction must rest on having a determinate character and knowing what it is, and that only the truth about God and happiness, if we somehow found it, could make us free. But the truth is not to be found by guessing at it, as religious prophets and men of genius have done, and then damning every one who does not agree. Human nature, for all its substantial fixity, is a living thing with many varieties and variations. All diversity of opinion is therefore not founded on ignorance; it may express a legitimate change of habit or interest. The classic and Christian synthesis from which we have broken loose was certainly premature, even if the only issue of our liberal experiments should be to lead us back to some such equilibrium. Let us hope at least that the new morality, when it comes, may be more broadly based than the old on knowledge of the world, not so absolute, not so meticulous, and not chanted so much in the monotone of an abstracted sage.

LIBERALISM AND CULTURE

Modern reformers, religious and political, have usually retained the classic theory of orthodoxy, namely, that there is one right or true system—democracy and free thought, for instance—which it is the reformer's duty to establish in the place of prevalent abuses. Certainly Luther and Calvin and the doctrinaires of the French Revolution only meant to substitute one orthodoxy for another, and what they set forth they regarded as valid for all men and forever. Nevertheless they had a greater success in discrediting the received system than in establishing their own, and the general effect of their reforms was to introduce the modern conception of liberty, the liberty of liberalism.

This consists in limiting the prescriptions of the law to a few points, for the most part negative, leaving it to the initiative and conscience of individuals to order their life and conversation as they like, provided only they do not interfere with the same freedom in others. In practice liberal countries have never reached this ideal of peaceful anarchy, but have continued to enforce state education, monogamy, the vested rights of property, and sometimes military service. But within whatever limits, liberty is understood to lie in the individual being left alone, so that he may express his personal impulses as he pleases in word and action.

A philosopher can readily see that this liberal ideal implies a certain view about the relations of man in the universe. It implies that the ultimate environment, divine or natural, is either chaotic in itself or undiscoverable by human science, and that human nature, too, is either radically various or only determinable in a few essentials, round which individual variations play *ad libitum*. For this reason no normal religion, science, art, or way of happiness can be prescribed. These remain always open, even in their foundations, for each man to arrange for himself. The more things are essentially unsettled and optional, the more liberty of this sort there may safely be in the world and the deeper it may run.

19

Liberalism and Culture

Man, however, is a gregarious animal, and much more so in his mind than in his body. He may like to go alone for a walk, but hates to stand alone in his opinions. And he is so imitative that what he thinks he most wishes to do is whatever he sees other people doing. Hence if compulsory organization disappears a thousand free and private organizations at once take its place. Virginal liberty is good only to be surrendered at the right time to a right influence. A state in which government is limited to police duty must allow churches, universities (with millionaires to found them), public sports, private charities, masonic or monastic orders, and every other sort of party institution, to flourish within it unhindered; otherwise that state would hardly be civilized and nothing of importance would ever be done in it. Yet the prevalence of such free associations will jeopardize the perfect liberty which individuals are supposed to enjoy. Private organizations are meddlesome; if they cannot impose themselves by force, they insinuate themselves by propaganda, and no paternal government ever exerted so pervasive and indiscreet an influence as they know how to acquire. Fashions in speech or clothes are harder to evade than any laws, and religion, when it is chosen and sectarian, eats more into the soul than when it is established and conventional. In a society honeycombed by private societies a man finds his life supervised, his opportunities pre-empted, his conscience intimidated, and his pocket drained. Everyone he meets informs him of a new duty and presents him with a new subscription list. At every turn he must choose between being incorporated or being ostracized. Indeed, the worst and most radical failure in his fabled liberty of choice is that he never had a choice about his environment or about his faculties, and has to take his luck as to his body, his mind, his position, his country, and his family. Even where he may cast a vote his vote is far from decisive. In electing a government, as in selecting a wife, only two or three candidates are commonly available, and the freeman's modest privilege is to declare hopefully which one he wants and then to put up with the one he gets.

Liberalism and Culture

If liberalism had been a primitive system, with no positive institutions behind it, it would have left human genius in the most depressed and forlorn condition. The organized part of life would have been a choice among little servitudes, and the free personal part would have been a blank. Fortunately, liberal ages have been secondary ages, inheriting the monuments, the feelings, and the social hierarchy of previous times, when men had lived in compulsory unison, having only one unquestioned religion, one style of art, one political order, one common spring of laughter and tears. Liberalism has come to remove the strain and the trammels of these traditions without as yet uprooting the traditions themselves. Most people retain their pre-liberal heritage and hardly remember that they are legally free to abandon it and to sample any and every other form of life. Liberalism does not go very deep; it is an adventitious principle, a mere loosening of an older structure. For that reason it brings to all who felt cramped and ill-suited much comfort and relief. It offers them an escape from all sorts of accidental tyrannies. It opens to them that sweet, scholarly, tenderly moral, critically superior attitude of mind which Matthew Arnold called culture.

Primitive, dragooned, unanimous ages cannot possess culture. What they possess is what the Germans call a *Kultur*, some type or other of manners, laws, implements, arts, religion. When these national possessions are perused and relished by some individual who does not take them for granted and who understands and judges them as if from outside, his acquaintance with them becomes an element in his culture; and if he is at home in many such forms of life and thought, his culture is the more perfect. It should ideally be culled from everywhere. Culture is a triumph of the individual over society. It is his way of profiting intellectually by a world he has not helped to make.

Culture requires liberalism for its foundation, and liberalism requires culture for its crown. It is culture that integrates in imagination the activities which liberalism so dangerously disperses in practice. Out of the public disarray of beliefs and efforts it gathers its private collection of curiosities, much as amateurs stock their museums with fragments of ancient works. It possesses a wealth of vicarious experience and historical insight which comforts it for having nothing of its own to contribute to history. The man of culture abounds in discriminating sentiments; he lives under the distant influence of exalted minds; his familiar thoughts at breakfast are intimate appreciations of poetry and art, and if his culture is really mellow, he sometimes smiles a little at his own culture.

Culture came into the modern world with the Renaissance, when personal humours and remote inspiration broke in upon the consecrated medieval mind. Piety and learning had their intrinsic charms, but, after all, they had been cultivated for the sake of ulterior duties and benefits, and in order to appropriate and hand down the revealed wisdom which opened the way to heaven. Culture, on the contrary, had no ulterior purpose, no forced unity. It was an aroma inhaled by those who walked in the evening in the garden of life. Far from being a means to religion, it threw religion also into the context of human experience, and touched its mysteries and quarrels with judgment and elegance. It liberated the studious mind from obligatory or national discipline, and as far as possible from all bonds of time, place, utility, and co-operation, kindling sympathies by preference with what was most exotic, and compensating the mind for the ignominious necessity of having to be, in practical matters, local and partisan. Culture was courteous, open, unconscious of self; it was the joy of living every life but one's own. And its moral side— for everything has its moral side—lay in the just judgments it fostered, the clear sense it awakened of the different qualities and values of things. The scale of values established by the man of culture might sometimes be fanciful or frivolous, but he was always most scrupulous, according to his lights, in distinguishing the better from the worse. This conscientiousness, after all, is the only form of morality that a liberal society can insist upon.

The days of liberalism are numbered. First the horrors of

competition discredited it, and now the trial of war, which it foolishly thought it could elude. The vogue of culture, too, has declined. We see that the man whose success is merely personal—the actor, the sophist, the millionaire, the aesthete —is incurably vulgar. The rightness of liberalism is exactly proportional to the diversity of human nature, to its vague hold on its ideals. Where this vagueness and play of variation stop, and they stop not far below the surface, the sphere of public organization should begin. It is in the subsoil of uniformity, of tradition, of dire necessity that human welfare is rooted, together with wisdom and unaffected art, and the flowers of culture that do not draw their sap from that soil are only paper flowers.

THE HUMAN SCALE

Great buildings often have great doors; but great doors are heavy to swing, and if left open they may let in too much cold or glare; so that we sometimes observe a small postern cut into one leaf of the large door for more convenient entrance and exit, and it is seldom or never that the monumental gates yawn in their somnolence. Here is the modest human scale reasserting itself in the midst of a titanic structure, but it reasserts itself with an ill grace and in the interests of frailty; the patch it makes seems unintended and ignominious.

Yet the human scale is not essentially petty; when it does not slip in as a sort of interloper it has nothing to apologize for. Between the infinite and the infinitesimal all sizes are equally central. The Greeks, the Saracens, the English, the Chinese, and Japanese instinctively retain the human scale in all that part of their work which is most characteristic of them and nearest to their affections. A Greek temple or the hall of an English mansion can be spacious and dignified enough, but they do not outrun familiar uses, and they lend their spaciousness and dignity to the mind, instead of crushing it. Everything about them has an air of friendliness and sufficiency; their elegance is not pompous, and if they are noble they are certainly not vast, cold, nor gilded.

The Saracens, Chinese, and Japanese in their various ways use the human scale with even greater refinement, for they apply it also in a sensuous and psychological direction. Not only is the size of their works moderate by preference, like their brief lyrics, but they exactly meet human sensibility by a great delicacy and concentration in design and a fragrant simplicity in workmanship. Everything they make is economical in its beauty and seems to say to us: 'I exist only to be enjoyed; there is nothing in me not merely delightful.' Here the human scale is not drawn from the human body so much as from the human soul; its faculties are treated with deference—I mean the faculties it really has, not

24

those, like reason, which a flattering philosophy may impute to it. An English country house which is a cottage in appearance may turn out on examination to be almost a palace in extent and appointments; there is no parade, yet there is great profusion—too much furniture, too many ornaments, too much food, too many flowers, too many people. Everything there is on the human scale except the quantity of things, which is oppressive. The Orientals are poorer, more voluptuous, and more sensitive to calligraphy; they leave empty spaces about them and enjoy one thing at a time and enjoy it longer.

One reason for this greater subtlety and mercifulness in the art of Orientals is perhaps the fiercer assault made on their senses by nature. The Englishman lives in a country which is itself on the human scale, clement at all seasons, charming with a gently inconstant atmospheric charm. The rare humanity of nature in his island permeates his being from boyhood up with a delight that is half sentimental, half physical and sporting. In his fields and moors he grows keen and fond of exertion; there too his friendships and his estimates of men are shaped unawares, as if under some silent superior influence. There he imbibes the impressions that make him tender to poetry. He may not require great subtlety in his poets, but he insists that their sentiment shall have been felt and their images seen, and while the obvious, even the shamelessly obvious, does not irritate him, he hates cheap sublimity and false notes. He respects experience and is master of it in his own field.

Thus the empty spaces with which a delicate art likes to surround itself are supplied for the Englishman by his comradeship with nature, his ranging habits, and the reticence of his imagination. There the unexpressed dimension, the background of pregnant silence, exists for him in all its power. For the Saracen, on the contrary, nature is an abyss: parched deserts, hard mountains, night with its overwhelming moon. Here the human scale is altogether transgressed; nature is cruel, alien, excessive, to be fled from with a veiled face. For a relief and solace he builds his house without windows; he makes his life simple, his religion a single phrase, his art exquisite and slight, like the jet of his fountain. It is sweet and necessary that the works of man should respect the human scale when everything in nature so infinitely transcends it.

Why the Egyptians loved things colossal I do not know, but the taste of the Romans for the grandiose is easier to understand. It seems to have been part and parcel of that yearning for the superhuman which filled late antiquity. This yearning took two distinct directions. Among the worldly it fostered imperialism, organization, rhetoric, portentous work, belief in the universality and eternity of Rome, and actual deification of emperors. Among the spiritually minded it led to a violent abstraction from the world, so that the soul in its inward solitude might feel itself inviolate and divine. The Christians at first belonged of course to the latter party; they detested the inflation of the empire, with its cold veneer of marble and of optimism; they were nothing if not humble and dead to the world. Their catacombs were perforce on the human scale, as a coffin is; but even when they emerged to the surface, they reduced rather than enlarged the temples and basilicas bequeathed to them by the pagans. Apart from a few imperial structures at Constantinople or Ravenna their churches for a thousand years kept to the human scale; often they were diminutive; when necessary they were spread out to hold multitudes, but remained low and in the nature of avenues to a tomb or a shrine. The centre was some sombre precinct, often subterranean, where the inward man might commune with the other world. The sacraments were received with a bowed head; they did not call for architectural vistas. The sumptuousness that in time encrusted these sanctuaries was that of a jewel—the Oriental, interior, concentrated sumptuousness of the cloistered arts. Yet the open-air pagan tradition was not dead. Roman works were everywhere, and not all in ruins, and love of display and of plastic grandiloquence lay hardly dormant in the breast of many. It required only a little prosperity to dispel the mystical humility and detachment which Christianity had brought with it at first; and the human scale of the Christian Greeks yielded at the first opportunity to the gigantic scale of the Romans. Spaces were cleared, vaults were raised, arches were made pointed in order that they might be wider and be poised higher, towers and spires were aimed at the clouds, usually getting only half-way, porches became immense caverns. Brunelleschi accomplished a *tour de force* in his dome and Michelangelo another in his, even more stupendous. These various strained models, straining in divergent directions, have kept artists uneasy and impotent ever since, except when under some benign influence they have recovered the human scale, and in domestic architecture or portrait painting have forgotten to be grand and have become felicitous.

The same movement is perhaps easier to survey in philosophy than in architecture. Scarcely had Socrates brought investigation down from the heavens and limited it to morals —a realm essentially on the human scale—when his pupils hastened to undo his work by projecting their moral system again into the sky, denaturalizing both morals and nature. They imagined a universe circling about man, tempering the light for his eyes and making absolute his childlike wishes and judgments. This was humanism out of scale and out of place, an attempt to cut not the works of man but the universe to human measure. It was the nemesis that overtook the Greeks for having become too complacently human. Earlier the monstrous had played a great part in their religion; henceforth, that surrounding immensity having been falsely humanized, their modest humanity itself had to be made monstrous to fill its place.

Hence we see the temples growing larger and larger, the dome introduced, things on the human scale piled on one another to make a sublime fabric, like Saint Sophia, triumphal arches on pedestals not to be passed through, vain columns like towers, with a statue poised on the summit like a weather-cock, and finally doors so large that they could not be opened and little doors had to be cut in them for men to use. So the human scale turned up again irrepressibly, but for the moment without its native dignity, because it had been stretched to compass a lifeless dignity quite other than its own.

CHARACTER AND OPINION IN
THE UNITED STATES

THE MORAL BACKGROUND

About the middle of the nineteenth century, in the quiet sunshine of provincial prosperity, New England had an Indian summer of the mind; and an agreeable reflective literature showed how brilliant that russet and yellow season could be. There were poets, historians, orators, preachers, most of whom had studied foreign literatures and had travelled; they demurely kept up with the times; they were universal humanists. But it was all a harvest of leaves; these worthies had an expurgated and barren conception of life; theirs was the purity of sweet old age. Sometimes they made attempts to rejuvenate their minds by broaching native subjects; they wished to prove how much matter for poetry the new world supplied, and they wrote *Rip Van Winkle*, *Hiawatha*, or *Evangeline*; but the inspiration did not seem much more American than that of Swift or Ossian or Chateaubriand. These cultivated writers lacked native roots and fresh sap because the American intellect itself lacked them. Their culture was half a pious survival, half an intentional acquirement; it was not the inevitable flowering of a fresh experience. Later there have been admirable analytic novelists who have depicted American life as it is, but rather bitterly, rather sadly; as if the joy and the illusion of it did not inspire them, but only an abstract interest in their own art. If anyone, like Walt Whitman, penetrated to the feelings and images which the American scene was able to breed out of itself, and filled them with a frank and broad afflatus of his own, there is no doubt that he misrepresented the conscious minds of cultivated Americans; in them the head as yet did not belong to the trunk.

Nevertheless, *belles-lettres* in the United States—which after all stretch beyond New England—have always had two points of contact with the great national experiment. One point of contact has been oratory, with that sort of poetry, patriotic, religious, or moral, which has the function of oratory. Eloquence is a republican art, as conversation is an aristocratic one. By eloquence at public meetings and dinners, in the pulpit or in the press, the impulses of the community could be brought to expression; consecrated maxims could be re-applied; the whole latent manliness and shrewdness of the nation could be mobilized. In the form of oratory reflection, rising out of the problems of action, could be turned to guide or to sanction action, and sometimes could attain, in so doing, a notable elevation of thought. Although Americans, and many other people, usually say that thought is for the sake of action, it has evidently been in these high moments, when action became incandescent in thought, that they have been most truly alive, intensively most active, and although *doing* nothing, have found at last that their existence was worth while. Reflection is itself a turn, and the top turn, given to life. Here is the second point at which literature in America has fused with the activities of the nation: it has paused to enjoy them. Every animal has his festive and ceremonious moments, when he poses or plumes himself or thinks; sometimes he even sings and flies aloft in a sort of ecstasy. Somewhat in the same way, when reflection in man becomes dominant, it may become passionate; it may create religion or philosophy—adventures often more thrilling than the humdrum experience they are supposed to interrupt.

This pure flame of mind is nothing new, superadded, or alien in America. It is notorious how metaphysical was the passion that drove the Puritans to those shores; they went there in the hope of living more perfectly in the spirit. And their pilgrim's progress was not finished when they had founded their churches in the wilderness; an endless migration of the mind was still before them, a flight from those new idols and servitudes which prosperity involves, and the eternal lure of spiritual freedom and truth. The moral world always contains undiscovered or thinly peopled continents

29

open to those who are more attached to what might or should be than to what already is. Americans are eminently prophets; they apply morals to public affairs; they are impatient and enthusiastic. Their judgments have highly speculative implications, which they often make explicit; they are men with principles, and fond of stating them. Moreover, they have an intense self-reliance; to exercise private judgment is not only a habit with them but a conscious duty. Not seldom personal conversions and mystical experiences throw their ingrained faith into novel forms, which may be very bold and radical. They are traditionally exercised about religion, and adrift on the subject more than any other people on earth; and if religion is a dreaming philosophy, and philosophy a waking religion, a people so wide awake and so religious as the old Yankees ought certainly to have been rich in philosophers.

In fact, philosophy in the good old sense of curiosity about the nature of things, with readiness to make the best of them, has not been absent from the practice of Americans or from their humorous moods; their humour and shrewdness are sly comments on the shortcomings of some polite convention that everybody accepts tacitly, yet feels to be insecure and contrary to the principles on which life is actually carried on. Nevertheless, with the shyness which simple competence often shows in the presence of conventional shams, these wits have not taken their native wisdom very seriously. They have not had the leisure nor the intellectual scope to think out and defend the implications of their homely perceptions. Their fresh insight has been whispered in parentheses and asides; it has been humbly banished, in alarm, from their solemn moments. What people have respected have been rather scraps of official philosophy, or entire systems, which they have inherited or imported, as they have respected operas and art museums. To be on speaking terms with these fine things was a part of social respectability, like having family silver. High thoughts must be at hand, like those candlesticks, probably candleless, sometimes displayed as a seemly ornament in a room blazing with electric light. Even in William James, spontaneous and stimulating as he was, a certain underlying discomfort was discernible; he had come out into the open, into what should have been the sunshine, but the vast shadow of the temple still stood between him and the sun. He was worried about what *ought* to be believed and the awful deprivations of disbelieving. What he called the cynical view of anything had first to be brushed aside, without stopping to consider whether it was not the true one; and he was bent on finding new and empirical reasons for clinging to free will, departed spirits, and tutelary gods. Nobody, except perhaps in this last decade, has tried to bridge the chasm between what he believes in daily life and the 'problems' of philosophy. Nature and science have not been ignored, and 'practice' in some schools has been constantly referred to; but instead of supplying philosophy with its data they have only constituted its difficulties; its function has been not to build on known facts but to explain them away. Hence a curious alternation and irrelevance, as between weekdays and Sabbaths, between American ways and American opinions.

That philosophy should be attached to tradition would be a great advantage, conducive to mutual understanding, to maturity, and to progress, if the tradition lay in the highway of truth. To deviate from it in that case would be to betray the fact that, while one might have a lively mind, one was not master of the subject. Unfortunately, in the nineteenth century, in America as elsewhere, the ruling tradition was not only erratic and far from the highway of truth, but the noonday of this tradition was over, and its classic forms were outgrown. A philosophy may have a high value, other than its truth to things, in its truth to method and to the genius of its author; it may be a feat of synthesis and imagination, like a great poem, expressing one of the eternal possibilities of being, although one which the creator happened to reject when he made this world. It is possible to be a master in false philosophy—easier, in fact, than to be a master in the truth, because a false philosophy can be made as simple and consistent as one pleases. Such had been the masters of the tradition prevalent in New England—Calvin, Hume, Fichte, not to mention others more relished because less pure; but one of the disadvantages of such perfection in error is that the illusion is harder to transmit to another age and country. If Jonathan Edwards, for instance, was a Calvinist of pristine force and perhaps the greatest *master* in false philosophy that America has yet produced, he paid the price by being abandoned, even in his lifetime, by his own sect, and seeing the world turn a deaf ear to his logic without so much as attempting to refute it. One of the peculiarities of recent speculation, especially in America, is that ideas are abandoned in virtue of a mere change of feeling, without any new evidence or new arguments. We do not nowadays refute our predecessors, we pleasantly bid them good-bye. Even if all our principles are unwittingly traditional we do not like to bow openly to authority. Hence masters like Calvin, Hume, or Fichte rose before their American admirers like formidable ghosts, foreign and unseizable. People refused to be encumbered with any system, even one of their own; they were content to imbibe more or less of the spirit of a philosophy and to let it play on such facts as happened to attract their attention. The originality even of Emerson and of William James was of this incidental character; they found new approaches to old beliefs or new expedients in old dilemmas. They were not in a scholastic sense pupils of anybody or masters in anything. They hated the scholastic way of saying what they meant, if they had heard of it; they insisted on a personal freshness of style, refusing to make their thought more precise than it happened to be spontaneously; and they lisped their logic, when the logic came.

We must remember that ever since the days of Socrates, and especially after the establishment of Christianity, the dice of thought have been loaded. Certain pledges have preceded inquiry and divided the possible conclusions beforehand into the acceptable and the inacceptable, the edifying and the shocking, the noble and the base. Wonder has no longer been the root of philosophy, but sometimes impatience at having been cheated and sometimes fear of being undeceived. The marvel of existence, in which the luminous and the opaque are so romantically mingled, no longer lay like a sea open to intellectual adventure, tempting the mind to conceive some bold and curious system of the universe, on the analogy of what had been so far discovered. Instead, people were confronted with an orthodoxy—though not always the same orthodoxy—whispering mysteries and brandishing anathemas. Their wits were absorbed in solving traditional problems, many of them artificial and such as the ruling orthodoxy had created by its gratuitous assumptions. Difficulties were therefore found in some perfectly obvious truths; and obvious fables, if they were hallowed by association, were seriously weighed in the balance against one another or against the facts; and many an actual thing was proved to be impossible, or was hidden under a false description. In conservative schools the student learned and tried to fathom the received solutions; in liberal schools he was perhaps invited to seek solutions of his own, but still to the old questions. Freedom, when nominally allowed, was a provisional freedom; if your wanderings did not somehow bring you back to orthodoxy you were a misguided being, no matter how disparate from the orthodox might be the field from which you fetched your little harvest; and if you could not be answered you were called superficial. Most spirits are cowed by such disparagement; but even those who snap their fingers at it do not escape; they can hardly help feeling that in calling a spade a spade they are petulant and naughty; or if their inspiration is too genuine for that, they still unwittingly shape their opinions in contrast to those that claim authority, and therefore on the same false lines—a terrible tax to pay to the errors of others; and it is only here and there that a very great and solitary mind, like that of Spinoza, can endure obloquy without bitterness or can pass through perverse controversies without contagion.

Under such circumstances it is obvious that speculation can be frank and happy only where orthodoxy has receded, abandoning a larger and larger field to unprejudiced inquiry; or else (as has happened among liberal Protestants), where the very heat of orthodoxy has melted, has absorbed the most alien substances, and is ready to bloom into anything that anybody finds attractive. This is the secret of that extraordinary vogue which the transcendental philosophy has had for nearly a century in Great Britain and America; it is a method which enables a man to renovate all his beliefs, scientific and religious, from the inside, giving them a new status and interpretation as phases of his own experience or imagination; so that he does not seem to himself to reject anything, and yet is bound to nothing, except to his creative self. Many too who have no inclination to practise this transcendental method—a personal, arduous, and futile art, which requires to be renewed at every moment—have been impressed with the results or the maxims of this or that transcendental philosopher, such as that every opinion leads on to another that reinterprets it, or every evil to some higher good that contains it; and they have managed to identify these views with what still seemed to them vital in religion.

In spite of this profound mutation at the core, and much paring at the edges, traditional belief in New England retained its continuity and its priestly unction; and religious teachers and philosophers could slip away from Calvinism and even from Christianity without any loss of elevation or austerity. They found it so pleasant and easy to elude the past that they really had no quarrel with it. The world, they felt, was a safe place, watched over by a kindly God, who exacted nothing but cheerfulness and goodwill from his children; and the American flag was a sort of rainbow in the sky, promising that all storms were over. Or if storms came, such as the Civil War, they would not be harder to weather than was necessary to test the national spirit and raise it to a new efficiency. The subtler dangers which we may now see threatening America had not yet come in sight—material restlessness was not yet ominous, the pressure of business enterprises was not yet out of scale with the old life or out of

key with the old moral harmonies. A new type of American
had not appeared—the untrained, pushing, cosmopolitan
orphan, cock-sure in manner but not too sure in his morality,
to whom the old Yankee, with his sour integrity, is almost
a foreigner. Was not 'increase', in the Bible, a synonym for
benefit? Was not 'abundance' the same, or almost the same,
as happiness?

Meantime the churches, a little ashamed of their past,
began to court the good opinion of so excellent a world.
Although called evangelical, they were far, very far, from
prophesying its end, or offering a refuge from it, or preaching
contempt for it; they existed only to serve it, and their
highest divine credential was that the world needed them.
Irreligion, dissoluteness, and pessimism—supposed naturally
to go together—could never prosper; they were incompatible
with efficiency. That was the supreme test. 'Be Christians,'
I once heard a president of Yale College cry to his assembled
pupils, 'be Christians and you will be successful.' Religion
was indispensable and sacred, when not carried too far; but
theology might well be unnecessary. Why distract this world
with talk of another? Enough for the day was the good thereof.
Religion should be disentangled as much as possible from
history and authority and metaphysics, and made to rest
honestly on one's fine feelings, on one's indomitable optimism and trust in life. Revelation was nothing miraculous,
given once for all in some remote age and foreign country;
it must come to us directly, and with greater authority now
than ever before. If evolution was to be taken seriously and to
include moral growth, the great men of the past could only
be stepping-stones to our own dignity. To grow was to contain and sum up all the good that had gone before, adding an
appropriate increment. Undoubtedly some early figures were
beautiful, and allowances had to be made for local influences
in Palestine, a place so much more primitive and backward
than Massachusetts. Jesus was a prophet more winsome and
nearer to ourselves than his predecessors; but how could any
one deny that the twenty centuries of progress since his time

must have raised a loftier pedestal for Emerson or Channing or Philips Brooks? It might somehow not be in good taste to put this feeling into clear words; one and perhaps two of these men would have deprecated it; nevertheless it beamed with refulgent self-satisfaction in the lives and maxims of most of their followers.

All this liberalism, however, never touched the centre of traditional orthodoxy, and those who, for all their modernness, felt that they inherited the faith of their fathers and were true to it were fundamentally right. There was still an orthodoxy among American highbrows at the end of the nineteenth century, dissent from which was felt to be scandalous; it consisted in holding that the universe exists and is governed for the sake of man or of the human spirit. This persuasion, arrogant as it might seem, is at bottom an expression of impotence rather than of pride. The soul is originally vegetative; it feels the weal and woe of what occurs within the body. With locomotion and the instinct to hunt and to flee, animals begin to notice external things also, but the chief point noticed about them is whether they are good or bad, friendly or hostile, far or near. The station of the animal and his interests thus become the measure of all things for him, in so far as he knows them; and this aspect of them is, by a primitive fatality, the heart of them to him. It is only reason that can discount these childish perspectives, neutralize the bias of each by collating it with the others, and masterfully conceive the field in which their common objects are deployed, discovering also the principle of foreshortening or projection which produces each perspective in turn. But reason is a later comer into this world, and weak; against its suasion stands the mighty resistance of habit and of moral presumption. It is in their interest, and to rehabilitate the warm vegetative autonomy of the primitive soul, that orthodox religion and philosophy labour in the western world—for the mind of India cannot be charged with this folly. Although inwardly these systems have not now a good conscience and do not feel very secure (for they are retrograde and sin against the light), yet outwardly they

are solemn and venerable; and they have incorporated a great
deal of moral wisdom with their egotism or humanism—
more than the Indians with their respect for the infinite. In
deifying human interests they have naturally studied and
expressed them justly, whereas those who perceive the relativity of human goods are tempted to scorn them—which is
itself unreasonable—and to sacrifice them all to the single
passion of worship or of despair. Hardly anybody, except
possibly the Greeks at their best, has realized the sweetness
and glory of being a rational animal.

The Jews, as we know, had come to think that it was the
creator of the world, the God of the universe, who had taken
them for his chosen people. Christians in turn had asserted
that it was God in person who, having become a man, had
founded their Church. According to this Hebraic tradition,
the dignity of man did not lie in being a mind (which he undoubtedly is) but in being a creature materially highly
favoured, with a longer life and a brighter destiny than
other creatures in the world. It is remarkable how deep, in
the Hebraic religions, is this interest in material existence;
so deep that we are surprised when we discover that, according to the insight of other races, this interest is the essence of
irreligion. Some detachment from existence and from hopes
of material splendour had indeed filtered into Christianity
through Platonism. Socrates and his disciples admired this
world, but they did not particularly covet it, or wish to live
long in it, or expect to improve it; what they cared for was an
idea or a good which they found expressed in it, something
outside it and timeless, in which the contemplative intellect
might be literally absorbed. This philosophy was no less
humanistic than that of the Jews, though in a less material
fashion: if it did not read the universe in terms of thrift, it
read it in terms of art. The pursuit of a good, such as is pre-
sumably aimed at in human action, was supposed to inspire
every movement in nature; and this good, for the sake of
which the very heavens revolved, was akin to the intellectual
happiness of a Greek sage. Nature was a philosopher in

pursuit of an idea. Natural science then took a moralizing
turn which it has not yet quite outgrown. Socrates required
of astronomy, if it was to be true science, that it should show
why *it was best* that the sun and moon should be as they are;
and Plato, refining on this, assures us that the eyes are placed
in the front of the head, rather than at the back, because the
front is the nobler quarter, and that the intestines are long in
order that we may have leisure between meals to study
philosophy. Curiously enough, the very enemies of final
causes sometimes catch this infection and attach absolute
values to facts in an opposite sense and in an inhuman interest;
and you often hear in America that whatever is is right. These
naturalists, while they rebuke the moralists for thinking that
nature is ruled magically for our good, think her adorable for
being ruled, in scorn of us, only by her own laws; and thus
we oscillate between egotism and idolatry.

The Reformation did not reform this belief in the cosmic
supremacy of man, or the humanity of God; on the contrary,
it took it (like so much else) in terrible German earnest, not
suffering it any longer to be accepted somewhat lightly as a
classical figure of speech or a mystery resting on revelation.
The human race, the chosen people, the Christian elect were
like tabernacle within tabernacle for the spirit; but in the
holy of holies was the spirit itself, one's own spirit and experience, which was the centre of everything. Protestant philosophy, exploring the domain of science and history with
confidence, and sure of finding the spirit walking there, was
too conscientious to misrepresent what it found. As the
terrible facts could not be altered they had to be undermined.
By turning psychology into metaphysics this could be accomplished, and we could reach the remarkable conclusion that
the human spirit was not so much the purpose of the universe
as its seat, and the only universe there was.

This conclusion, which sums up idealism on its critical or
scientific side, would not of itself give much comfort to
religious minds, that usually crave massive support rather
than sublime independence; it leads to the heroic egotism of

Fichte or Nietzsche rather than to any green pastures beside any still waters. But the critical element in idealism can be used to destroy belief in the natural world; and by so doing it can open the way to another sort of idealism, not at all critical, which might be called the higher superstition. This views the world as an oracle or charade, concealing a dramatic unity, or formula, or maxim, which all experience exists to illustrate. The habit of regarding existence as a riddle, with a surprising solution which we think we have found, should be the source of rather mixed emotions; the facts remain as they were, and rival solutions may at any time suggest themselves; and the one we have hit on may not, after all, be particularly comforting. The Christian may find himself turned by it into a heathen, the humanist into a pantheist, and the hope with which we instinctively faced life may be chastened into mere conformity. Nevertheless, however chilling and inhuman our higher superstition may prove, it will make us feel that we are masters of a mystical secret, that we have a faith to defend, and that, like all philosophers, we have taken a ticket in a lottery, in which if we hit on the truth, even if it seems a blank, we shall have drawn the first prize.

Orthodoxy in New England, even so transformed and attenuated, did not of course hold the field alone. There are materialists by instinct in every age and country; there are always private gentlemen whom the clergy and the professors cannot deceive. Here and there a medical or scientific man, or a man of letters, will draw from his special pursuits some hint of the nature of things at large; or a political radical will nurse undying wrath against all opinions not tartly hostile to Church and state. But these clever people are not organized, they are not always given to writing, nor speculative enough to make a system out of their convictions. The enthusiasts and the pedagogues naturally flock to the other camp. The very competence which scientific people and connoisseurs have in their special fields disinclines them to generalize, or renders their generalizations one-sided; so that their speculations are extraordinarily weak and stammering. Both by what they represent and by what they ignore they are isolated and deprived of influence, since only those who are at home in a subject can feel the force of analogies drawn from that field, whereas anyone can be swayed by sentimental and moral appeals, by rhetoric and unction. Furthermore, in America the materialistic school is without that support from popular passions which it draws in many European countries from its associations with anticlericalism or with revolutionary politics; and it also lacks the maturity, self-confidence, and refinement proper in older societies to the great body of Epicurean and disenchanted opinion, where for centuries wits, critics, minor philosophers, and men of the world have chuckled together over their Horace, their Voltaire, and their Gibbon. The horror which the theologians have of infidelity passes therefore into the average American mind unmitigated by the suspicion that anything pleasant could lie in that quarter, much less the open way to nature and truth and a secure happiness.

There is another handicap, of a more technical sort, under which naturalistic philosophy labours in America, as it does in England; it has been crossed by scepticism about the validity of perception and has become almost identical with psychology. Of course, for anyone who thinks naturalistically (as the British empiricists did in the beginning, like every unsophisticated mortal), psychology is the description of a very superficial and incidental complication in the animal kingdom: it treats of the curious sensibility and volatile thoughts awakened in the mind by the growth and fortunes of the body. In noting these thoughts and feelings, we can observe how far they constitute true knowledge of the world in which they arise, how far they ignore it, and how far they play with it, by virtue of the poetry and the syntax of discourse which they add out of their own exuberance; for fancy is a very fertile, treacherous thing, as every one finds when he dreams. But dreams run over into waking life, and sometimes seem to permeate and to underlie it; and it was just this suspicion that he might be dreaming awake, that discourse and tradition

might be making a fool of him, that prompted the hard-
headed Briton, even before the Reformation, to appeal from
conventional beliefs to 'experience'. He was anxious to clear
away those sophistries and impostures of which he was particularly apprehensive, in view of the somewhat foreign
character of his culture and religion. Experience, he thought,
would bear unimpeachable witness to the nature of things;
for by experience he understood knowledge produced by direct
contact with the object. Taken in this sense, experience is a
method of discovery, an exercise of intelligence; it is the same
observation of things, strict, cumulative, and analytic, which
produces the natural sciences. It rests on naturalistic assumptions (since we know when and where we find our data) and
could not fail to end in materialism. What prevented British
empiricism from coming to this obvious conclusion was a
peculiarity of the national temperament. The Englishman is
not only distrustful of too much reasoning and too much
theory (and science and materialism involve a good deal of
both), but he is also fond of musing and of withdrawing into
his inner man. Accordingly his empiricism took an introspective form; like Hamlet he stopped at the *how*; he began
to think about thinking. His first care was now to arrest
experience as he underwent it; though its presence could not
be denied, it came in such a questionable shape that it could
not be taken at its word. This mere presence of experience,
this ghostly apparition to the inner man, was all that empirical
philosophy could now profess to discover. Far from being an
exercise of intelligence, it retracted all understanding, all
interpretation, all instinctive faith; far from furnishing a sure
record of the truths of nature, it furnished a set of pathological
facts, the passive subject-matter of psychology. These now
seemed the only facts admissible, and psychology, for the
philosophers, became the only science. Experience could discover nothing, but all discoveries had to be retracted, so that
they should revert to the fact of experience and terminate
there. Evidently when the naturalistic background and meaning of experience have dropped out in this way, empiricism is

a form of idealism, since whatever objects we can come upon will all be *a priori* and *a fortiori* and *sensu eminentiori* ideal in the mind. The irony of logic actually made English empiricism, understood in this psychological way, the starting-point for transcendentalism and for German philosophy.

Between these two senses of the word experience, meaning sometimes contact with things and at other times absolute feeling, the empirical school in England and America has been helplessly torn, without ever showing the courage or the self-knowledge to choose between them. I think we may say that on the whole their view has been this: that feelings or ideas were absolute atoms of existence, without any ground or source, so that the elements of their universe were all mental; but they conceived these physical elements to be deployed in a physical time and even (since there were many simultaneous series of them) in some sort of space. These philosophers were accordingly idealists about substance but naturalists about the order and relations of existences; and experience on their lips meant feeling when they were thinking of particulars, but when they were thinking broadly, in matters of history or science, experience meant the universal nebula or cataract which these feelings composed—itself no object of experience, but one believed in and very imperfectly presented in imagination. These men believed in nature, and were materialists at heart and to all practical purposes; but they were shy intellectually, and seemed to think they ran less risk of error in holding a thing covertly than in openly professing it.

If anyone, like Herbert Spencer, kept psychology in its place and in that respect remained a pure naturalist, he often forfeited this advantage by enveloping the positive information he derived from the sciences in a whirlwind of generalizations. The higher superstition, the notion that nature dances to the tune of some comprehensive formula or some magic rhyme, thus reappeared among those who claimed to speak for natural science. In their romantic sympathy with nature they attributed to her an excessive sympathy with themselves; they overlooked her infinite complications and continual irony, and candidly believed they could measure her with their thumb-rules. Why should philosophers drag a toy-net of words, fit to catch butterflies, through the sea of being, and expect to land all the fish in it? Why not take note simply of what the particular sciences can as yet tell us of the world? Certainly, when put together, they already yield a very wonderful, very true, and very sufficient picture of it. Are we impatient of knowing everything? But even if science was much enlarged it would have limits, both in penetration and in extent; and there would always remain, I will not say an infinity of unsolved problems (because 'problems' are created by our impatience or our contradictions), but an infinity of undiscovered facts. Nature is like a beautiful woman that may be as delightfully and as truly known at a certain distance as upon a closer view; as to knowing her through and through, that is nonsense in both cases, and might not reward our pains. The love of all-inclusiveness is as dangerous in philosophy as in art. The savour of nature can be enjoyed by us only through our own senses and insight, and an outline map of the entire universe, even if it was not fabulously concocted, would not tell us much that was worth knowing about the outlying parts of it. Without suggesting for a moment that the proper study of mankind is man only—for it may be landscape or mathematics—we may safely say that their proper study is what lies within their range and is interesting to them. For this reason the moralists who consider principally human life and paint nature only as a background to their figures are apt to be better philosophers than the speculative naturalists. In human life we are at home, and our views on it, if one-sided, are for that very reason expressive of our character and fortunes. An unfortunate peculiarity of naturalistic philosophers is that usually they have but cursory and wretched notions of the inner life of the mind; they are dead to patriotism and to religion, they hate poetry and fancy and passion and even philosophy itself; and therefore (especially if their science too, as often happens, is borrowed and vague) we need not wonder if the academic and cultivated world despises them, and harks back to the mythology of Plato or Aristotle or Hegel, who at least were conversant with the spirit of man.

Philosophers are very severe towards other philosophers because they expect too much. Even under the most favourable circumstances no mortal can be asked to seize the truth in its wholeness or at its centre. As the senses open to us only partial perspectives, taken from one point of view, and report the facts in symbols which, far from being adequate to the full nature of what surrounds us, resemble the coloured signals of danger or of free way which a railway engine-driver peers at in the night, so our speculation, which is a sort of panoramic sense, approaches things peripherally and expresses them humanly. But how doubly dyed in this subjectivity must our thought be when an orthodoxy dominant for ages has twisted the universe into the service of moral interests, and when even the heretics are entangled in a scepticism so partial and arbitrary that it substitutes psychology, the most derivative and dubious of sciences, for the direct intelligent reading of experience! But this strain of subjectivity is not in all respects an evil; it is a warm purple dye. When a way of thinking is deeply rooted in the soil, and embodies the instincts or even the characteristic errors of a people, it has a value quite independent of its truth; it constitutes a phase of human life and can powerfully affect the intellectual drama in which it figures...Men of intense feeling—and others will hardly count—are not mirrors but lights. If pure truth happened to be what they passionately desired, they would seek it single-mindedly, and in matters within their competence they would probably find it; but the desire for pure truth, like any other, must wait to be satisfied until its organ is ripe and the conditions are favourable. The nineteenth century was not a time and America was not a place where such an achievement could be expected. There the wisest felt themselves to be, as they were, questioners and apostles rather than serene philosophers. We should not pay them the doubtful compliment of attributing to them merits alien to their tradition and scope, as if the nobleness they actually possessed—their conscience, vigour, timeliness, and influence—were not enough.

THE ACADEMIC ENVIRONMENT

...The tendency to gather and to breed philosophers in universities does not belong to ages of free and humane reflection: it is scholastic and proper to the Middle Ages and to Germany. And the reason is not far to seek. When there is a philosophical orthodoxy, and speculation is expected to be a reasoned defence of some funded inspiration, it becomes itself corporate and traditional, and requires centres of teaching, endowment, and propaganda. Fundamental questions have been settled by the Church, the government, or the *Zeitgeist*, and the function of the professor, himself bred in that school, is to transmit its lore to the next generation, with such original touches of insight or eloquence as he may command. To maintain and elucidate such a tradition, all the schools and universities of Christendom were originally founded; and if philosophy seemed sometimes to occupy but a small place in them—as for instance in the old-fashioned American college—it was only because the entire discipline and instruction of the place were permeated with a particular system of faith and morals, which it was almost superfluous to teach in the abstract. In those universities where philosophical controversy is rife, its traditional and scholastic character is no less obvious; it lives less on meditation than on debate, and turns on proofs, objections, paradoxes, or expedients for seeming to re-establish everything that had come to seem clearly false, by some ingenious change of front or some twist of dialectic. Its subject-matter is not so much what is known of the world, as what often very ignorant philosophers have said in answer to one another; or else, when the age is out of patience with scholasticism, orthodoxy may take refuge in intuition, and for fear of the letter without the spirit, may excuse itself from considering at all what is logical or probable, in order to embrace whatever seems most

welcome and comforting. The sweet homilies of the professors
then become clerical, genteel, and feminine.

Harvard College had been founded to rear Puritan divines,
and as Calvinism gradually dissolved, it left a void there and
as it were a mould, which a philosophy expressing the same
instincts in a world intellectually transformed could flow into
and fill almost without knowing it. Corporate bodies are like
persons, long vaguely swayed by early impressions they may
have forgotten. Even when changes come over the spirit of
their dream, a sense of the mission to which they were first
dedicated lingers about them, and may revive, like the anti-
quarian and poetic Catholicism of Oxford in the nineteenth
century. In academic America the Platonic and Catholic
traditions had never been planted; it was only the Calvinistic
tradition, when revived in some modern disguise, that could
stir there the secret cord of reverence and enthusiasm. Harvard
was the seminary and academy for the inner circle of Bosto-
nians, and naturally responded to all the liberal and literary
movements of which Boston was the centre. In religion it
became first Unitarian and afterwards neutral; in philosophy
it might long have been satisfied with what other New
England colleges found sufficient, namely such lofty views as
the president, usually a clergyman, could introduce into his
baccalaureate sermons, or into the course of lectures he might
give for seniors on the evidences of Christianity or on the
theory of evolution. Such philosophical initiation had sufficed
for the distinguished literary men of the middle of the century,
and even for so deep a sage as Emerson. But things cannot
stand still, and Boston, as is well known, is not an ordinary
place. When the impulse to domestic literary expression
seemed to be exhausted, intellectual ambition took other
forms. It was an age of science, of philology, of historical
learning, and the laurels of Germany would not let Boston
sleep. As it had a great public library, and hoped to have a
great art museum, might it not have a great university?
Harvard in one sense was a university already, in that the
college (although there was only one) was surrounded by a

group of professional schools, notably those of law and medicine, in which studies requisite for the service of the community, and leading potentially to brilliant careers, were
carried on with conspicuous success. The number of these
professional schools might have been enlarged, as has been
actually done later, until training in all the professions had
been provided. But it happens that the descriptive sciences,
languages, mathematics, and philosophy are not studies useful
for any profession, except that of teaching these very subjects
over again; and there was no practical way of introducing
them into the Harvard system except to graft them upon the
curriculum of the college; otherwise neither money nor
students could have been found for so much ornamental
learning.

This circumstance, external and irrelevant as it may seem,
I think had a great influence over the temper and quality of
the Harvard philosophers; for it mingled responsibility for
the education of youth, and much labour in it, with their pure
speculation. Teaching is a delightful paternal art, and especially teaching intelligent and warm-hearted youngsters, as
most American collegians are; but it is an art like acting,
where the performance, often rehearsed, must be adapted to
an audience hearing it only once. The speaker must make
concessions to their impatience, their taste, their capacity,
their prejudices, their ultimate good; he must neither bore
nor perplex nor demoralize them. His thoughts must be such
as can flow daily, and be set down in notes; they must come
when the bell rings and stop appropriately when the bell rings
a second time. The best that is in him, as Mephistopheles says
in *Faust*, he dare not tell them; and as the substance of this
possession is spiritual, to withhold is often to lose it. For it is
not merely a matter of fearing not to be understood, or giving
offence; in the presence of a hundred youthful upturned faces
a man cannot, without diffidence, speak in his own person, of
his own thoughts; he needs support, in order to exert influence with a good conscience; unless he feels that he is the
vehicle of a massive tradition, he will become bitter, or

flippant, or aggressive; if he is to teach with good grace and modesty and authority, it must not be he that speaks, but science or humanity that is speaking in him.

Now the state of Harvard College, and of American education generally, at the time to which I refer, had this remarkable effect on the philosophers there: it made their sense of social responsibility acute, because they were consciously teaching and guiding the community, as if they had been clergymen; and it made no less acute their moral loneliness, isolation, and forced self-reliance, because they were like clergymen without a Church, and not only had no common philosophic doctrine to transmit, but were expected not to have one. They were invited to be at once genuine philosophers and popular professors; and the degree to which some of them managed to unite these contraries is remarkable, especially if we consider the character of the academic public they had to serve and to please. While the sentiments of most Americans in politics and morals, if a little vague, are very conservative, their democratic instincts, and the force of circumstances, have produced a system of education which anticipates all that the most extreme revolution could bring about; and while no one dreams of forcibly suppressing private property, religion, or the family, American education ignores these things, and proceeds as much as possible as if they did not exist. The child passes very young into a free school, established and managed by the municipal authorities; the teachers, even for the older boys, are chiefly unmarried women, sensitive, faithful, and feeble; their influence helps to establish that separation which is so characteristic of America between things intellectual, which remain wrapped in a feminine veil and, as it were, under glass, and the rough business and passions of life. The lessons are ambitious in range, but are made as easy, as interesting, and as optional as possible; the stress is divided between what the child likes now and what he is going to need in his trade or profession. The young people are sympathetically encouraged to instruct themselves and to educate one another. They romp and make fun like

48

young monkeys, they flirt and have their private 'brain-storms' like little supermen and superwomen. They are tremendously in earnest about their college intrigues and intercollegiate athletic wars. They are fond, often compassionately fond, of their parents, and home is all the more sacred to them in that they are seldom there. They enjoy a surprising independence in habits, friendships, and opinions. Brothers and sisters often choose different religions. The street, the school, the young people's club, the magazine, the popular novel, furnish their mental pabulum. The force of example, and of passing custom is all the more irresistible in this absence of authority and tradition; for this sort of independence rather diminishes the power of being original, by supplying a slenderer basis and a thinner soil from which originality might spring. Uniformity is established spontaneously without discipline, as in the popular speech and ethics of every nation. Against this tendency to uniformity the efforts of a cultivated minority to maintain a certain distinction and infuse it into their lives and minds are not very successful. They have secondary schools for their boys in which the teachers are men, and even boarding-schools in the country, more or less Gothic in aspect and English in regimen; there are other semi-foreign institutions and circles, Catholic or Jewish, in which religion is the dominant consideration. There is also the society of the very rich, with cosmopolitan leanings and a vivacious interest in artistic undertakings and personalities. But all these distinctions, important as they may seem to those who cultivate them, are a mere shimmer and ripple on the surface of American life; and for an observer who sees things in perspective they almost disappear. By a merciful dispensation of nature, the pupils of these choice establishments, the moment they plunge into business or politics, acquire the protective colouring of their environment and become indistinguishable from the generic American. Their native disposition was after all the national one, their attempted special education was perfunctory, and the influence of their public activities and surroundings is overwhelming. American life is a powerful solvent. As it stamps the immigrant, almost before he can speak English, with an unmistakable muscular tension, cheery self-confidence, and habitual challenge in the voice and eyes, so it seems to neutralize every intellectual element, however tough and alien it may be, and to fuse it in the native good-will, complacency, thoughtlessness, and optimism.

Consider, for instance, the American Catholics, of whom there are nominally many millions, and who often seem to retain their ancestral faith sincerely and affectionately. This faith took shape during the decline of the Roman Empire; it is full of large disillusions about this world and minute illusions about the other. It is ancient, metaphysical, poetic, elaborate, ascetic, autocratic, and intolerant. It confronts the boastful natural man, such as the American is, with a thousand denials and menaces. Everything in American life is at the antipodes to such a system. Yet the American Catholic is entirely at peace. His tone in everything, even in religion, is cheerfully American. It is wonderful how silently, amicably, and happily he lives in a community whose spirit is profoundy hostile to that of his religion. He seems to take stock in his Church as he might in a gold mine—sure it is a grand, dazzling, unique thing; and perhaps he masks, even to himself, his purely imaginative ardour about it, with the pretext that it is sure to make his fortune both in this life and in the next. His Church, he will tell you, is a first-rate Church to belong to; the priests are fine fellows, like the policemen; the Sisters are dear noble women, like his own sisters; his parish is flourishing, and always rebuilding its church and founding new schools, orphan asylums, sodalities, confraternities, perpetual adoration societies. No parish can raise so much money for any object, or if there are temporary troubles, the fact still remains that America has three Cardinals and that the Catholic religion is the biggest religion on earth. Attachment to his Church in such a temper brings him into no serious conflict with his Protestant neighbours. They live and meet on common ground. Their respective religions pass among them for family matters, private and sacred, with no political implications.

Such was the education and such the atmosphere of intellectual innocence which prevailed in the public—mostly undergraduates—to which the Harvard philosophers adapted their teaching and to some extent their philosophy. The students were intelligent, ambitious, remarkably able to 'do things'; they were keen about the matters that had already entered into their lives, and invincibly happy in their ignorance of everything else. A gentle contempt for the past permeated their judgments. They were not accustomed to the notion of authority, nor aware that it might have legitimate grounds; they instinctively disbelieved in the superiority of what was out of reach. About high questions of politics and religion their minds were open but vague; they seemed not to think them of practical importance; they acquiesced in people having any views they liked on such subjects; the fluent and fervid enthusiasms so common among European students, prophesying about politics, philosophy, and art, were entirely unknown among them. Instead they had absorbing local traditions of their own, athletic and social, and their college life was their true education, an education in friendship, co-operation, and freedom. In the 1880s a good deal of old-fashioned shabbiness and jollity lingered about Harvard. Boston and Cambridge in those days resembled in some ways the London of Dickens: the same dismal wealth, the same speechifying, the same anxious respectability, the same sordid back streets, with their air of shiftlessness and decay, the same odd figures and loud humour, and, to add a touch of horror, the monstrous suspicion that some of the inhabitants might be secretly wicked. Life, for the undergraduates, was full of droll incidents and broad farce; it drifted good-naturedly from one commonplace thing to another. Standing packed in the tinkling horse-car, their coat collars above their ears and their feet deep in the winter straw, they jogged in a long half-hour to Boston, there to enjoy the delights of female society, the theatre, or a good dinner. And in the summer days, for Class Day and Commencement, feminine and elderly Boston would return the visit, led by the governor of Massachusetts in his hired carriage-and-four, and by the local orators and poets, brimming with jokes and conventional sentiments, and eager not so much to speed the youngsters on their career, as to air their own wit, and warm their hearts with punch and with collective memories of youth. It was an idyllic, haphazard, humoristic existence, without fine imagination, without any familiar infusion of scholarship, without articulate religion: a flutter of intelligence in a void, flying into trivial play, in order to drop back, as soon as college days were over, into the drudgery of affairs. There was the love of beauty, but without the sight of it; for the bits of pleasant landscape or the works of art which might break the ugliness of the foreground were a sort of aesthetic miscellany, enjoyed as one enjoys a museum; there was nothing in which the spirit of beauty was deeply interfused, charged with passion and discipline and intricate familiar associations with delicate and noble things. Of course, the sky is above every country, and New England had brilliant sunsets and deep snows, and sea and woods were at hand for the holidays; and it was notable how much even what a homely art or accident might have done for the towns was studied and admired. Old corners were pointed out where the dingy red brick had lost its rigidity and taken on a mossy tinge, and where here and there a pane of glass, surviving all tenants and housemaids, had turned violet in the sunlight of a hundred years; and most precious of all were the high thin elms, spreading aloft, looped and drooping over old streets and commons. And yet it seemed somehow as if the sentiment lavished on these things had been intended by nature for something else, for something more important. Not only had the mind of the nation been originally somewhat chilled and impoverished by Protestantism, by migration to a new world, by absorption in material tasks, but what fine sensibility lingered in an older generation was not easily transmitted to the young. The young had their own ways, which on principle were to be fostered and respected; and one of their instincts was to associate only with those of their own age and calibre. The young were simply young, and the old simply old, as among peasants. Teachers and pupils seemed animals of different species, useful and well disposed towards each other, like a cow and a milkmaid; periodic contributions could pass between them, but not conversation. This circumstance shows how much American intelligence is absorbed in what is not intellectual. Their tasks and their pleasures divide people of different ages; what can unite them is ideas, impersonal interests, liberal arts. Without these they cannot forget their mutual inferiority.

Certainly those four college years, judged by any external standard, were trivial and wasted; but Americans, although so practical in their adult masculine undertakings, are slow to take umbrage at the elaborate playfulness of their wives and children. With the touching humility of strength, they seem to say to themselves, 'Let the dear creatures have their fling, and be happy: what else are we old fellows slaving for?' And certainly the joy of life is the crown of it; but have American ladies and collegians achieved the joy of life? Is that the summit?

William James had a theory that if some scientific widower, with a child about to learn to walk, could be persuaded to allow the child's feet to be blistered, it would turn out, when the blisters were healed, that the child would walk as well as if he had practised and had many a fall; because the machinery necessary for walking would have matured in him automatically, just as the machinery for breathing does in the womb. The case of the old-fashioned American college may serve to support this theory. It blistered young men's heads for four years and prevented them from practising anything useful; yet at the end they were found able to do most things as well, or twice as well, as their contemporaries who had been all that time apprenticed and chained to a desk. Manhood and sagacity ripen of themselves; it suffices not to repress or distort them. The college liberated the young man from the pursuit of money, from hypocrisy, from the control of women. He could grow for a time according to his nature, and if this growth was not guided by much superior wisdom or deep study, it was not warped by any serious perversion; and if the intellectual world did not permanently entice him, are we so sure that in philosophy, for instance, it had anything to offer that was very solid in itself, or humanly very important? At least he learned that such things existed, and gathered a shrewd notion of what they could do for a man, and what they might make of him.

When Harvard was reformed—and I believe all the colleges are reformed now—the immediate object was not to refine college life or render it more scholarly, though for certain circles this was accomplished incidentally; the object was rather to extend the scope of instruction, and make it more advanced. It is natural that every great city, the capital of any nation or region, should wish to possess a university in the literal sense of the word—an encyclopaedic institute, or group of institutes, to teach and foster all the professions, all the arts, and all the sciences. Such a university need have nothing to do with education, with the transmission of a particular moral and intellectual tradition. Education might be courteously presupposed. The teacher would not be a man with his hand on a lad's shoulder, his son or young brother; he would be an expert in some science, delivering lectures for public instruction, while perhaps privately carrying on investigations with the aid of a few disciples whom he would be training in his specialty. There would be no reason why either the professors or the auditors in such an institution should live together or should have much in common in religion, morals, or breeding, or should even speak the same language. On the contrary, if only each was competent in his way, the more miscellaneous their types the more perfect would these render their *universitas*. The public addressed, also, need not be restricted, any more than the public at a church or a theatre or a town library, by any requirements as to age, sex, race, or attainments. They would come on their own responsibility, to pursue what studies they chose, and so long as they found them profitable. Nor need there be any limit as to the subjects broached, or any division of them into faculties or departments, except for convenience in administration. One of the functions of professors would be to invent new subjects, because this world is so complex and the play of the human mind upon it is so external and iridescent, that, as men's interests and attitude vary, fresh unities and fresh aspects are always discernible in everything.

As Harvard University developed, all these characteristics appeared in it in a more or less marked degree; but the transformation was never complete. The centre of it remained a college, with its local constituency and rooted traditions, and its thousand undergraduates needing to be educated. Experts in every science and money to pay them were not at hand, and the foreign talent that could be attracted did not always prove morally or socially digestible. The browsing undergraduate could simply range with a looser tether, and he was reinforced by a fringe of graduates who had not yet had enough, or who were attracted from other colleges. These graduates came to form a sort of normal school for future professors, stamped as in Germany with a Ph.D.; and the teachers in each subject became a committee charged with something of the functions of a registry office, to find places for their nurslings. The university could thus acquire a national and even an international function, drawing in distinguished talent and youthful ambition from everywhere, and sending forth in various directions its apostles of light and learning.

I think it is intelligible that in such a place and at such a crisis philosophy should have played a conspicuous part, and also that it should have had an ambiguous character. There had to be, explicit or implicit, a philosophy for the college. A place where all polite Boston has been educated for centuries cannot belie its moral principles and religious questionings; it must transmit its austere, faithful, reforming spirit. But at the same time there had now to be a philosophy for the university. A chief part of that traditional faith was the faith in freedom, in inquiry; and it was necessary, in the very interests of the traditional philosophy, to take account of all that was being said in the world, and to incorporate the spirit of the times in the spirit of the fathers. Accordingly, no single abstract opinion was particularly tabooed at Harvard; granted industry, sobriety, and some semblance of theism, no professor was expected to agree with any other. I believe the authorities would have been well pleased, for the sake of completeness, to have added a Buddhist, a Moslem, and a Catholic scholastic to the philosophical faculty, if only suitable sages could have been found, house-trained, as it were, and able to keep pace with the academic machine and to attract a sufficient number of pupils. But this official freedom was not true freedom, there was no happiness in it. A slight smell of brimstone lingered in the air. You might think what you liked, but you must consecrate your belief or your unbelief to the common task of encouraging everybody and helping everything on. You might almost be an atheist, if you were troubled enough about it. The atmosphere was not that of intelligence nor of science, it was that of duty.

In the academic life and methods of the university there was the same incomplete transformation. The teaching required was for the most part college teaching, in college subjects, such as might well have been entrusted to tutors; but it was given by professors in the form of lectures, excessive in number and too often repeated; and they were listened to by absent-minded youths, ill grounded in the humanities, and not keenly alive to intellectual interests. The graduates (like the young ladies) were more attentive and anxious not to miss anything, but they were no better prepared and often less intelligent; and there is no dunce like a mature dunce. Accordingly, the professor of philosophy had to swim against rather a powerful current. Sometimes he succumbed to the reality; and if, for instance, he happened to mention Darwin, and felt a blank before him, he would add in a parenthesis, 'Darwin, Charles, author of the *Origin of Species*, 1859; epoch-making work.' At other times he might lose himself altogether in the ideal and imagine that he was publishing immortal thoughts to the true university, to the world at large, and was feeling an exhilarating contact with masses of mankind, themselves quickened by his message. He might see in his mind's eye rows of learned men and women before him, familiar with every doubt, hardened to every conflict of opinion, ready for any revolution, whose minds nothing he could say could possibly shock, or disintegrate any further; on the contrary, the naked truth, which is gentle in its austerity, might come to them as a blessed deliverance, and he might fancy himself for a moment a sort of hero from the realms of light descending into the nether regions and throwing a sop of reason into the jaws of snarling prejudice and frantic error. Or if the class was small, and only two or three were gathered together, he might imagine instead that he was sowing seeds of wisdom, warmed by affection, in the minds of genuine disciples, future tabernacles of the truth. It is possible that if the reality had corresponded more nearly with these dreams, and Harvard had actually been an adult university, philosophers there might have distilled their doctrines into a greater purity. As it was, Harvard philosophy had an opposite merit: it represented faithfully the complex inspiration of the place and hour. As the university was a local Puritan college opening its windows to the scientific world, so at least the two most gifted of its philosophers were men of intense feeling, religious and romantic, but attentive to the facts of nature and the currents of worldly opinion; and each of them felt himself bound by two different responsibilities, that of describing things as they are, and that of finding them propitious to certain preconceived human desires. And while they shared this double allegiance, they differed very much in temper, education, and taste. William James was what is called an empiricist, Josiah Royce an idealist; they were excellent friends and greatly influenced each other, and the very diversity between them rendered their conjunction typical of the state of philosophy in England and America, divided between the old British and the German schools. As if all this intellectual complication had not been enough, they were obliged to divide their energies externally, giving to their daily tasks as professors and pedagogues what duty demanded, and only the remainder to scholarship, reflection, and literary work. Even this distracting circumstance, however, had its compensations. College work was a human bond, a common practical interest; it helped to keep up that circulation of the blood which made the whole Harvard school of philosophy a vital unit, and co-operative in its freedom. There was a general momentum in it, half institutional, half moral, a single troubled, noble, exciting life. Everyone was labouring with the contradiction he felt in things, and perhaps in himself; all were determined to find some honest way out of it, or at least to bear it bravely. It was a fresh morning in the life of reason, cloudy but brightening.

MATERIALISM AND IDEALISM IN AMERICAN LIFE

The language and traditions common to England and America are like other family bonds: they draw kindred together at the greater crises in life, but they also occasion at times a little friction and fault-finding. The groundwork of the two societies is so similar, that each nation, feeling almost at home with the other, and almost able to understand its speech, may instinctively resent what hinders it from feeling at home altogether. Differences will tend to seem anomalies that have slipped in by mistake and through somebody's fault. Each will judge the other by his own standards, not feeling, as in the presence of complete foreigners, that he must make an effort of imagination and put himself in another man's shoes.

In matters of morals, manners, and art, the danger of comparisons is not merely that they may prove invidious, by ranging qualities in an order of merit which might wound somebody's vanity; the danger is rather that comparisons may distort comprehension, because in truth good qualities are all different in kind, and free lives are different in spirit. Comparison is the expedient of those who cannot reach the heart of the things compared; and no philosophy is more external and egotistical than that which places the essence of a thing in its relation to something else. In reality, at the centre of every natural being there is something individual and incommensurable, a seed with its native impulses and aspirations, shaping themselves as best they can in their given environment. Variation is a consequence of freedom, and the slight but radical diversity of souls in turn makes freedom requisite. Instead of instituting in his mind any comparisons between the United States and other nations, I would accordingly urge the reader to forget himself and, in so far as such a thing may be possible for him or for me, to transport himself ideally with me into the outer circumstances of American life, the better to feel its inner temper, and to see how inevitably the American shapes his feelings and judgments, honestly reporting all things as they appear from his new and unobstructed station.

I speak of the American in the singular, as if there were not millions of them, north and south, east and west, of both sexes, of all ages, and of various races, professions, and religions. Of course the one American I speak of is mythical; but to speak in parables is inevitable in such a subject, and it is perhaps as well to do so frankly. There is a sort of poetic ineptitude in all human discourse when it tries to deal with natural and existing things. Practical men may not notice it, but in fact human discourse is intrinsically addressed not to natural existing things but to ideal essences, poetic or logical terms which thought may define and play with. When fortune or necessity diverts our attention from this congenial ideal sport to crude facts and pressing issues, we turn our frail poetic ideas into symbols for those terrible irruptive things. In that paper money of our own stamping, the legal tender of the mind, we are obliged to reckon all the movements and values of the world. The universal American I speak of is one of these symbols; and I should be still speaking in symbols and creating moral units and a false simplicity, if I spoke of classes pedantically subdivided, or individuals ideally integrated and defined. As it happens, the symbolic American

can be made largely adequate to the facts; because, if there are immense differences between individual Americans—for some Americans are black—yet there is a great uniformity in their environment, customs, temper, and thoughts. They have all been uprooted from their several soils and ancestries and plunged together into one vortex, whirling irresistibly in a space otherwise quite empty. To be an American is of itself almost a moral condition, an education, and a career. Hence a single ideal figment can cover a large part of what each American is in his character, and almost the whole of what most Americans are in their social outlook and political judgments.

The discovery of the new world exercised a sort of selection among the inhabitants of Europe. All the colonists, except the negroes, were voluntary exiles. The fortunate, the deeply rooted, and the lazy remained at home; the wilder instincts or dissatisfaction of others tempted them beyond the horizon. The American is accordingly the most adventurous, or the descendant of the most adventurous, of Europeans. It is in his blood to be socially a radical, though perhaps not intellectually. What has existed in the past, especially in the remote past, seems to him not only not authoritative, but irrelevant, inferior, and outworn. He finds it rather a sorry waste of time to think about the past at all. But his enthusiasm for the future is profound; he can conceive of no more decisive way of recommending an opinion or a practice than to say that it is what everybody is coming to adopt. This expectation of what he approves, or approval of what he expects, makes up his optimism. It is the necessary faith of the pioneer.

Such a temperament is, of course, not maintained in the nation merely by inheritance. Inheritance notoriously tends to restore the average of a race, and plays incidentally many a trick of atavism. What maintains this temperament and makes it national is social contagion or pressure—something immensely strong in democracies. The luckless American who is born a conservative, or who is drawn to poetic subtlety, pious retreats, or gay passions, nevertheless has the categori-

cal excellence of work, growth, enterprise, reform, and prosperity dinned into his ears: every door is open in this direction
and shut in the other; so that he either folds up his heart and
withers in a corner—in remote places you sometimes find
such a solitary gaunt idealist—or else he flies to Oxford or
Florence or Montmartre to save his soul—or perhaps not to
save it.

The optimism of the pioneer is not limited to his view of
himself and his own future: it starts from that; but feeling
assured, safe, and cheery within, he looks with smiling and
most kindly eyes on everything and everybody about him.
Individualism, roughness, and self-trust are supposed to go
with selfishness and a cold heart; but I suspect that is a
prejudice. It is rather dependence, insecurity, and mutual
jostling that poison our placid gregarious brotherhood; and
fanciful passionate demands upon people's affections, when
they are disappointed, as they soon must be, breed ill will
and a final meanness. The milk of human kindness is less apt
to turn sour if the vessel that holds it stands steady, cool, and
separate, and is not too often uncorked. In his affections the
American is seldom passionate, often deep, and always kindly.
If it were given to me look into the depths of a man's heart,
and I did not find goodwill at the bottom, I should say without any hesitation, You are not an American. But as the
American is an individualist, his goodwill is not officious.
His instinct is to think well of everybody, and to wish everybody well, but in a spirit of rough comradeship, expecting
every man to stand on his own legs and to be helpful in his
turn. When he has given his neighbour a chance he thinks he
has done enough for him; but he feels it is an absolute duty
to do that. It will take some hammering to drive a coddling
socialism into America.

As self-trust may pass into self-sufficiency, so optimism,
kindness, and good will may grow into a habit of doting on
everything. To the good American many subjects are sacred:
sex is sacred, women are sacred, children are sacred, business
is sacred, America is sacred, masonic lodges and college

clubs are sacred. This feeling grows out of the good opinion
he wishes to have of these things, and serves to maintain it.
If he did not regard all these things as sacred he might come
to doubt sometimes if they were wholly good. Of this kind,
too, is the idealism of single ladies in reduced circumstances
who can see the soul of beauty in ugly things, and are perfectly
happy because their old dog has such pathetic eyes, their
minister is so eloquent, their garden with its three sunflowers
is so pleasant, their dead friends were so devoted, and their
distant relations are so rich.

Consider now the great emptiness of America: not merely
the primitive physical emptiness, surviving in some regions,
and the continental spacing of the chief natural features, but
also the moral emptiness of a settlement where men and even
houses are easily moved about, and no one, almost, lives where
he was born or believes what he has been taught. Not that
the American has jettisoned these impedimenta in anger;
they have simply slipped from him as he moves. Great empty
spaces bring a sort of freedom to both soul and body. You
may pitch your tent where you will; or if ever you decide to
build anything, it can be in a style of your own devising. You
have room, fresh materials, few models, and no critics. You
trust your own experience, not only because you must, but
because you find you may do so safely and prosperously; the
forces that determine fortune are not yet too complicated for
one man to explore. Your detachable condition makes you
lavish with money and cheerfully experimental; you lose little
if you lose all, since you remain completely yourself. At the
same time your absolute initiative gives you practice in coping
with novel situations, and in being original; it teaches you
shrewd management. Your life and mind will become dry and
direct, with few decorative flourishes. In your works everything will be stark and pragmatic; you will not understand
why anybody should make those little sacrifices to instinct or
custom which we call grace. The fine arts will seem to you
academic luxuries, fit to amuse the ladies, like Greek and
Sanskrit; for while you will perfectly appreciate generosity

in men's purposes, you will not admit that the execution of
these purposes can be anything but business. Unfortunately
the essence of the fine arts is that the execution should be
generous too, and delightful in itself; therefore the fine arts
will suffer, not so much in their express professional pursuit—
for then they become practical tasks and a kind of business—
as in that diffused charm which qualifies all human action
when men are artists by nature. Elaboration, which is something to accomplish, will be preferred to simplicity, which is
something to rest in; manners will suffer somewhat; speech
will suffer horribly. For the American the urgency of his
novel attack upon matter, his zeal in gathering its fruits,
precludes meanderings in primrose paths; devices must be
short cuts, and symbols must be mere symbols. If his wife
wants luxuries, of course she may have them; and if he has
vices, that can be provided for too; but they must all be set
down under those headings in his ledgers.

At the same time, the American is imaginative; for where
life is intense, imagination is intense also. Were he not
imaginative he would not live so much in the future. But his
imagination is practical, and the future it forecasts is immediate; it works with the clearest and least ambiguous terms
known to his experience, in terms of number, measure, con-
trivance, economy, and speed. He is an idealist working on
matter. Understanding as he does the material potentialities
of things, he is successful in invention, conservative in reform,
and quick in emergencies. All his life he jumps into the train
after it has started and jumps out before it has stopped; and
he never once gets left behind, or breaks a leg. There is an
enthusiasm in his sympathetic handling of material forces
which goes far to cancel the illiberal character which it might
otherwise assume. The good workman hardly distinguishes
his artistic intention from the potency in himself and in things
which is about to realise that intention. Accordingly his ideals
fall into the form of premonitions and prophecies; and his
studious prophecies often come true. So do the happy work-
manlike ideals of the American. When a poor boy, perhaps,

he dreams of an education, and presently he gets an education, or at least a degree; he dreams of growing rich, and he grows rich—only more slowly and modestly, perhaps, than he expected; he dreams of marrying his Rebecca and, even if he marries a Leah instead, he ultimately finds in Leah his Rebecca after all. He dreams of helping to carry on and to accelerate the movement of a vast, seething, progressive society, and he actually does so. Ideals clinging so close to nature are almost sure of fulfilment; the American beams with a certain self-confidence and sense of mastery; he feels that God and nature are working with him.

Idealism in the American accordingly goes hand in hand with present contentment and with foresight of what the future very likely will actually bring. He is not a revolutionist; he believes he is already on the right track and moving towards an excellent destiny. In revolutionists, on the contrary, idealism is founded on dissatisfaction and expresses it. What exists seems to them an absurd jumble of irrational accidents and bad habits, and they want the future to be based on reason and to be the pellucid embodiment of all their maxims. All their zeal is for something radically different from the actual and (if they only knew it) from the possible; it is ideally simple, and they love it and believe in it because their nature craves it. They think life would be set free by the destruction of all its organs. They are therefore extreme idealists in the region of hope, but not at all, as poets and artists are, in the region of perception and memory. In the atmosphere of civilized life they miss all the refraction and all the fragrance; so that in their conception of actual things they are apt to be crude realists; and their ignorance and inexperience of the moral world, unless it comes of ill luck, indicates their incapacity for education. Now incapacity for education, when united with great inner vitality, is one root of idealism. It is what condemns us all, in the region of sense, to substitute perpetually what we are capable of imagining for what things may be in themselves; it is what condemns us, wherever it extends, to think *a priori*;

it is what keeps us bravely and incorrigibly pursuing what we call the good—that is, what would fulfil the demands of our nature—however little provision the fates may have made for it. But the want of insight on the part of revolutionists touching the past and the present infects in an important particular their idealism about the future; it renders their dreams of the future unrealizable. For in human beings—this may not be true of other animals, more perfectly preformed—experience is necessary to pertinent and concrete thinking; even our primitive instincts are blind until they stumble upon some occasion that solicits them; and they can be much transformed or deranged by their first partial satisfactions. Therefore a man who does not idealize his experience, but idealizes *a priori*, is incapable of true prophecy; when he dreams he raves, and the more he criticizes the less he helps. American idealism, on the contrary, is nothing if not helpful, nothing if not pertinent to practicable transformations; and when the American frets, it is because whatever is useless and impertinent, be it idealism or inertia, irritates him; for it frustrates the good results which he sees might so easily have been obtained.

The American is wonderfully alive; and his vitality, not having often found a suitable outlet, makes him appear agitated on the surface; he is always letting off an unnecessarily loud blast of incidental steam. Yet his vitality is not superficial; it is inwardly prompted, and as sensitive and quick as a magnetic needle. He is inquisitive, and ready with an answer to any question that he may put to himself of his own accord; but if you try to pour instruction into him, on matters that do not touch his own spontaneous life, he shows the most extraordinary powers of resistance and oblivescence; so that he often is remarkably expert in some directions and surprisingly obtuse in others. He seems to bear lightly the sorrowful burden of human knowledge. In a word, he is young.

What sense is there in this feeling, which we all have, that the American is young? His country is blessed with as many elderly people as any other, and his descent from Adam, or from the Darwinian rival of Adam, cannot be shorter than that of his European cousins. Nor are his ideas always very fresh. Trite and rigid bits of morality and religion, with much seemly and antique political lore, remain axiomatic in him, as in the mind of a child; he may carry all this about with an unquestioning familiarity which does not comport under standing. To keep traditional sentiments in this way insulated and uncriticized is itself a sign of youth. A good young man is naturally conservative and loyal on all those subjects which his experience has not brought to a test; advanced opinions on politics, marriage, or literature are comparatively rare in America; they are left for the ladies to discuss, and usually to condemn, while the men get on with their work. In spite of what is old-fashioned in his more general ideas, the American is unmistakably young; and this, I should say, for two reasons: one, that he is chiefly occupied with his immediate environment, and the other, that his reactions upon it are inwardly prompted, spontaneous, and full of vivacity and self-trust. His views are not yet lengthened; his will is not yet broken or transformed...

In America there is a tacit optimistic assumption about existence, to the effect that the more existence the better. The soulless critic might urge that quantity is only a physical category, implying no excellence, but at best an abundance of opportunities both for good and for evil. Yet the young soul, being curious and hungry, views existence *a priori* under the form of the good; its instinct to live implies a faith that most things it can become or see or do will be worth while. Respect for quantity is accordingly something more than the childish joy and wonder at bigness; it is the fisherman's joy in a big haul, the good uses of which he can take for granted. Such optimism is amiable. Nature cannot afford that we should begin by being too calculating or wise, and she encourages us by the pleasure she attaches to our functions in advance of their fruits, and often in excess of them; as the angler enjoys catching his fish more than eating it, and often, waiting patiently for the fish to bite, misses his own supper. The pioneer must devote himself to preparations; he must work for the future, and it is healthy and dutiful of him to love his work for its own sake. At the same time, unless reference to an ultimate purpose is at least virtual in all his activities, he runs the danger of becoming a living automaton, vain and ignominious in its mechanical constancy. Idealism about work can hide an intense materialism about life. Man, if he is a rational being, cannot live by bread alone nor be a labourer merely; he must eat and work in view of an ideal harmony which overarches all his days, and which is realized in the way they hang together, or in some ideal issue which they have in common. Otherwise, though his technical philosophy may call itself idealism, he is a materialist in morals; he esteems things, and esteems himself, for mechanical uses and energies...

The circumstances of his life hitherto have necessarily driven the American into moral materialism; for in his dealings with material things he can hardly stop to enjoy their sensible aspects, which are ideal, nor proceed at once to their ultimate uses, which are ideal too. He is practical as against the poet, and worldly as against the clear philosopher or the saint. The most striking expression of this materialism is usually supposed to be his love of the almighty dollar; but that is a foreign and unintelligent view. The American talks about money, because that is the symbol and measure he has at hand for success, intelligence, and power; but as to money itself he makes, loses, spends, and gives it away with a very light heart. To my mind the most striking expression of his materialism is his singular preoccupation with quantity. If, for instance, you visit Niagara Falls, you may expect to hear how many cubic feet or metric tons of water are precipitated per second over the cataract; how many cities and towns (with the number of their inhabitants) derive light and motive power from it; and the annual value of the further industries that might very well be carried on by the same means, without visibly depleting the world's greatest wonder or injuring the tourist trade. That is what I confidently expected to hear on arriving at the adjoining town of Buffalo; but I was deceived. The first thing I heard instead was that there are more miles

of asphalt pavement in Buffalo than in any city in the world.
Nor is this insistence on quantity confined to men of business.
The president of Harvard College, seeing me once by chance
soon after the beginning of a term, inquired how my classes
were getting on; and when I replied that I thought they were
getting on well, that my men seemed to be keen and intelligent, he stopped me as if I was about to waste his time.
'I meant,' said he, '*what is the number* of students in your
classes?'

Here I think we may perceive that this love of quantity often
has a silent partner, which is diffidence as to quality. The
democratic conscience recoils before anything that savours of
privilege; and lest it should concede an unmerited privilege
to any pursuit or person, it reduces all things as far as possible
to the common denominator of quantity. Numbers cannot lie:
but if it came to comparing the ideal beauties of philosophy
with those of Anglo-Saxon, who should decide? All studies
are good—why else have universities?—but those must be
most encouraged which attract the greatest number of students.
Hence the president's question. Democratic faith, in its diffidence about quality, throws the reins of education upon the
pupil's neck, as Don Quixote threw the reins on the neck of
Rocinante, and bids his divine instinct choose its own way...

ENGLISH LIBERTY IN AMERICA

The straits of Dover, which one may sometimes see across,
have sufficed so to isolate England that it has never moved
quite in step with the rest of Europe in politics, morals, or art.
No wonder that the Atlantic Ocean, although it has favoured
a mixed emigration and cheap intercourse, should have cut off
America so effectually that all the people there, even those of
Latin origin, have become curiously different from any kind
of European. In vain are they reputed to have the same religions or to speak the same languages as their cousins in the
old world; everything has changed its accent, spirit, and
value. Flora and fauna have been intoxicated by that un-

touched soil and fresh tonic air, and by those vast spaces; in spite of their hereditary differences of species they have all acquired the same crude savour and defiant aspect. In comparison with their European prototypes they seem tough, meagre, bold, and ugly. In the United States, apart from the fact that most of the early colonists belonged to an exceptional type of Englishman, the scale and speed of life have made everything strangely un-English. There is cheeriness instead of doggedness, confidence instead of circumspection; there is a desire to quizz and to dazzle rather than a fear of being mistaken or of being shocked; there is a pervasive cordiality, exaggeration, and farcical humour; and in the presence of the Englishman, when by chance he turns up or is thought of, there is an invincible impatience and irritation that his point of view should be so fixed, his mind so literal, and the freight he carries so excessive (when you are sailing in ballast yourself), and that he should seem to take so little notice of changes in the wind to which you are nervously sensitive.

Nevertheless there is one gift or habit, native to England, that has not only been preserved in America unchanged, but has found there a more favourable atmosphere in which to manifest its true nature—I mean the spirit of free co-operation. The root of it is free individuality, which is deeply seated in the English inner man; there is an indomitable instinct or mind in him which he perpetually consults and reveres, slow and embarrassed as his expression of it may be. But this free individuality in the Englishman is crossed and biased by a large residue of social servitude. The Church and the aristocracy, entanglement in custom and privilege, mistrust and bitterness about particular grievances, warp the inner man and enlist him against his interests in alien causes; the straits of Dover were too narrow, the shadow of a hostile continent was too oppressive, the English sod was soaked with too many dews and cut by too many hedges, for each individual, being quite master of himself, to confront every other individual without fear or prejudice, and to unite with him in the free pursuit of whatever aims they might find that they had in common. Yet this slow co-operation of free men, this liberty in democracy—the only sort that America possesses or believes in—is wholly English in its personal basis, its reserve, its tenacity, its empiricism, its public spirit, and its assurance of its own rightness; and it deserves to be called English always, to whatever countries it may spread.

The omnipresence in America of this spirit of co-operation, responsibility, and growth is very remarkable. Far from being neutralized by American dash and bravura, or lost in the opposite instincts of so many alien races, it seems to be adopted at once in the most mixed circles and in the most novel predicaments. In America social servitude is reduced to a minimum; in fact we may almost say that it is reduced to subjecting children to their mothers and to a common public education, agencies that are absolutely indispensable to produce the individual and enable him to exercise his personal initiative effectually; for after all, whatever metaphysical egotism may say, one cannot vote to be created. But once created, weaned, and taught to read and write, the young American can easily shoulder his knapsack and choose his own way in the world. He is as yet very little trammelled by want of opportunity, and he has no roots to speak of in place, class, or religion. Where individuality is so free, co-operation, when it is justified, can be all the more quick and hearty. Everywhere co-operation is taken for granted, as something that no one would be so mean or so short-sighted as to refuse. Together with the will to work and to prosper, it is of the essence of Americanism, and is accepted as such by all the unkempt polyglot peoples that turn to the new world with the pathetic but manly purpose of beginning life on a new principle. Every political body, every public meeting, every club, or college, or athletic team, is full of it. Out it comes whenever there is an accident in the street or a division in a church, or a great unexpected emergency like the late war. The general instinct is to run and help, to assume direction, to pull through somehow by mutual adaptation, and by seizing on the readiest practical measures and working compromises. Each man joins in and gives a helping hand, without a preconceived plan or a prior motive. Even the leader, when he is a natural leader and not a professional, has nothing up his sleeve to force on the rest, in their obvious goodwill and mental blankness. All meet in a genuine spirit of consultation, eager to persuade but ready to be persuaded, with a cheery confidence in their average ability, when a point comes up and is clearly put before them, to decide it for the time being, and to move on. It is implicitly agreed, in every case, that disputed questions shall be put to a vote, and that the minority will loyally acquiesce in the decision of the majority and build henceforth upon it, without a thought of ever retracting it.

Such a way of proceeding seems in America a matter of course, because it is bred in the bone, or imposed by that permeating social contagion which is so irresistible in a natural democracy. But if we consider human nature at large and the practice of most nations, we shall see that it is a very rare, wonderful, and unstable convention. It implies a rather unimaginative optimistic assumption that at bottom all men's interests are similar and compatible, and a rather heroic public spirit—such that no special interest, in so far as it has to be overruled, shall rebel and try to maintain itself absolutely. In America hitherto these conditions happen to have been actually fulfilled in an unusual measure. Interests have been very similar—to exploit business opportunities and organize public services useful to all; and these similar interests have been also compatible and harmonious. A neighbour, even a competitor, where the field is so large and so little pre-empted, has more often proved a resource than a danger. The rich have helped the public more than they have fleeced it, and they have been emulated more than hated or served by the enterprising poor. To abolish millionaires would have been to dash one's own hopes. The most opposite systems of religion and education could look smilingly upon one another's prosperity, because the country could afford these superficial luxuries, having a constitutional religion and

71

education of its own, which everybody drank in unconsciously
and which assured the moral cohesion of the people. Impulses
of reason and kindness, which are potential in all men, under
such circumstances can become effective; people can help one
another with no great sacrifice to themselves, and minorities
can dismiss their special plans without sorrow, and cheerfully
follow the crowd down another road. It was because life in
America was naturally more co-operative and more plastic
than in England that the spirit of English liberty, which
demands co-operation and plasticity, could appear there more
boldly and universally than it ever did at home.

English liberty is a method, not a goal. It is related to the
value of human life very much as the police are related to
public morals or commerce to wealth; and it is not accident
that the Anglo-Saxon race excels in commerce and in the
commercial as distinguished from the artistic side of industry,
and that having policed itself successfully it is beginning to
police the world at large. It is all an eminence in temper,
good will, reliability, accommodation. Probably some other
races, such as the Jews and Arabs, make individually better
merchants, more shrewd, patient, and loving of their art.
Englishmen and Americans often seem to miss or force opportunities, to play for quick returns, or to settle down into
ponderous corporations; for successful men they are not particularly observant, constant, or economical. But the superiority
of the Oriental is confined to his private craft; he has not the
spirit of partnership. In English civilization the individual is
neutralized; it does not matter so much even in high places
if he is rather stupid or rather cheap; public spirit sustains him,
and he becomes its instrument all the more readily, perhaps,
for not being very distinguished or clear-headed in himself.
The community prospers; comfort and science, good manners
and generous feelings are diffused among the people, without
the aid of that foresight and cunning direction which sometimes give a temporary advantage to a rival system like the
German. In the end, adaptation to the world at large, where
so much is hidden and unintelligible, is only possible piece-

meal, by groping with a genuine indetermination in one's aims. Its very looseness gives the English method its lien on the future. To dominate the world co-operation is better than policy, and empiricism safer than inspiration. Anglo-Saxon imperialism is unintended; military conquests are incidental to it and often not maintained; it subsists by a mechanical equilibrium of habits and interests, in which every colony, province, or protectorate has a different status. It has a commercial and missionary quality, and is essentially an invitation to pull together—an invitation which many nations may be incapable of accepting or even of understanding, or which they may deeply scorn, because it involves a surrender of absolute liberty on their part; but whether accepted or rejected, it is an offer of co-operation, a project for a limited partnership, not a complete plan of life to be imposed on anybody.

It is a wise instinct, in dealing with foreigners or with material things (which are foreigners to the mind), to limit oneself in this way to establishing external relations, partial mutual adjustments, with a great residuum of independence and reserve; if you attempt more you will achieve less; your interpretations will become chimerical and your regimen odious. So deep-seated is this prudent instinct in the English nature that it appears even at home; most of the concrete things which English genius has produced are expedients. Its spiritual treasures are hardly possessions, except as character is a possession; they are rather a standard of life, a promise, an insurance. English poetry and fiction form an exception; the very incoherence and artlessness which they share with so much else that is English lend them an absolute value as an expression. . . But apart from the literature that simply utters the inner man, no one considering the English language, the English Church, or English philosophy, or considering the common law and parliamentary government, would take them for perfect realizations of art or truth or an ideal polity. Institutions so jumbled and limping could never have been planned; they can never be transferred to another setting, or adopted bodily; but special circumstances and contrary currents have given them birth, and they are accepted and prized, where they are native, for keeping the door open to a great volume and variety of goods, at a moderate cost of danger and absurdity.

Of course no product of mind is *merely* an expedient; all are concomitantly expressions of temperament; there is something in their manner of being practical which is poetical and catches the rhythm of the heart. In this way anything foreign —and almost all the elements of civilization in England and America are foreign—when it is adopted and acclimatized, takes on a native accent, especially on English lips; like the Latin words in the language, it becomes thoroughly English in texture. The English Bible, again, with its archaic homeliness and majesty, sets the mind brooding, not less than the old ballad most redolent of the native past and the native imagination; it fills the memory with solemn and pungent phrases; and this incidental spirit of poetry in which it comes to be clothed is a self-revelation perhaps more pertinent and welcome to the people than the alien revelations it professes to transmit. English law and parliaments, too, would be very unjustly judged if judged as practical contrivances only; they satisfy at the same time the moral interest people have in uttering and enforcing their feelings. These institutions are ceremonious, almost sacramental; they are instinct with a dramatic spirit deeper and more vital than their utility. Englishmen and Americans love debate; they love sitting round a table as if in consultation, even when the chairman has pulled the wires and settled everything beforehand, and when each of the participants listens only to his own remarks and votes according to his party. They love committees and commissions; they love public dinners with after-dinner speeches, those stammering compounds of facetiousness, platitude, and business. How distressing such speeches usually are, and how helplessly prolonged, does not escape anybody; yet everyone demands them notwithstanding, because in pumping them up or sitting through them he feels he is leading the political life. A public man must show himself in public, even if not to advantage. The moral expressiveness of such institutions also helps to redeem their clumsy procedure; they would not be useful, nor work at all as they should, if people did not smack their lips over them and feel a profound pleasure in carrying them out. Without the English spirit, without the faculty of making themselves believe in public what they never feel in private, without the habit of clubbing together and facing facts, and feeling duty in a cautious, consultative, experimental way, English liberties forfeit their practical value; as we see when they are extended to a volatile histrionic people like the Irish, or when a jury in France, instead of pronouncing simply on matters of fact and the credibility of witnesses, rushes in the heat of its patriotism to carry out, by its verdict, some political policy.

The practice of English liberty presupposes two things: that all concerned are fundamentally unanimous, and that each has a plastic nature, which he is willing to modify. If fundamental unanimity is lacking and all are not making in the same general direction, there can be no honest co-operation, no satisfying compromise. Every concession, under such circumstances, would be a temporary one, to be retracted at the first favourable moment; it would amount to a mutilation of one's essential nature, a partial surrender of life, liberty, and happiness, tolerable for a time, perhaps, as the lesser of two evils, but involving a perpetual sullen opposition and hatred. To put things to a vote, and to accept unreservedly the decision of the majority, are points essential to the English system; but they would be absurd if fundamental agreement were not presupposed. Every decision that the majority could conceivably arrive at must leave it still possible for the minority to live and prosper, even if not exactly in the way they wished. Were this not the case, a decision by vote would be as alien a fatality to any minority as the decree of a foreign tyrant, and at every election the right of rebellion would come into play. In a hearty and sound democracy all questions at issue must be minor matters; fundamentals must have been silently agreed upon and taken for granted when the democracy arose. To leave a decision to the majority is like leaving it to chance—a fatal procedure unless one is willing to have it either way. You must be able to risk losing the toss; and if you do you will acquiesce all the more readily in the result, because, unless the winners cheated at the game, they had no more influence on it than yourself—namely none, or very little. You acquiesce in democracy on the same conditions and for the same reasons, and perhaps a little more cheerfully, because there is an infinitesimally better chance of winning on the average; but even then the enormity of the risk involved would be intolerable if anything of vital importance was at stake. It is therefore actually required that juries, whose decisions may really be of moment, should be unanimous; and parliaments and elections are never more satisfactory than when a wave of national feeling runs through them and there is no longer any minority nor any need of voting . . .

The levelling tendency of English liberty (inevitable if plastic natures are to co-operate and to make permanent concessions to one another's instincts) comes out more clearly in America than in England itself. In England there are still castles and rural retreats, there are still social islands within the Island, where special classes may nurse particular allegiances. America is all one prairie, swept by a universal tornado. Although it has always thought itself in an eminent sense the land of freedom, even when it was covered with slaves, there is no country in which people live under more overpowering compulsions. The prohibitions, although important and growing, are not yet, perhaps, so many or so blatant as in some other countries; but prohibitions are less galling than compulsions. What can be forbidden specifically —bigamy, for instance, or heresy—may be avoided by a prudent man without renouncing the whole movement of life and mind which, if carried beyond a certain point, would end in those trespasses against convention. He can indulge in hypothesis or gallantry, without falling foul of the positive law, which indeed may even stimulate his interest and ingenuity by suggesting some indirect means of satisfaction. On the other hand, what is exacted cuts deeper; it creates habits which overlay nature, and every faculty is atrophied that does not conform with them. If, for instance, I am compelled to be in an office (and up to business, too) from early morning to late afternoon, with long journeys in thundering and sweltering trains before and after and a flying shot at a quick lunch between, I am caught and held both in soul and body; and except for the freedom to work and to rise by that work—which may be very interesting in itself—I am not suffered to exist morally at all. My evenings will be drowsy, my Sundays tedious, and after a few days' holiday I shall be wishing to get back to business. Here is as narrow a path left open to freedom as is left open in a monastic establishment, where bell and book keep your attention fixed at all hours upon the hard work of salvation—an infinite vista, certainly, if your soul was not made to look another way. Those, too, who may escape this crushing routine—the invalids, the ladies, the fops—are none the less prevented by it from doing anything else with success or with a good conscience; the bubbles also must swim with the stream. Even what is best in American life is compulsory—the idealism, the zeal, the beautiful happy unison of its great moments. You must wave, you must cheer, you must push with the irresistible crowd; otherwise you will feel like a traitor, a soulless outcast, a deserted ship high and dry on the shore. In America there is but one way of being saved, though it is not peculiar to any of the official religions, which themselves must silently conform to the national orthodoxy, or else become impotent and merely ornamental. This national faith and morality are vague in idea, but inexorable in spirit; they are the gospel of work and the belief in progress. By them, in a country where all men are free, every man finds that what most matters has been settled for him beforehand.

Nevertheless, American life *is* free as a whole, because it is mobile, because every atom that swims in it has a momentum of its own which is felt and respected throughout the mass,

like the weight of an atom in the solar system, even if the
deflection it may cause is infinitesimal. In temper America is
docile and not at all tyrannical; it has not predetermined its
career, and its merciless momentum is a passive resultant.
Like some Mississippi or Niagara, it rolls its myriad drops
gently onward, being but the suction and pressure which they
exercise on one another. Any tremulous thought or playful
experiment anywhere may be a first symptom of great changes
and may seem to precipitate the cataract in a new direction.
Any snowflake in a boy's sky may become the centre for his
boule de neige, his prodigious fortune; but the monster will
melt as easily as it grew, and leaves nobody poorer for having
existed. In America there is duty everywhere, but everywhere
also there is light. I do not mean superior understanding or
even moderately wide knowledge, but openness to light, an
evident joy in seeing things clearly and doing them briskly,
which would amount to a veritable triumph of art and reason
if the affairs in which it came into play were contral and
important. The American may give an exorbitant value to
subsidiary things, but his error comes of haste in praising
what he possesses, and trusting the first praises he hears. He
can detect sharp practices, because he is capable of them, but
vanity or wickedness in the ultimate aims of a man, including
himself, he cannot detect, because he is ingenuous in that
sphere. He thinks life splendid and blameless, without stopping to consider how far folly and malice may be inherent in it.
He feels that he himself has nothing to dread, nothing to hide
or apologize for; and if he is arrogant in his ignorance, there
is often a twinkle in his eye when he is most boastful. Perhaps
he suspects that he is making a fool of himself, and he chal-
lenges the world to prove it; and his innocence is quickly gone
when he is once convinced that it exists. Accordingly the
American orthodoxy, though imperious, is not unyielding.
It has a keener sense for destiny than for policy. It is confident
of a happy and triumphant future, which it would be shameful
in any man to refuse to work for and to share; but it cannot
prefigure what that bright future is to be. While it works

feverishly in outward matters, inwardly it only watches and waits; and it feels tenderly towards the unexpressed impulses in its bosom, like a mother towards her unborn young.

There is a mystical conviction, expressed in Anglo-Saxon life and philosophy, that our labours, even when they end in failure, contribute to some ulterior achievement in which it is well they should be submerged. This Anglo-Saxon piety, in the form of trust and adaptability, reaches somewhat the same insight that more speculative religions have reached through asceticism, the insight that we must renounce our wills and deny ourselves. But to have a will remains essential to animals, and having a will we must kick against the pricks, even if philosophy thinks it foolish of us. The spirit in which parties and nations beyond the pale of English liberty confront one another is not motherly nor brotherly nor Christian. Their valorousness and morality consist in their indomitable egotism. The liberty they want is absolute liberty, a desire which is quite primitive. It may be identified with the love of life which animates all creation, or the pursuit of happiness which all men would be engaged in if they were rational. Indeed, it might even be identified with the first law of motion, that all bodies, if left free, persevere in that state of rest, or of motion in a straight line, in which they happen to find themselves. The enemies of this primitive freedom are all such external forces as make it deviate from the course it is in the habit of taking or is inclined to take; and when people begin to reflect upon their condition, they protest against this alien tyranny, and contrast in fancy what they would do if they were free with what under duress they are actually doing. All human struggles are inspired by what, in this sense, is the love of freedom. Even craving for power and possessions may be regarded as the love of a free life on a larger scale, for which more instruments and resources are needed. The apologists of absolute will are not slow, for instance, to tell us that Germany in her laborious ambitions has been pursuing the highest form of freedom, which can be attained only by organizing all the resources of the world, and the souls of all the subsidiary nations, around one luminous centre of direction and self-consciousness, such as the Prussian government was eminently fitted to furnish. Freedom to exercise absolute will methodically seems to them much better than English liberty, because it knows what it wants, pursues it intelligently, and does not rely for success on some measure of goodness in mankind at large. English liberty is so trustful! It moves by a series of checks, mutual concessions, and limited satisfactions, it counts on chivalry, sportsmanship, brotherly love, and on that rarest and least lucrative of virtues, fair-mindedness: it is a broad-based, stupid, blind adventure, groping towards an unknown goal. Who but an Englishman would think of such a thing! A fanatic, a poet, a doctrinaire, a dilettante—anyone who has a fixed aim and clear passions—will not relish English liberty. It will seem a bitter irony to him to give the name of liberty to something so muffled, exacting and oppressive. In fact English liberty is a positive infringement and surrender of the freedom most fought for and most praised in the past. It makes impossible the sort of liberty for which the Spartans died at Thermopylae, or the Christian martyrs in the arena, or the Protestant reformers at the stake; for these people all died because they would not co-operate, because they were not plastic and would never consent to lead the life dear or at least customary to other men. They insisted on being utterly different and independent and inflexible in their chosen systems, and aspired either to destroy the society around them or at least to insulate themselves in the midst of it, and live a jealous, private, unstained life of their own within their city walls or mystical conclaves. Anyone who passionately loves his particular country or passionately believes in his particular religion cannot be content with less liberty or more democracy than that; he must be free to live absolutely according to his ideal, and no hostile votes, no alien interests, must call on him to deviate from it by one iota. Such was the claim to religious liberty which has played so large a part in the revolutions and divisions of the western world. Every new heresy professed to be orthodoxy itself, purified and restored; and woe to all backsliders from the reformed faith! Even the popes, without thinking to be ironical, have often raised a wail for liberty. Such, too, was the aspiration of those medieval cities and barons who fought for their liberties and rights. Such was the aspiration even of the American declaration of independence and the American constitution: cast-iron documents, if only the spirit of co-operative English liberty had not been there to expand, embosom, soften, or transform them. So the French Revolution and the Russian one of today have aimed at establishing society once for all on some eternally just principle, and at abolishing all traditions, interests, faiths, and even words that did not belong to their system. Liberty, for all these pensive or rabid apostles of liberty, meant liberty for themselves to be just so, and to remain just so for ever, together with the most vehement defiance of anybody who might ask them, for the sake of harmony, to be a little different. They summoned every man to become free in exactly their own fashion, or have his head cut off...

Moral Philosophy

THE GENTEEL TRADITION IN
AMERICAN PHILOSOPHY[1]

Ladies and Gentlemen,—The privilege of addressing you to-day is very welcome to me, not merely for the honour of it, which is great, nor for the pleasures of travel, which are many, when it is California that one is visiting for the first time, but also because there is something I have long wanted to say which this occasion seems particularly favourable for saying. America is still a young country, and this part of it is especially so; and it would have been nothing extraordinary if, in this young country, material preoccupations had altogether absorbed people's minds, and they had been too much engrossed in living to reflect upon life, or to have any philosophy. The opposite, however, is the case. Not only have you already found time to philosophize in California, as your society proves, but the eastern colonists from the very beginning were a sophisticated race. As much as in clearing the land and fighting the Indians, they were occupied, as they expressed it, in wrestling with the Lord. The country was new, but the race was tried, chastened, and full of solemn memories. It was an old wine in new bottles; and America did not have to wait for its present universities, with their departments of academic philosophy, in order to possess a living philosophy—to have a distinct vision of the universe and definite convictions about human destiny.

Now this situation is a singular and remarkable one, and has many consequences, not all of which are equally fortunate. America is a young country with an old mentality: it has enjoyed the advantages of a child carefully brought up and thoroughly indoctrinated; it has been a wise child. But a wise child, an old head on young shoulders, always has a comic and an unpromising side. The wisdom is a little thin and verbal,

---

[1] Address delivered before the Philosophical Union of the University of California, 25 August 1911.

not aware of its full meaning and grounds; and physical and emotional growth may be stunted by it, or even deranged. Or when the child is too vigorous for that, he will develop a fresh mentality of his own, out of his observations and actual instincts; and this fresh mentality will interfere with the traditional mentality, and tend to reduce it to something perfunctory, conventional, and perhaps secretly despised. A philosopy is not genuine unless it inspires and expresses the life of those who cherish it. I do not think the hereditary philosophy of America has done much to atrophy the natural activities of the inhabitants; the wise child has not missed the joys of youth or of manhood; but what has happened is that the hereditary philosophy has grown stale, and that the academic philosophy afterwards developed has caught the stale odour from it. America is not simply, as I said a moment ago, a young country with an old mentality: it is a country with two mentalities, one a survival of the beliefs and standards of the fathers, the other an expression of the instincts, practice, and discoveries of the younger generations. In all the higher things of the mind—in religion, in literature, in the moral emotions—it is the hereditary spirit that still prevails, so much so that Mr Bernard Shaw finds that America is a hundred years behind the times. The truth is that one half of the American mind, that not occupied intensely in practical affairs, has remained, I will not say high and dry, but slightly becalmed; it has floated gently in the backwater, while, alongside, in invention and industry and social organization, the other half of the mind was leaping down a sort of Niagara Rapids. This division may be found symbolized in American architecture: a neat reproduction of the colonial mansion— with some modern comforts introduced surreptitiously— stands beside the skyscraper. The American Will inhabits the skyscraper; the American Intellect inhabits the colonial mansion. The one is the sphere of the American man; the other, at least predominantly, of the American woman. The one is all aggressive enterprise; the other is all genteel tradition.

Now, with your permission, I should like to analyse more

fully how this interesting situation has arisen, how it is qualified, and whither it tends. And in the first place we should remember what, precisely, that philosophy was which the first settlers brought with them into the country. In strictness there was more than one; but we may confine our attention to what I will call Calvinism, since it is on this that the current academic philosophy has been grafted. I do not mean exactly the Calvinism of Calvin, or even of Jonathan Edwards; for in their systems there was much that was not pure philosophy, but rather faith in the externals and history of revelation. Jewish and Christian revelation was interpreted by these men, however, in the spirit of a particular philosophy, which might have arisen under any sky, and been associated with any other religion as well as with Protestant Christianity. In fact, the philosophical principle of Calvinism appears also in the Koran, in Spinoza, and in Cardinal Newman; and persons with no very distinctive Christian belief, like Carlyle or like Professor Royce, may be nevertheless, philosophically, perfect Calvinists. Calvinism, taken in this sense, is an expression of the agonized conscience. It is a view of the world which an agonized conscience readily embraces, if it takes itself seriously, as, being agonized, of course it must. Calvinism, essentially, asserts three things: that sin exists, that sin is punished, and that it is beautiful that sin should exist to be punished. The heart of the Calvinist is therefore divided between tragic concern at his own miserable condition, and tragic exultation about the universe at large. He oscillates between a profound abasement and a paradoxical elation of the spirit. To be a Calvinist philosophically is to feel a fierce pleasure in the existence of misery, especially of one's own, in that this misery seems to manifest the fact that the Absolute is irresponsible or infinite or holy. Human nature, it feels, is totally depraved: to have the instincts and motives that we necessarily have is a great scandal, and we must suffer for it; but that scandal is requisite, since otherwise the serious importance of being as we ought to be would not have been vindicated.

To those of us who have not an agonized conscience this

87

system may seem fantastic and even unintelligible; yet it is logically and intently thought out from its emotional premises. It can take permanent possession of a deep mind here and there, and under certain conditions it can become epidemic. Imagine, for instance, a small nation with an intense vitality, but on the verge of ruin, ecstatic and distressful, having a strict and minute code of laws, that paints life in sharp and violent chiaroscuro, all pure righteousness and black abominations, and exaggerating the consequences of both perhaps to infinity. Such a people were the Jews after the exile, and again the early Protestants. If such a people is philosophical at all, it will not improbably be Calvinistic. Even in the early American communities many of these conditions were fulfilled. The nation was small and isolated; it lived under pressure and constant trial; it was acquainted with but a small range of goods and evils. Vigilance over conduct and an absolute demand for personal integrity were not merely traditional things, but things that practical sages, like Franklin and Washington, recommended to their countrymen, because they were virtues that justified themselves visibly by their fruits. But soon these happy results themselves helped to relax the pressure of external circumstances, and indirectly the pressure of the agonized conscience within. The nation became numerous; it ceased to be either ecstatic or distressful; the high social morality which on the whole it preserved took another colour; people remained honest and helpful out of good sense and good will rather than out of scrupulous adherence to any fixed principles. They retained their instinct for order, and often created order with surprising quickness; but the sanctity of law, to be obeyed for its own sake, began to escape them; it seemed too unpractical a notion, and not quite serious. In fact, the second and native-born American mentality began to take shape. The sense of sin totally evaporated. Nature, in the words of Emerson, was all beauty and commodity; and while operating on it laboriously, and drawing quick returns, the American began to drink in inspiration from it aesthetically. At the same time, in so broad a

continent, he had elbow-room. His neighbours helped more
than they hindered him; he wished their number to increase.
Goodwill became the great American virtue; and a passion
arose for counting heads, and square miles, and cubic feet, and
minutes saved—as if there had been anything to save them for.
How strange to the American now that saying of Jonathan
Edwards, that men are naturally God's enemies! Yet that is
an axiom to any intelligent Calvinist, though the words he
uses may be different. If you told the modern American that
he is totally depraved, he would think you were joking, as he
himself usually is. He is convinced that he always has been,
and always will be, victorious and blameless.

Calvinism thus lost its basis in American life. Some
emotional natures, indeed, reverted in their religious revivals
or private searchings of heart to the sources of the tradition;
for any of the radical points of view in philosophy may cease
to be prevalent, but none can cease to be possible. Other
natures, more sensitive to the moral and literary influences
of the world, preferred to abandon parts of their philosophy,
hoping thus to reduce the distance which should separate the
remainder from real life.

Meantime, if anybody arose with a special sensibility or a
technical genius, he was in great straits; not being fed sufficiently by the world, he was driven in upon his own resources.
The three American writers whose personal endowment was
perhaps the finest—Poe, Hawthorne, and Emerson—had all
a certain starved and abstract quality. They could not retail
the genteel tradition; they were too keen, too perceptive, and
too independent for that. But life offered them little digestible material, nor were they naturally voracious. They were
fastidious, and under the circumstances they were starved.
Emerson, to be sure, fed on books. There was a great
catholicity in his reading; and he showed a fine tact in his
comments, and in his way of appropriating what he read. But
he read transcendentally, not historically, to learn what he
himself felt, not what others might have felt before him.
And to feed on books, for a philosopher or a poet, is still to

starve. Books can help him to acquire form, or to avoid pitfalls; they cannot supply him with substance, if he is to have any. Therefore the genius of Poe and Hawthorne, and even of Emerson, was employed on a sort of inner play, or digestion of vacancy. It was a refined labour, but it was in danger of being morbid, or tinkling, or self-indulgent. It was a play of intra-mental rhymes. Their mind was like an old music-box, full of tender echoes and quaint fancies. These fancies expressed their personal genius sincerely, as dreams may; but they were arbitrary fancies in comparison with what a real observer would have said in the premises. Their manner, in a word, was subjective. In their own persons they escaped the mediocrity of the genteel tradition, but they supplied nothing to supplant it in other minds.

The churches, likewise, although they modified their spirit, had no philosophy to offer save a new emphasis on parts of what Calvinism contained. The theology of Calvin, we must remember, had much in it besides philosophical Calvinism. A Christian tenderness, and a hope of grace for the individual, came to mitigate its sardonic optimism; and it was these evangelical elements that the Calvinistic churches now emphasized, seldom and with blushes referring to hell fire or infant damnation. Yet philosophic Calvinism, with a theory of life that would perfectly justify hell fire and infant damnation if they happened to exist, still dominates the traditional metaphysics. It is an ingredient, and the decisive ingredient, in what calls itself idealism. But in order to see just what part Calvinism plays in current idealism, it will be necessary to distinguish the other chief element in that complex system, namely, transcendentalism.

Transcendentalism is the philosophy which the romantic era produced in Germany, and independently, I believe, in America also. Transcendentalism proper, like romanticism, is not any particular set of dogmas about what things exist; it is not a system of the universe regarded as a fact, or as a collection of facts. It is a method, a point of view, from which any world, no matter what it might contain, could be ap-

proached by a self-conscious observer. Transcendentalism is
systematic subjectivism. It studies the perspectives of knowledge as they radiate from the self; it is a plan of those avenues
of inference by which our ideas of things must be reached,
if they are to afford any systematic or distant vistas. In other
words, transcendentalism is the critical logic of science. Knowledge, it says, has a station, as in a watch-tower; it is always
seated here and now, in the self of the moment. The past and
the future, things inferred and things conceived, lie around it,
painted as upon a panorama. They cannot be lighted up save
by some centrifugal ray of attention and present interest, by
some active operation of the mind.

This is hardly the occasion for developing or explaining
this delicate insight; suffice it to say, lest you should think
later that I disparage transcendentalism, that as a method I
regard it as correct and, when once suggested, unforgettable.
I regard it as the chief contribution made in modern times to
speculation. But it is a method only, an attitude we may always
assume if we like and that will always be legitimate. It is no
answer, and involves no particular answer, to the question:
What exists; in what order is what exists produced; what is to
exist in the future? This question must be answered by observing the object, and tracing humbly the movement of the
object. It cannot be answered at all by harping on the fact that
this object, if discovered, must be discovered by somebody,
and by somebody who has an interest in discovering it. Yet
the Germans who first gained the full transcendental insight
were romantic people; they were more or less frankly poets;
they were colossal egotists, and wished to make not only
their own knowledge but the whole universe centre about
themselves. And full as they were of their romantic isolation
and romantic liberty, it occurred to them to imagine that all
reality might be a transcendental self and a romantic dreamer
like themselves; nay, that it might be just their own transcendental self and their own romantic dreams extended indefinitely. Transcendental logic, the method of discovery for
the mind, was to become also the method of evolution in

91

nature and history. Transcendental method, so abused, produced transcendental myth. A conscientious critique of knowledge was turned into a sham system of nature. We must therefore distinguish sharply the transcendental grammar of the intellect, which is significant and potentially correct, from the various transcendental systems of the universe, which are chimeras.

In both its parts, however, transcendentalism had much to recommend it to American philosophers, for the transcendental method appealed to the individualistic and revolutionary temper of their youth, while transcendental myths enabled them to find a new status for their inherited theology, and to give what parts of it they cared to preserve some semblance of philosophical backing. This last was the use to which the transcendental method was put by Kant himself, who first brought it into vogue, before the terrible weapon had got out of hand, and become the instrument of pure romanticism. Kant came, he himself said, to remove knowledge in order to make room for faith, which in his case meant faith in Calvinism. In other words, he applied the transcendental method to matters of fact, reducing them thereby to human ideas, in order to give to the Calvinistic postulates of conscience a metaphysical validity. For Kant had a genteel tradition of his own, which he wished to remove to a place of safety, feeling that the empirical world had become too hot for it; and this place of safety was the region of transcendental myth. I need hardly say how perfectly this expedient suited the needs of philosophers in America, and it is no accident if the influence of Kant soon became dominant here. To embrace this philosophy was regarded as a sign of profound metaphysical insight, although the most mediocre minds found no difficulty in embracing it. In truth it was a sign of having been brought up in the genteel tradition, of feeling it weak, and of wishing to save it.

But the transcendental method, in its way, was also sympathetic to the American mind. It embodied, in a radical form, the spirit of Protestantism as distinguished from its inherited doctrines; it was autonomous, undismayed, calmly revolutionary; it felt that Will was deeper than Intellect; it focused everything here and now, and asked all things to show their credentials at the bar of the young self, and to prove their value for this latest born moment. These things are truly American; they would be characteristic of any young society with a keen and discursive intelligence, and they are strikingly exemplified in the thought and in the person of Emerson. They constitute what he called self-trust. Self-trust, like other transcendental attitudes, may be expressed in metaphysical fables. The romantic spirit may imagine itself to be an absolute force, evoking and moulding the plastic world to express its varying moods. But for a pioneer who is actually a world-builder this metaphysical illusion has a partial warrant in historical fact; far more warrant than it could boast of in the fixed and articulated society of Europe, among the moon-struck rebels and sulking poets of the romantic era. Emerson was a shrewd Yankee, by instinct on the winning side; he was a cheery, child-like soul, impervious to the evidence of evil, as of everything that it did not suit his transcendental individuality to appreciate or to notice. More, perhaps, than anybody that has ever lived, he practised the transcendental method in all its purity. He had no system. He opened his eyes on the world every morning with a fresh sincerity, marking how things seemed to him then, or what they suggested to his spontaneous fancy. This fancy, for being spontaneous, was not always novel; it was guided by the habits and training of his mind, which were those of a preacher. Yet he never insisted on his notions so as to turn them into settled dogmas; he felt in his bones that they were myths. Sometimes, indeed, the bad example of other transcendentalists, less true than he to their method, or the pressing questions of unintelligent people, or the instinct we all have to think our ideas final, led him to the very verge of system-making; but he stopped short. Had he made a system out of his notion of Compensation, or the Over-Soul, or Spiritual Laws, the result would have been as thin and forced as it is in other transcendental systems. But he coveted truth; and he returned to experience, to history, to poetry, to the natural science of his day, for new starting-points and hints toward fresh transcendental musings.

To covet truth is a very distinguished passion. Every philosopher says he is pursuing the truth, but this is seldom the case. As Mr Bertrand Russell has observed, one reason why philosophers often fail to reach the truth is that often they do not desire to reach it. Those who are genuinely concerned in discovering what happens to be true are rather the men of science, the naturalists, the historians; and ordinarily they discover it, according to their lights. The truths they find are never complete, and are not always important; but they are integral parts of the truth, facts and circumstances that help to fill in the picture, and that no later interpretation can invalidate or afford to contradict. But professional philosophers are usually only apologists: that is, they are absorbed in defending some vested illusion or some eloquent idea. Like lawyers or detectives, they study the case for which they are retained, to see how much evidence or semblance of evidence they can gather for the defence, and how much prejudice they can raise against the witnesses for the prosecution; for they know they are defending prisoners suspected by the world, and perhaps by their own good sense, of falsification. They do not covet truth, but victory and the dispelling of their own doubts. What they defend is some system, that is, some view about the totality of things, of which men are actually ignorant. No system would have ever been framed if people had been simply interested in knowing what is true, whatever it may be. What produces systems is the interest in maintaining against all comers that some favourite or inherited idea of ours is sufficient and right. A system may contain an account of many things which, in detail, are true enough; but as a system, covering infinite possibilities that neither our experience nor our logic can prejudge, it must be a work of imagination and a piece of human soliloquy. It may be expressive of human experience, it may be poetical; but how should anyone who really coveted truth suppose that it was true?

Emerson had no system; and his coveting truth had another exceptional consequence: he was detached, unworldly, contemplative. When he came out of the conventicle or the reform meeting, or out of the rapturous close atmosphere of the lecture-room, he heard nature whispering to him: 'Why so hot, little sir?' No doubt the spirit or energy of the world is what is acting in us, as the sea is what rises in every little wave; but it passes through us, and cry out as we may, it will move on. Our privilege is to have perceived it as it moves. Our dignity is not in what we do, but in what we understand. The whole world is doing things. We are turning in that vortex; yet within us is silent observation, the speculative eye before which all passes, which bridges the distances and compares the combatants. On this side of his genius Emerson broke away from all conditions of age or country and represented nothing except intelligence itself.

There was another element in Emerson, curiously combined with transcendentalism, namely, his love and respect for nature. Nature, for the transcendentalist, is precious because it is his own work, a mirror in which he looks at himself and says (like a poet relishing his own verses), 'What a genius I am! Who would have thought there was such stuff in me?' And the philosophical egotist finds in his doctrine a ready explanation of whatever beauty and commodity nature actually has. No wonder, he says to himself, that nature is sympathetic, since I made it. And such a view, one-sided and even fatuous as it may be, undoubtedly sharpens the vision of a poet and a moralist to all that is inspiriting and symbolic in the natural world. Emerson was particularly ingenious and clear-sighted in feeling the spiritual uses of fellowship with the elements. This is something in which all Teutonic poetry is rich and which forms, I think, the most genuine and spontaneous part of modern taste, and especially of American taste. Just as some people are naturally enthralled and refreshed by music, so others are by landscape. Music and landscape make up the spiritual resources of those who cannot or dare not express their unfulfilled ideals in words. Serious poetry, profound religion (Calvinism, for instance), are the joys of an unhappiness that confesses itself; but when a genteel tradition forbids people to confess that they are unhappy, serious poetry and profound religion are closed by that; and since human life, in its depths, cannot then express itself openly, imagination is driven for comfort into abstract arts, where human circumstances are lost sight of, and human problems dissolve in a purer medium. The pressure of care is thus relieved, without its quietus being found in intelligence. To understand oneself is the classic form of consolation; to elude oneself is the romantic. In the presence of music or landscape human experience eludes itself; and thus romanticism is the bond between transcendental and naturalistic sentiment. The winds and clouds come to minister to the solitary ego.

Have there been, we may ask, any successful efforts to escape from the genteel tradition, and to express something worth expressing behind its back? This might well not have occurred as yet; but America is so precocious, it has been trained by the genteel tradition to be so wise for its years, that some indications of a truly native philosophy and poetry are already to be found. I might mention the humorists, of whom you here in California have had your share. The humorists, however, only half escape the genteel tradition; their humour would lose its savour if they had wholly escaped it. They point to what contradicts it in the facts; but not in order to abandon the genteel tradition, for they have nothing solid to put in its place. When they point out how ill many facts fit into it, they do not clearly conceive that this militates against the standard, but think it a funny perversity in the facts. Of course, did they earnestly respect the genteel tradition, such an incongruity would seem to them sad, rather than ludicrous. Perhaps the prevalence of humour in America, in and out of season, may be taken as one more evidence that the genteel tradition is present pervasively, but everywhere weak. Similarly in Italy, during the Renaissance, the Catholic tradition could not be banished from the intellect, since there was nothing articulate to take its place; yet its hold on the heart was singularly relaxed. The consequence was that humorists could regale themselves with the foibles of monks and of cardinals, with the credulity of fools, and the bogus miracles of the saints; not intending to deny the theory of the Church, but caring for it so little at heart that they could find it infinitely amusing that it should be contradicted in men's lives and that no harm should come of it. So when Mark Twain says, 'I was born of poor but dishonest parents', the humour depends on the parody of the genteel Anglo-Saxon convention that it is disreputable to be poor; but to hint at the hollowness of it would not be amusing if it did not remain at bottom one's habitual conviction.

The one American writer who has left the genteel tradition entirely behind is perhaps Walt Whitman. For this reason educated Americans find him rather an unpalatable person, who they sincerely protest ought not to be taken for a representative of their culture; and he certainly should not, because their culture is so genteel and traditional. But the foreigner may sometimes think otherwise, since he is looking for what may have arisen in America to express, not the polite and conventional American mind, but the spirit and the inarticulate principles that animate the community, on which its own genteel mentality seems to sit rather lightly. When the foreigner opens the pages of Walt Whitman, he thinks that he has come at last upon something representative and original. In Walt Whitman democracy is carried into psychology and morals. The various sights, moods, and emotions are given each one vote; they are declared to be all free and equal, and the innumerable commonplace moments of life are suffered to speak like the others. Those moments formerly reputed great are not excluded, but they are made to march in the ranks with their companions—plain foot-soldiers and servants of the hour. Nor does the refusal to discriminate stop there; we must carry our principle further down, to the animals, to inanimate nature, to the cosmos as a whole. Whitman became a pantheist; but his pantheism, unlike that of the Stoics and of

97

Spinoza, was unintellectual, lazy, and self-indulgent; for he simply felt jovially that everything real was good enough, and that he was good enough himself. In him Bohemia rebelled against the genteel tradition; but the reconstruction that alone can justify revolution did not ensue. His attitude, in principle, was utterly disintegrating; his poetic genius fell back to the lowest level, perhaps, to which it is possible for poetic genius to fall. He reduced his imagination to a passive sensorium for the registering of impressions. No element of construction remained in it, and therefore no element of penetration. But his scope was wide; and his lazy, desultory apprehension was poetical. His work, for the very reason that it is so rudimentary, contains a beginning, or rather many beginnings, that might possibly grow into a noble moral imagination, a worthy filling for the human mind. An American in the nineteenth century who completely disregarded the genteel tradition could hardly have done more.

But there is another distinguished man, lately lost to this country, who has given some rude shocks to this tradition and who, as much as Whitman, may be regarded as representing the genuine, the long silent American mind—I mean William James. He and his brother Henry were as tightly swaddled in the genteel tradition as any infant geniuses could be, for they were born before 1850, and in a Swedenborgian household. Yet they burst those bands almost entirely. The ways in which the two brothers freed themselves, however, are interestingly different. Mr Henry James has done it by adopting the point of view of the outer world, and by turning the genteel American tradition, as he turns everything else, into a subject-matter for analysis. For him it is a curious habit of mind, intimately comprehended, to be compared with other habits of mind, also well known to him. Thus he has overcome the genteel tradition in the classic way, by understanding it. With William James too this infusion of worldly insight and European sympathies was a potent influence, especially in his earlier days; but the chief source of his liberty was another. It was his personal spontaneity, similar to that of Emerson, and his personal vitality, similar to that of nobody else. Convictions and ideas came to him, so to speak, from the subsoil. He had a prophetic sympathy with the dawning sentiments of the age, with the moods of the dumb majority. His scattered words caught fire in many parts of the world. His way of thinking and feeling represented the true America, and represented in a measure the whole ultra-modern, radical world. Thus he eluded the genteel tradition in the romantic way, by continuing it into its opposite. The romantic mind, glorified in Hegel's dialectic (which is not dialectic at all, but a sort of tragi-comic history of experience), is always rendering its thoughts unrecognizable through the infusion of new insights, and through the insensible transformation of the moral feeling that accompanies them, till at last it has completely reversed its old judgments under cover of expanding them. Thus the genteel tradition was led a merry dance when it fell again into the hands of a genuine and vigorous romanticist like William James. He restored their revolutionary force to its neutralized elements, by picking them out afresh, and emphasizing them separately, according to his personal predilections.

For one thing, William James kept his mind and heart wide open to all that might seem, to polite minds, odd, personal, or visionary in religion and philosophy. He gave a sincerely respectful hearing to sentimentalists, mystics, spiritualists, wizards, cranks, quacks, and impostors—for it is hard to draw the line, and James was not willing to draw it prematurely. He thought, with his usual modesty, that any of these might have something to teach him. The lame, the halt, the blind, and those speaking with tongues could come to him with the certainty of finding sympathy; and if they were not healed, at least they were comforted, that a famous professor should take them so seriously; and they began to feel that after all to have only one leg, or one hand, or one eye, or to have three, might be in itself no less beauteous than to have just two, like the stolid majority. Thus William James became the friend and helper of those groping, nervous, half-educated, spiritually disinherited, passionately hungry individuals of which

America is full. He became, at the same time, their spokesman and representative before the learned world; and he made it a chief part of his vocation to recast what the learned world has to offer, so that as far as possible it might serve the needs and interests of these people.

Yet the normal practical masculine American, too, had a friend in William James. There is a feeling abroad now, to which biology and Darwinism lend some colour, that theory is simply an instrument for practice, and intelligence merely a help toward material survival. Bears, it is said, have fur and claws, but poor naked man is condemned to be intelligent, or he will perish. This feeling William James embodied in that theory of thought and of truth which he called pragmatism. Intelligence, he thought, is no miraculous, idle faculty, by which we mirror passively any or everything that happens to be true, reduplicating the real world to no purpose. Intelligence has its roots and its issue in the context of events; it is one kind of practical adjustment, an experimental act, a form of vital tension. It does not essentially serve to picture other parts of reality, but to connect them. This view was not worked out by William James in its psychological and historical details; unfortunately he developed it chiefly in controversy against its opposite, which he called intellectualism, and which he hated with all the hatred of which his kind heart was capable. Intellectualism, as he conceived it, was pure pedantry; it impoverished and verbalized everything, and tied up nature in red tape. Ideas and rules that may have been occasionally useful it put in the place of the full-blooded irrational movement of life which had called them into being; and these abstractions, so soon obsolete, it strove to fix and to worship for ever. Thus all creeds and theories and all formal precepts sink in the estimation of the pragmatist to a local and temporary grammar of action; a grammar that must be changed slowly by time, and may be changed quickly by genius. To know things as a whole, or as they are eternally, if there is anything eternal in them, is not only beyond our powers, but would prove worthless, and perhaps even fatal to our lives.

Ideas are not mirrors, they are weapons; their function is to prepare us to meet events, as future experience may unroll them. Those ideas that disappoint us are false ideas; those to which events are true are true themselves.

This may seem a very utilitarian view of the mind; and I confess I think it a partial one, since the logical force of beliefs and ideas, their truth or falsehood as assertions, has been overlooked altogether, or confused with the vital force of the material processes which these ideas express. It is an external view only, which marks the place and conditions of the mind in nature, but neglects its specific essence; as if a jewel were defined as a round hole in a ring. Nevertheless, the more materialistic the pragmatist's theory of the mind is, the more vitalistic his theory of nature will have to become. If the intellect is a device produced in organic bodies to expedite their processes, these organic bodies must have interests and a chosen direction in their life; otherwise their life could not be expedited, nor could anything be useful to it. In other words—and this is a third point at which the philosophy of William James has played havoc with the genteel tradition, while ostensibly defending it—nature must be conceived anthropomorphically and in psychological terms. Its purposes are not to be static harmonies, self-unfolding destinies, the logic of spirit, the spirit of logic, or any other formal method and abstract law; its purposes are to be concrete endeavours, finite efforts of souls living in an environment which they transform and by which they, too, are affected. A spirit, the divine spirit as much as the human, as this new animism conceives it, is a romantic adventurer. Its future is undetermined. Its scope, its duration, and the quality of its life are all contingent. This spirit grows; it buds and sends forth feelers, sounding the depths around for such other centres of force or life as may exist there. It has a vital momentum, but no predetermined goal. It uses its past as a stepping-stone, or rather as a diving-board, but has an absolutely fresh will at each moment to plunge this way or that into the unknown. The universe is an experiment; it is unfinished. It has no ultimate or total nature, because it has no end. It embodies no formula or statable law; any formula is at best a poor abstraction, describing what, in some region and for some time, may be the most striking characteristic of existence; the law is a description *a posteriori* of the habit things have chosen to acquire, and which they may possibly throw off altogether. What a day may bring forth is uncertain; uncertain even to God. Omniscience is impossible; time is real; what had been omniscience hitherto might discover something more today. 'There shall be news,' William James was fond of saying with rapture, quoting from the unpublished poem of an obscure friend, 'there shall be news in heaven!' There is almost certainly, he thought, a God now; there may be several gods, who might exist together, or one after the other. We might, by our conspiring sympathies, help to make a new one. Much in us is doubtless immortal; we survive death for some time in a recognizable form; but what our career and transformations may be in the sequel we cannot tell, although we may help to determine them by our daily choices. Observation must be continual if our ideas are to remain true. Eternal vigilance is the price of knowledge; perpetual hazard, perpetual experiment keep quick the edge of life.

This is, so far as I know, a new philosophical vista; it is a conception never before presented, although implied, perhaps, in various quarters, as in Norse and even Greek mythology. It is a vision radically empirical and radically romantic; and as William James himself used to say, the visions and not the arguments of a philosopher are the interesting and influential things about him. William James, rather too generously, attributed this vision to M. Bergson, and regarded him in consequence as a philosopher of the first rank, whose thought was to be one of the turning-points in history. M. Bergson had killed intellectualism. It was his book on creative evolution, said James with humorous emphasis, that had come at last to '*écraser l'infâme*'. We may suspect, notwithstanding, that intellectualism, infamous and crushed, will survive the blow; and if the author of the Book of Ecclesiastes were now alive, and heard that there shall be news in heaven, he would doubtless say that there may possibly be news there, but that under the sun there is nothing new—not even radical empiricism or radical romanticism, which from the beginning of the world has been the philosophy of those who as yet had had little experience; for to the blinking little child it is not merely something in the world that is new daily, but everything is new all day.

I am not concerned with the rights and wrongs of that controversy; my point is only that William James, in this genial evolutionary view of the world, has given a rude shock to the genteel tradition. What! The world a gradual improvisation? Creation unpremeditated? God a sort of young poet or struggling artist? William James is an advocate of theism; pragmatism adds one to the evidences of religion; that is excellent. But is not the cool abstract piety of the genteel getting more than it asks for? This empirical naturalistic God is too crude and positive a force; he will work miracles, he will answer prayers, he may inhabit distinct places, and have distinct conditions under which alone he can operate; he is a neighbouring being, whom we can act upon, and rely upon for specific aids, as upon a personal friend, or a physician, or an insurance company. How disconcerting! Is not this new theology a little like superstition? And yet how interesting, how exciting, if it should happen to be true! I am far from wishing to suggest that such a view seems to me more probable than conventional idealism or than Christian orthodoxy. All three are in the region of dramatic system-making and myth to which probabilities are irrelevant. If one man says the moon is sister to the sun, and another that she is his daughter, the question is not which notion is more probable, but whether either of them is at all expressive. The so-called evidences are devised afterwards, when faith and imagination have prejudged the issue. The force of William James's new theology, or romantic cosmology, lies only in this: that it has broken the spell of the genteel tradition, and enticed faith in a new direction, which on second thoughts may prove no less alluring than the old. The important fact is not that the new fancy might possibly be true—who shall know that?—but that it has entered the heart of a leading American to conceive and to cherish it. The genteel tradition cannot be dislodged by these insurrections; there are circles to which it is still congenial, and where it will be preserved. But it has been challenged and (what is perhaps more insidious) it has been discovered. No one need be browbeaten any longer into accepting it. No one need be afraid, for instance, that his fate is sealed because some young prig may call him a dualist; the pint would call the quart a dualist, if you tried to pour the quart into him. We need not be afraid of being less profound, for being direct and sincere. The intellectual world may be traversed in many directions; the whole has not been surveyed; there is a great career in it open to talent. That is a sort of knell, that tolls the passing of the genteel tradition. Something else is now in the field; something else can appeal to the imagination, and be a thousand times more idealistic than academic idealism, which is often simply a way of whitewashing and adoring things as they are. The illegitimate monopoly which the genteel tradition had established over what ought to be assumed and what ought to be hoped for has been broken down by the first-born of the family, by the genius of the race. Henceforth there can hardly be the same peace and the same pleasure in hugging the old proprieties. Hegel will be to the next generation what Sir William Hamilton was to the last. Nothing will have been disproved, but everything will have been abandoned. An honest man has spoken, and the cant of the genteel tradition has become harder for young lips to repeat.

With this I have finished such a sketch as I am here able to offer you of the genteel tradition in American philosophy. The subject is complex, and calls for many an excursus and qualifying footnote; yet I think the main outlines are clear enough. The chief fountains of this tradition were Calvinism and transcendentalism. Both were living fountains; but to keep them alive they required, one an agonized conscience, and the other a radical subjective criticism of knowledge. When these rare metaphysical preoccupations disappeared—and the American atmosphere is not favourable to either of them—the two systems ceased to be inwardly understood; they subsisted as sacred mysteries only; and the combination of the two in some transcendental system of the universe (a contradiction in principle) was doubly artificial. Besides, it could hardly be held with a single mind. Natural science, history, the beliefs implied in labour and invention, could not be disregarded altogether; so that the transcendental philosopher was condemned to a double allegiance, and to not letting his left hand know the bluff that his right hand was making. Nevertheless, the difficulty in bringing practical inarticulate convictions to expression is very great, and the genteel tradition has subsisted in the academic mind for want of anything equally academic to take its place.

The academic mind, however, has had its flanks turned. On the one side came the revolt of the Bohemian temperament, with its poetry of crude naturalism; on the other side came an impassioned empiricism, welcoming popular religious witnesses to the unseen, reducing science to an instrument of success in action, and declaring the universe to be wild and young, and not to be harnessed by the logic of any school.

This revolution, I should think, might well find an echo among you, who live in a thriving society, and in the presence of a virgin and prodigious world. When you transform nature to your uses, when you experiment with her forces, and reduce them to industrial agents, you cannot feel that nature was made by you or for you, for then these adjustments would have been pre-established. Much less can you feel it when she destroys your labour of years in a momentary spasm. You must feel, rather, that you are an offshoot of her life; one brave little force among her immense forces. When you escape, as you love to do, to your forests and your sierras, I am sure again that you do not feel you made them, or that they were made for you. They have grown, as you have grown, only more massively and more slowly. In their non-

human beauty and peace they stir the subhuman depths and
the superhuman possibilities of your own spirit. It is no transcendental logic that they teach; and they give no sign of any
deliberate morality seated in the world. It is rather the vanity
and superficiality of all logic, the needlessness of argument,
the relativity of morals, the strength of time, the fertility of
matter, the variety, the unspeakable variety, of possible life.
Everything is measurable and conditioned, indefinitely repeated, yet, in repetition, twisted somewhat from its old form.
Everywhere is beauty and nowhere permanence, everywhere
an incipient harmony, nowhere an intention, nor a responsibility, nor a plan. It is the irresistible suasion of this daily
spectacle, it is the daily discipline of contact with things, so
different from the verbal discipline of the schools, that will,
I trust, inspire the philosophy of your children. A Californian
whom I had recently the pleasure of meeting observed that,
if the philosophers had lived among your mountains, their
systems would have been different from what they are.
Certainly, I should say, very different from what those systems are which the European genteel tradition has handed
down since Socrates; for these systems are egotistical; directly
or indirectly they are anthropocentric, and inspired by the
conceited notion that man, or human reason, or the human
distinction between good and evil, is the centre and pivot of
the universe. That is what the mountains and the woods
should make you at last ashamed to assert. From what, indeed,
does the society of nature liberate you, that you find it so
sweet? It is hardly (is it?) that you wish to forget your past,
or your friends, or that you have any secret contempt for
your present ambitions. You respect these, you respect them
perhaps too much; you are not suffered by the genteel tradition to criticize or to reform them at all radically. No; it is the
yoke of this genteel tradition itself that these primeval soli-
tudes lift from your shoulders. They suspend your forced
sense of your own importance not merely as individuals, but
even as men. They allow you, in one happy moment, at once
to play and to worship, to take yourselves simply, humbly,

for what you are, and to salute the wild, indifferent, non-censorious infinity of nature. You are admonished that what you can do avails little materially, and in the end nothing. At the same time, through wonder and pleasure, you are taught speculation. You learn what you are really fitted to do, and where lie your natural dignity and joy, namely, in representing many things, without being them, and in letting your imagination, through sympathy, celebrate and echo their life. Because the peculiarity of man is that his machinery for reaction on external things has involved an imaginative transcript of these things, which is preserved and suspended in his fancy; and the interest and beauty of this inward landscape, rather than any fortunes that may await his body in the outer world, constitute his proper happiness. By their mind, its scope, quality, and temper, we estimate men, for by the mind only do we exist as men, and are more than so many storage-batteries for material energy. Let us therefore be frankly human. Let us be content to live in the mind.

PLOTINUS AND THE NATURE
OF EVIL[1]

The age of Plotinus was in many ways the opposite of our
own. In the last days of antiquity the only great enterprises
open to men were spiritual and internal to the soul. Not
that the philosophers would have been unwilling to make
themselves comfortable in the world and to govern it (as the
conservatives would like to do now) in the spirit of their
inherited polity and religion; but the ruffians, christened and
unchristened, had got out of hand and would not let them.
To the ruffians, accordingly, they sadly abandoned the world,
and turned to chastening their unused passions and pondering
on supernatural things: for if there was a 'general loss of
nerve',* there was no loss of intellectual fire. The tide of
metaphysical religion was then rising which is ebbing now, and
earth-loving Christians of today are naturally out of sympathy
with the rapt consolations of those last earth-spurning pagans.

He [Fuller] maintains that the theory of evil is on the
horns of a dilemma between naturalism and mysticism. We
may choose to be naturalists; but then we must hold, he
thinks, that all kinds of good are equal and incommensurable,
anything perfect after its kind being as perfect as anything else
can be. No hierarchy of goods will be admissible in which one
good should be better than another in kind. Everyone should
be perfectly satisfied with his own nature and be incapable
of regarding any different endowment as more desirable.
Mr Fuller views this naturalistic ideal with some enthusiasm.
Could it be realized everyone would be a god, perfect after
his kind, without the least suspicion of envy of any other
being, and the welkin would ring with a chorus of universal
self-satisfaction.

[1] Review of B. A. G. Fuller, *The Problem of Evil in Plotinus*.
* See the preface to Professor Gilbert Murray's *Four Stages of Greek Religion*.

After all, this is not so fantastic a proposal; men faithfully carry it out in considering all other animals, even winged ones, hopelessly inferior to themselves, and thinking no God worthy of the name who should not be endowed with a human consciousness and with human principles of justice and economy. Even special tribes of men have their specific ideals; I know of no nation, and hardly of a province, that does not think itself the best in the world. 'I was born in Aragon', runs a Spanish ditty, 'because such was the will of God; still, if I had had my choice, I should have been born in Aragon.' Could a Bostonian feel differently? And who has not been struck by the weary contempt our radical friends express for any heaven that should not call for reform? The naturalist in ethics should give his blessing impartially to all such homespun ideals, although, I should say, only on two conditions: first, that these ideals be radically sincere and adequate to the actual nature and capacities of the creatures that accept them (as most conventional and religious ideals are not); and, second, that, in natural philosophy, everyone should admit the similar vital status and internal authority of all the ideals in competition. This last requirement, which sounds so preternaturally liberal, is also often fulfilled in practice. Animals are not blamed for their instincts, even if inconvenient to us, but rather admired; and this occurs precisely in so far as the irrelevance of their nature to the human is realized imaginatively. Animals do not speak; they do not compel us to rehearse in words sentiments abhorrent to our nature and habits. Therefore, they do not exasperate us or rouse in us that fanatical impulse to persecute which expresses our deep and just desire to be uncontradicted and at peace within ourselves. Had animals spoken, the Inquisition would have had a pretty work on its hands.

If this ethical naturalism offends us, with its democracy of disparate ideals, Mr Fuller will allow us no refuge except in ethical mysticism. Every good except the highest must then be imperfect in our sight; evil will be identical with finitude, and the hierarchy of ascending goods will be simply a series of diminishing evils. The stages of natural happiness will become so many stages of spiritual misery. Virtue will be the consciousness of sin, sin the original condition of life and existence. Paradoxical as it may seem, we shall be optimists notwithstanding; for it will be clear to us that evil is an epithet blindly used, and that the consciousness of sin and unworthiness is merely a needful illusion, whatever we call evil being in itself a modicum of good and an integrating element in the greatest good possible. Our optimism, as Mr Bradley once candidly put it, will consist in maintaining that 'the world is the best possible world, and everything in it is a necesary evil'.

Such is the alternative before which Mr Fuller's analysis places us—and his analysis is very incisive: either all excellences are absolute and incomparable, or there is no excellence but one. Before resigning myself to this choice, however, I should like to consider one or two circumstances that may affect the question. Why, for instance, do actual naturalists so seldom remark this parity and independence among various perfections, which Mr Fuller's ideal naturalist proclaims so loudly? We have just seen that almost everyone thinks his chosen type of perfection alone good, or by far the best. Does not the reason lie in this, that the parity among ideals is in truth a natural parity only, a parity in a field beneath or beyond all moral comparison? Moral comparisons are possible only in view of each ideal, and after some ideal has been virtually set up. The living dispositions by which various ideals are determined are pre-moral; they cannot be said to be equal morally because they are biological facts only, without any moral status at all. The values which may be assigned to them eventually are assigned by some one of them, already in operation, in proportion as they are useful, congenial, or stimulating to its own expression. Hence each nature ordinarily pronounces itself to be good, but imperfect, since it stumbles and creaks as it goes, and it pronounces other natures to be good or bad by turns and in various degrees, according to their kinship or co-operation with itself.

This naturalism in respect to ethics is not itself an ethical system; it is no pronouncement on the better and the worse. It is a biological and historical doctrine, a part of naturalism in general. What it asserts is that moral distinctions are natural, that they arise and vary with the endeavours and interests of living beings. The various ideals and types of perfection themselves, if a vital interest finds them propitious or antipathetic, are qualified and graded morally in view of that interest; and they could not otherwise be judged at all. Truly, as Mr Fuller says, among various perfections one is as perfect as another, and a perfect glove is as truly perfect as a perfect family: but I, being a naturalist, do not feel compelled to assert in consequence that a perfect family is not the greater good. Perfections may be differently prized, though each be as perfect as every other, because various sorts of perfect objects are not of equal consequence to a given animal nor in a given ideal. So when Mr Benedetto Croce tells us that all expressions, if successful, are equally perfect works of art, and that a perfect Neapolitan sigh is aesthetically equal to the *Iliad*, I should be far from wishing to contradict him; only I should feel that the aesthetic quality so defined was interesting to aesthetes only, and that man must continue to value and to compare works of art on far more humane and complex principles. Just because goods are relative to living interests, each interest may establish a hierarchy among the several goods it recognizes, according to the depth and force of its need for them. Various kinds of good are incommensurable only when the living interests that posit them are wholly disparate. Thus, it might be impossible to compare the intrinsic value of a perfect gnat with that of a perfect elephant or the intrinsic value of mere love with that of mere knowledge; yet the gnat and the elephant, love and knowledge, might perfectly well have comparable and unequal values for the interests and in the environment of a third party; and they might even be inwardly subordinated in the imagination of some god capable of sympathizing perfectly with both and of weaving these distinct experiences together.

111

This privilege, native to every creature, of arranging different perfections imagined by it in a scale of ascending values, relieves the naturalist of the charge of indifference and anarchy in morals; for the naturalist has a nature of his own, and if he learns to know himself, he will have a clear and dogmatic system of ethics. The same circumstance relieves Plotinus of the charge Mr Fuller brings against him of confusing kinds with degrees of perfection; for Plotinus conceived that the universe was but a single living creature, with no wholly disparate interests existing in it, since all things had been created by the magic of a single good, and by nature converged upon it, though at various removes; so that the respective perfections of all these stages were thoroughly relevant to one another, and definitely subordinated in the life and meaning of the whole. It was as if in a written sentence we urged that the perfection of each letter was incomparable with that of each word, and not a stage towards it, and so, again, of each word in respect of the perfection of the sense and syntax. Not that these kinds of perfection ought to merge or pass into one another, so that the letters should cease to be letters or the words words; yet if in truth, as Plotinus fancied, the sense of the whole alone had operated to produce those elements, it would follow that in their several spheres their perfections had different degrees of importance and of affinity to the perfection of the whole. Extrinsically all would be collated and ordered serially in the cosmic life, and internally each higher stage would contain and project out of itself the nature of the lower, as our meanings seem to precipitate our words, and our words to determine and, as it were, to emit their letters.

No doubt this view of nature is wrong and reverses the actual order of genesis, in which grunts and gurglings come first and meanings, such as they are, float through the mind later—for the consciousness of them is fluid and evanescent —carried and alone fixed by their sensuous vehicle; but the contrary mythical view is the one proper to rhetoricians and idealists, and it is not for us to throw stones at Plotinus for not piercing an illusion which was fundamental in his nation and in his school, and to which most of us are still subject. Mr Fuller is one of the honourable exceptions; he perceives that protoplasm is susceptible of development in alternative as well as in progressive ways; that moralities, like arts and languages, radiate from a common centre, but diverge, the most elaborate being the farthest apart; and that life is essentially centrifugal, multiple, and variable in its ideals. Some ethical profusion appears in the civilizations known to us, and in each man, before he has learned the needful renunciations; but if we allow our fancy to range over the unknown parts of the universe, the natural heterogeneity of the good becomes simply overpowering. Furthermore, the types of good, extensible indefinitely at the periphery, are always subtly changing at the core. Human nature is not altogether fixed, and human goodness and what man can look upon as good vary with it. Plotinus, in supposing that the good was single and *a priori*, in fancying it to be the creative power, encouraged himself to ignore the greater part of its possible forms. He shut himself up, with his sect, in imaginative intolerance. And incidentally he missed the true explanation of the origin of evil, which lies in the natural conflict of many powers and many ideals. This error, though grave and dangerous, is intelligible in a mere moralist become a metaphysician (as all Platonists are) because it obeys the suasion of the moral life itself. In each man, as in the world at large, there is actually some variety of ideals. Each feels himself called upon to pursue the satisfaction of diverse faculties and opposed passions. But this moral multifariousness, when he reflects, becomes his peculiar torment, his bad conscience. Reason requires him to assume integrity, if he has it not. He is biologically but a single being, an indivisible engine, and he cannot work in two directions at once without disrupting his life and rendering himself incapable of any perfect achievement. Harmony, unity of direction, thus become his necessary method. The better man he is, the more strictly he imposes it on his wayward impulses. Now let ill luck compel such a moral man, such a legislator over himself and plotter of inward policy, to become a natural philosopher. Will he not inevitably say that the secret of the world is a morality like his own? Will he not instinctively make a legislator of God and a single city out of the cosmos, and a moral symbol even of the landscape? His Socratic wisdom in life will become his Platonic folly in science.

Mr Fuller's only consistent mystic, like his only consistent naturalist, is also rather an idol of the class-room than a type found in history, and I cannot much blame Plotinus if his spectrum was not confined to ultra-violet rays. To believe that the life of God is best, even to aspire to rest wholly in it, if all other resting-places fail, hardly requires us to assert that in itself everything not God is evil. What falls short of the supreme may not be a sufficing good for a soul insatiable and touched with divinity; but every soul need not be of that temper, and even one that is may consistently delight in the various images and echoes of the Beloved which it finds in created things. Ought a mystic to lament that he was ever so far separated from God as to be able to love him? Be that as it may, such actual mystics as Plotinus and St Francis were not kept from hatred of finitude merely by an inconsistency; they were kept from it by their first principles; they were kept from it by the very springs of their devotion, by the tenderness and wonder which filled them in the presence of the creation. The Christian in his whole being, and the Neo-Platonist in all but the whole of it, was permeated by humility. To be separated, to be inferior, to have always before and above him something not himself that he could adore, was essential to his nature and even to his celestial happiness. The beatific vision was still dualistic; it was a contemplation, a reception of influence, an ecstasy of wonder and love. Of course the life of God was in itself better than that of the saint, and the humility of the saint implied that he recognized that fact; but his humility prevented him at the same time from desiring that that fact should be otherwise. The mere existence of finitude and separation was accordingly no evil but a good, although this good was inferior to that other good in the imitation or worship of which it arose. Mr Fuller's ideal mystic would not be a pious enthusiast at all, but a sort of self-torturing Lucifer, unwilling not to be God. He would be like an artist cursing his works because they could not be identical with their model. Such a passion is intelligible but misguided; like that of Pygmalion, it is surely not the only consistent expression of an artistic temperament.

If we turn now to Mr Fuller's other principal theme, the actual philosophy of Plotinus, we cannot help feeling that to pose that dilemma between an abstract naturalist and an abstract mystic was not the happiest way of approaching it. Plotinus, Mr Fuller himself says, 'denied the dilemma'; and yet he adds that it 'is the key to a proper understanding of his treatment of his problem'. Is this likely? The problem that preoccupied Plotinus and his age was not how to explain the existence of evil or how to justify the ways of God; it was rather to rise above evil, to decipher a divine image in the worn and degraded lineaments of things, and to save the soul from a temporal and sensuous life to which evil was native. I know that Mr Fuller can quote many a phrase that seems to countenance now the one now the other of his two ultimate alternatives. Plotinus was a learned, respectable man, almost a professor; he addressed a sophisticated, over-literary public; and the training of ancient rhetoricians, which has descended to Christian preachers, encouraged the use of miscellaneous arguments and maxims, no matter what philosophy they might imply, if only they had an edifying sound or could serve to rebuke some pernicious adversary. Plotinus was not above this eclecticism in the detail of his controversies, but it would be doing him a great injustice to suppose that he was eclectic in his general thought or that his small pilferings from the Stoics and from others impeded the vigorous flight of his heart and imagination towards their congenial goal. The Neo-Platonists tended to regard as orthodox all philosophers who accepted Homer, much as the Hindus regarded as orthodox all systems that accepted the Vedas, however different they might be technically; only the atheists, i.e. the Epicureans and the Christians, were tabooed. Everything else with a national and noble stamp was swept in; but the current that engulfed it all was impetuous and single enough. It made unmistakably for salvation.

The first impulse of men in the presence of evil is to resist and try to abolish it; but when evil is seen to be ineradicable in the world, their next impulse is to elude it in their own persons, so recasting their habits as to be strengthened against it and to lay up their chief treasures beyond its reach. This was the universal effort of the later Greek moralists and of Plotinus among them. He had no courage for such a legislative vision as that of Plato's *Republic*; but the chastening lessons of the *Gorgias*, the *Phaedo*, and the *Phaedrus* were deeply graven in his heart. If he ever spoke of civic bonds and the beauty of the body, or of the world, it was only by rote, because the classical Hellenic tradition required it. His spontaneous ideal was to quit the body and the state and the cosmos, leaving behind all martial passions and sensuous images, to find bliss beyond them, in union with what created beings might borrow, but could not keep, of divine beauty and peace.

This is the mystic experience which, when expressed in a cosmic allegory, yields the Plotinian system of emanation. The transcendence of aspiration, divining the ideal behind the actual, becomes, when reversed in a myth, an emanation of the actual from the ideal. Hence the values of the terms remain what they had been in the original experience. The sensible is truly good, for it was deeply loved; it is a true image and hint of the ideal, since it revealed it; but at the same time it is inadequate, since to rest in it was impossible, and the love which it unlocked overflowed it. The manifestation is never good intransitively and as only significant of its own being; it has become a sacramental vehicle of grace. At the same time the deity signified is proved to be good and gracious, since he is what the enthusiast beholds and is enraptured by in his image. I know that in practice a devotion that passes from individuals to the ideal is seldom an honest devotion. Platonic love has the reputation of being either frigid or hypocritical, or perhaps both at once; when it really exists, it is commonly only a sort of abstract sensuality or aestheticism, at once selfish and visionary. Yet in its origin, and in the experience of the few in whom it is a spontaneous religion, Platonic love is precisely the opposite of all that. It is a passion for individuals so intense, so arresting, so disproportionate to their poor human merits, that it seems and is the revelation of an essence greater than theirs, of something that, could we live always in its presence, would render us supremely happy.

A touch of this transcendence is present in all romantic passion; for the sluices of the soul are opened, and a flood of potential joy is let loose which overflows the narrow channel of any particular friendship. It is this extreme sensitiveness to what instinctively charms, this piercing shaft of natural beauty, that drives the genuine Platonist from the individual to the ideal, from an exceeding love of things that must prove inadequate to the thought of something adequate that would justify that love. So that if there is anything morbid in Platonic love, it is not its unnatural coldness, but its disproportionate fervour, not the barren egoism of it, but its suicidal self-surrender; for the Platonic lover loves so religiously that his love must needs carry him beyond its initial object, and beyond himself.

When we view the system of Plotinus from this side, which is the genuine side of it, can we urge that in consistency everything not the supreme good should have been pronounced an evil? Has the lovely creature we first fell in love with become an evil, because that frail charm may have awakened and bound us to higher loyalties? To transcend an affection in this way is not to destroy but to understand it. The all-transcending aspiration of Plotinus, in leaving the earth and the stars and the intellect behind, did not need to dishonour these instruments of grace; on the contrary, in feeling them to be instruments of grace, it could add a divine sanction to their native allurements, as if a bridegroom became the priest at his own wedding. Platonism is a Hellenism transfigured by Socratic faith, a paganism in which the twelve cosmic gods have found a master, the good, and become its twelve apostles.

So much in justification of the sentiment of Plotinus that nature is good, although the supernatural is better. When we come to his occasional apologies not for finite goods but for positive evils, his arguments are as lame and the principle of them as immoral as in other theodicies: and here I can only utter a loud Amen to all Mr Fuller's criticisms. The trick (whoever invented it) of calling finite good 'metaphysical evil' was devilish in its guile; for as we can easily show that this sort of 'evil' is good, and the prerequisite of all moral discrimination, we may thereby so confuse and disarm our conscience as to entertain the notion that true evils, too, might be good. But they are not. In thwarting or injuring any determinate creature (an absolute point of origin for values) they are bad irretrievably. No doubt the same material object or event which is bad for one man may be good for another, as is the issue of a battle; but that does not make it good in itself, nor good altogether, nor better for the man it destroys; nor can this man find it good while he retains his vital strength and his native shade of humanity. Pantheism, in teaching that the world ought to be full of horrors, since so it is, accepts the most savage of ideals; yet it is often embraced by the most tender-minded people, to spare themselves the distress of admitting that anything is horrible after all. Plotinus, however, was no pantheist, and his God, who created the world by a virtue that flowed, as it were, from the hem of his garment, was not responsible for the world, nor glorified by the evils in it, nor even cognizant of their existence. Plotinus could not explain the origin of evil; in fact he could not explain the origin of anything, his whole natural philosophy being unnatural, and merely a moral allegory. We must not assimilate unduly the Platonic eschatology to the Hebraic. In the latter, evil was originally an accident, which God parried dramatically, capping it with a greater good. This deity, as at first conceived, was by no means omnipotent in the sense of being the only force at work in things, and having a calm eternal vision of them in their ultimate destiny. He was omnipotent only in the rhetorical sense that he could bring about practically anything he chose; a Titanic magician (such as Michael Angelo painted him), he could dart from place to place, and set right anything that in his absence might have taken a turn that displeased him. For things, although he might once have created them, all had a will and a way of their own; they made a great pother, and it was no sinecure to keep them in hand, and drive them all abreast. Afterwards the theologians, influenced by Greek and Oriental philosophies, found this dramatic notion of Providence crude, and tried to rationalize it. They thought God ought to be the serene author and spectator of the drama in which the popular imagination had made him a passionate actor; he must have foreseen and planned all the villainies and tears in it, in order to obtain a more moving effect at the end, when the tears should be dried, and the villainies punished or forgiven. Thus the evil that to religious sentiment seemed to offend God, according to religious theory really subserved his purposes: and having shifted their ground and contradicted their premises, the theologians had the 'problem of evil' on their hands; and they still have it.

For the Platonist, however, the matter was not so hopelessly tangled. Evil he thought a weakness, an ignorance, a confusion which the influence of the divine life, if we could only appropriate it, was always ready to cure. Salvation was a return to nature, to what the spirit that works in us demands; and while none of the functions or organs which this spirit gathers about it was evil in itself, they stood in need of strict subordination. The only happy life for each function, for each level of endowment, lay in serving the one above it; the flesh must serve the heart, the heart the intellect, the intellect the single ultimate good. The standard of excellence for each faculty and for each creature was not placed, as in naturalism, in self-preservation and a congenial routine at that particular

119

level; it was placed outside in the higher excellence it immediately subserved. Not (let me repeat) that the vocation of each creature or faculty was to *become* the next higher; there was no such restless evolution in this hierarchy. But the life of each came from above, and could be fully received only by obedience and fidelity. So morality was made aristocratic. The joy of everybody could lie only in service, not in that service of equals or inferiors which a democratic morality now enjoins, but in a sort of feudal devotion to a master brighter, purer, and stronger than ourselves. Plotinus was a very great prophet, although he thought little about the future. He caught completely the inspiration of his age and laid down in advance the essential principles of Byzantine art, of alchemy, of demonology, of medieval astrology and theology, of ascetic discipline, and even of feudal loyalty and romantic enchantment.

But what of 'the problem of evil'? Such a problem properly exists only for the theologians I was just speaking of, who teach a deliberate planning and creation of the world *ex nihilo*, or for pantheists like the Stoics, who, in spite of their pantheism, wish to give universal authority to a particular ethics. It does not exist for the naturalist, because for him both good and evil are relative to finite interests necessarily at war in this crowded world. Nor does it exist for the Platonist, to whom it is obvious that the good is far away and that it was not the good that removed the good where it is absent. The problem of darkness does not exist for a man gazing at the stars. No doubt the darkness is there, fundamental, pervasive, and unconquerable except at the pin-points where the stars twinkle; but the problem is not why there is such darkness, but what is the light that breaks through it so remarkably; and granting this light, why we have eyes to see it and hearts to be gladdened by it. This truly idealistic and moral question Plotinus answers sublimely, saying that our hearts are themselves sparks, scattered by that celestial flame, that rush by nature to rejoin their element. This answer of the Platonic sage, for all its sublimity, cannot be imposed on anyone who is made sincerely happy by eating, fighting, loving, talking, and peering curiously about, or whose genius and situation, for any reason, carry him towards some different point of the moral compass. The Platonic good is the goal of a very special aspiration, now largely in abeyance. But things come round in this world; the ruffians may be upon us some day when we least expect it, and philosophy may have to retire again to the sanctuary. Even then we should search the books of Plotinus in vain for any solution of the artificial problem concerning the existence of evil; but if we searched them for a thread out of the natural labyrinth of evil, we might possibly find it.

THE PHILOSOPHY OF
M. HENRI BERGSON

The most representative and remarkable of living philosophers is M. Henri Bergson. Both the form and the substance of his works attract universal attention. His ideas are pleasing and bold, and at least in form wonderfully original; he is persuasive without argument and mystical without conventionality; he moves in the atmosphere of science and free thought, yet seems to transcend them and to be secretly religious. An undercurrent of zeal and even of prophecy seems to animate his subtle analyses and his surprising fancies. He is eloquent, and to a public rather sick of the half-education it has received and eager for some inspiriting novelty he seems more eloquent than he is. He uses the French language (and little else is French about him) in the manner of the more recent artists in words, retaining the precision of phrase and the measured judgments which are traditional in French literature, yet managing to envelop everything in a penumbra of emotional suggestion. Each expression of an idea is complete in itself; yet these expressions are often varied and constantly metaphorical, so that we are led to feel that much in that idea has remained unexpressed and is indeed inexpressible.

Studied and insinuating as M. Bergson is in his style, he is no less elaborate in his learning. In the history of philosophy, in mathematics and physics, and especially in natural history he has taken great pains to survey the ground and to assimilate the views and spirit of the most recent scholars. He might be called outright an expert in all these subjects, were it not for a certain externality and want of radical sympathy in his way of conceiving them. A genuine historian of philosophy, for instance, would love to rehearse the views of great thinkers, would feel their eternal plausibility, and in interpreting them would think of himself as little as they ever thought of him. But M. Bergson evidently regards Plato or Kant as persons who did or did not prepare the way for some Bergsonian insight. The theory of evolution, taken enthusiastically, is apt to exercise an evil influence on the moral estimation of things. First the evolutionist asserts that later things grow out of earlier, which is true of things in their causes and basis, but not in their values; as modern Greece proceeds out of ancient Greece materially but does not exactly crown it. The evolutionist, however, proceeds to assume that later things are necessarily better than what they have grown out of: and this is false altogether. This fallacy reinforces very unfortunately that inevitable esteem which people have for their own opinions, and which must always vitiate the history of philosophy when it is a philosopher that writes it. A false subordination comes to be established among systems, as if they moved in single file and all had the last, the author's system, for their secret goal. In Hegel, for instance, this conceit is conspicuous, in spite of his mastery in the dramatic presentation of points of view, for his way of reconstructing history was, on the surface, very sympathetic. He too, like M. Bergson, proceeded from learning to intuition, and feigned at every turn to identify himself with what he was describing, especially if this was a philosophical attitude or temper. Yet in reality his historical judgments were forced and brutal: Greece was but a stepping-stone to Prussia, Plato and Spinoza found their higher synthesis in himself, and (though he may not say so frankly) Jesus Christ and St Francis realized their better selves in Luther. Actual spiritual life, the thoughts, affections, and pleasures of individuals, passed with Hegel for so much moonshine; the true spirit was 'objective', it was simply the movement of those circumstances in which actual spirit arose. He was accordingly contemptuous of everything intrinsically good, and his idealism consisted in forcing the natural world into a formula of evolution and then worshipping it as the embodiment of the living God. But under the guise of optimism and belief in a cosmic reason this is mere idolatry of success—a malign superstition, by which all moral independence is crushed out and conscience enslaved to chronology; and it is no marvel if, somewhat to relieve this subjection, history in turn was expurgated, marshalled, and distorted, that it might pass muster for the work of the Holy Ghost.

In truth the value of spiritual life is intrinsic and centred at every point. It is never wholly recoverable. To recover it at all, an historian must have a certain detachment and ingenuousness; knowing the dignity and simplicity of his own mind, he must courteously attribute the same dignity and simplicity to others, unless their avowed attitude prevents; this is to be an intelligent critic and to write history like a gentleman. The truth, which all philosophers alike are seeking, is eternal. It lies as near to one age as to another; the means of discovery alone change, and not always for the better. The course of evolution is no test of what is true or good; else nothing could be good intrinsically nor true simply and ultimately; on the contrary, it is the approach to truth and excellence anywhere, like the approach of tree tops to the sky, that tests the value of evolution, and determines whether it is moving upward or downward or in a circle.

M. Bergson accordingly misses fire when, for instance, in order utterly to damn a view which he has been criticizing, and which may be open to objection on other grounds, he cries that those who hold it '*retardent sur Kant*'; as if a clock were the compass of the mind, and he who was one minute late was one point off the course. Kant was a hard, honest thinker, more sinned against than sinning, from whom a great many people in the nineteenth century have taken their point of departure, departing as far as they chose; but if a straight line of progress could be traced at all through the labyrinth of philosophy, Kant would not lie in that line. His thought is essentially excentric and sophisticated, being largely based on two inherited blunders, which a truly progressive philosophy would have to begin by avoiding, thus leaving Kant on one side, and weathering his philosophy, as one might Scylla or Charybdis. The one blunder was that of the English malicious psychology which had maintained since the time of Locke that the ideas in the mind are the only objects of knowledge, instead of being the knowledge of objects. The other blunder was that of Protestantism which, in groping after that moral freedom which is so ineradicable a need of a pure spirit, thought to find it in a revision of revelation, tradition, and prejudice, so as to be able to cling to these a little longer. How should a system so local, so accidental, and so unstable as Kant's be prescribed as a sort of catechism for all humanity? The tree of knowledge has many branches, and all its fruits are not condemned to hang for ever from that one gnarled and contorted bough. M. Bergson himself 'lags behind' Kant on those points on which his better insight requires it, as, for instance, on the reality of time; but with regard to his own philosophy I am afraid he thinks that all previous systems empty into it, which is hardly true, and that all future systems must flow out of it, which is hardly necessary.

The embarrassment that qualifies M. Bergson's attainments in mathematics and physics has another and more personal source. He understands, but he trembles. Non-human immensities frighten him, as they did Pascal. He suffers from cosmic agoraphobia. We might think empty space an innocent harmless thing, a mere opportunity to move, which ought to be highly prized by all devotees of motion. But M. Bergson is instinctively a mystic, and his philosophy deliberately discredits the existence of anything except in immediacy, that is, as an experience of the heart. What he dreads in space is that the heart should be possessed by it, and transformed into it. He dreads that the imagination should be fascinated by the homogeneous and static, hypnotized by geometry, and actually lost in *Auseinandersein*. This would be a real death and petrifaction of consciousness, frozen into contemplation of a monotonous infinite void. What is warm and desirable is rather the sense of variety and succession, as if all visions radiated from the occupied focus or hearth of the self. The more concentration at this habitable point, with the more mental perspectives opening backwards and forwards through time; in a word, the more personal and historical the

apparition, the better it would be. Things must be reduced
again to what they seem; it is vain and terrible to take them
for what we find they are. M. Bergson is at bottom an
apologist for very old human prejudices, an apologist for
animal illusion. His whole labour is a plea for some vague
but comfortable faith which he dreads to have stolen from him
by the progress of art and knowledge. There is a certain
trepidation, a certain suppressed instinct to snap at and sting
the hated oppressor, as if some desperate small being were at
bay before a horrible monster. M. Bergson is afraid of space,
of mathematics, of necessity, and of eternity; he is afraid of the
intellect and the possible discoveries of science; he is afraid of
nothingness and death. These fears may prevent him from
being a philosopher in the old and noble sense of the word;
but they sharpen his sense for many a psychological problem,
and make him the spokesman of many an inarticulate soul.
Animal timidity and animal illusion are deep in the heart of all
of us. Practice may compel us to bow to the conventions of the
intellect, as to those of polite society; but secretly, in our
moments of immersion in ourselves, we may find them a great
nuisance, even a vain nightmare. Could we only listen un-
disturbed to the beat of protoplasm in our hearts, would not
that oracle solve all the riddles of the universe, or at least
avoid them?

To protect this inner conviction, however, it is necessary
for the mystic to sally forth and attack the enemy on his own
ground. If he refuted physics and mathematics simply out of
his own faith, he might be accused of ignorance of the subject.
He will therefore study it conscientiously, yet with a certain
irritation and haste to be done with it, somewhat as a Jesuit
might study Protestant theology. Such a student, however,
is apt to lose his pains; for in retracing a free inquiry in his
servile spirit, he remains deeply ignorant, not indeed of its
form, but of its nature and value. Why, for instance, has
M. Bergson such a horror of mechanical physics? He seems
to think it a black art, dealing in unholy abstractions, and
rather dangerous to salvation, and he keeps his metaphysical

exorcisms and antidotes always at hand, to render it innocuous, at least to his own soul. But physical science never solicited of anybody that he should be wholly absorbed in the contemplation of atoms, and worship them; that we must worship and lose ourselves in reality, whatever reality may be, is a mystic aberration, which physical science does nothing to foster. Nor does any critical physicist suppose that what he describes is the whole of the object; he merely notes the occasions on which its sensible qualities appear, and calculates events. Because the calculable side of nature is his province, he does not deny that events have other aspects—the psychic and the moral, for instance—no less real in their way, in terms of which calculation would indeed be impossible. If he chances to call the calculable elements of nature her substance, as it is proper to do, that name is given without passion; he may perfectly well proclaim with Goethe that it is in the accidents, in the *farbiger Abglanz*, that we have our life. And if it be for his freedom that the mystic trembles, I imagine any man of science would be content with M. Bergson's assertion that true freedom is the *sense* of freedom, and that in any intelligible statement of the situation, even the most indeterministic, this freedom disappears; for it is an immediate experience, not any scheme of relation between events.

The horror of mechanical physics arises, then, from attributing to that science pretensions and extensions which it does not have; it arises from the habits of theology and metaphysics being imported inopportunely into science. Similarly, when M. Bergson mentions mathematics, he seems to be thinking of the supposed authority it exercises—one of Kant's confusions—over the empirical world, and trying to limit and subordinate that authority, lest movement should somehow be removed from nature, and vagueness from human thought. But nature and human thought are what they are; they have enough affinity to mathematics, as it happens, to suggest that study to our minds, and to give those who go deep into it a great, though partial, mastery over things.

Nevertheless, a true mathematician is satisfied with the hypothetical and ideal cogency of his science, and puts its dignity in that. Moreover, M. Bergson has the too pragmatic notion that the use of mathematics is to keep our accounts straight in this business world; whereas its inherent use is emancipating and Platonic, in that it shows us the possibility of other worlds, less contingent and perturbed than this one. If he allows himself any excursus from his beloved immediacy, it is only in the interests of practice; he little knows the pleasures of a liberal mind, ranging over the congenial realm of internal accuracy and ideal truth, where it can possess itself of what treasures it likes in perfect security and freedom. An artist in his workmanship, M. Bergson is not an artist in his allegiance; he has no respect for what is merely ideal.

For this very reason, perhaps, he is more at home in natural history than in the exact sciences. He has the gift of observation, and can suggest vividly the actual appearance of natural processes, in contrast to the verbal paraphrase of these processes which is sometimes taken to explain them. He is content to stop at habit without formulating laws; he refuses to assume that the large obvious cycles of change in things can be reduced to mechanism, that is, to minute included cycles repeated *ad libitum*. He may sometimes defend this refusal by sophisticated arguments, as when he says that mechanism would require the last stage of the universe to be simultaneous with the first, forgetting that the unit of mechanism is not a mathematical equation but some observed typical event. The refusal itself, however, would be honest scepticism enough were it made with no *arrière pensée*, but simply in view of the immense complexity of the facts and the extreme simplicity of the mechanical hypothesis. In such a situation, to halt at appearances might seem the mark of a true naturalist and a true empiricist not misled by speculative haste and the human passion for system and simplification. At the first reading, M. Bergson's *Evolution créatrice* may well dazzle the professional naturalist and seem to him an illuminating confession of the nature and limits of his science; yet a second reading, I have good authority for saying, may as easily reverse that impression. M. Bergson never reviews his facts in order to understand them, but only if possible to discredit others who may have fancied they understood. He raises difficulties, he marks the problems that confront the naturalist, and the inadequacy of explanations that may have been suggested. Such criticism would be a valuable beginning if it were followed by the suggestion of some new solution; but the suggestion only is that no solution is possible, that the phenomena of life are simply miraculous, and that it is in the tendency or vocation of the animal, not in its body or its past, that we must see the ground of what goes on before us.

With such a philosophy of science, it is evident that all progress in the understanding of nature would cease, as it ceased after Aristotle. The attempt would again be abandoned to reduce gross and obvious cycles of change, such as generation, growth, and death, to minute latent cycles, so that natural history should offer a picturesque approach to universal physics. If for the magic power of types, invoked by Aristotle, we substituted with M. Bergson the magic power of the *élan vital,* that is, of evolution in general, we should be referring events not to finer, more familiar, more pervasive processes, but to one all-embracing process, unique and always incomplete. Our understanding would end in something far vaguer and looser than what our observation began with. Aristotle at least could refer particulars to their specific types, as medicine and social science are still glad enough to do, to help them in guessing and in making a learned show before the public. But if divination and eloquence—for science is out of the question—were to invoke nothing but a fluid tendency to grow, we should be left with a flat history of phenomena and no means of prediction or even classification. All knowledge would be reduced to gossip, infinitely diffuse, perhaps enlisting our dramatic feelings, but yielding no intellectual mastery of experience, no practical competence, and no moral lesson. The world would be a serial novel, to be continued for ever, and all men mere novel-readers.

Nothing is more familiar to philosophers nowadays than that criticism of knowledge by which we are thrown back upon the appearances from which science starts, upon what is known to children and savages, whilst all that which long experience and reason may infer from those appearances is set down as so much hypothesis; and indeed it is through hypothesis that latent being, if such there be, comes before the mind at all. Now such criticism of knowledge might have been straightforward and ingenuous. It might have simply disclosed the fact, very salutary to meditate upon, that the whole frame of nature, with the minds that animate it, is disclosed to us by intelligence; that if we were not intelligent our sensations would exist for us without meaning anything, as they exist for idiots. The criticism of knowledge, however, has usually been taken maliciously, in the sense that it is the idiots only that are not deceived; for any interpretation of sensation is a mental figment, and while experience may have any extent it will it cannot possibly, they say, have expressive value; it cannot reveal anything going on beneath. Intelligence and science are accordingly declared to have no penetration, no power to disclose what is latent, for nothing latent exists; they can at best furnish symbols for past or future sensations and the order in which they arise; they can be seven-league boots for striding over the surface of sentience.

This negative dogmatism as to knowledge was rendered harmless and futile by the English philosophers, in that they maintained at the same time that everything happens exactly *as if* the intellect were a true instrument of discovery, and *as if* a material world underlay our experience and furnished all its occasions. Hume, Mill, and Huxley were scientific at heart, and full of the intelligence they dissected; they seemed to cry to nature: Though thou dost not exist, yet will I trust in thee. Their idealism was a theoretical scruple rather than a passionate superstition. Not so M. Bergson; he is not so simple as to invoke the malicious criticism of knowledge in order to go on thinking rationalistically. Reason and science make him deeply uncomfortable. His point accordingly is not merely that mechanism is a hypothesis, but that it is a wrong hypothesis. Events do not come as if mechanism brought them about; they come, at least in the organic world, as if a magic destiny, an inscrutable ungovernable effort, were driving them on.

Thus M. Bergson introduces metaphysics into natural history; he invokes, in what is supposed to be science, the agency of a power, called the *élan vital*, on a level with the 'Will' of Schopenhauer or the 'Unknowable Force' of Herbert Spencer. But there is a scientific vitalism also, which it is well to distinguish from the metaphysical sort. The point at issue between vitalism and mechanism in biology is whether the living processes in nature can be resolved into a combination of the material. The material processes will always remain vital, if we take this word in a descriptive and poetic sense; for they will contain a movement having a certain idiosyncrasy and taking a certain time, like the fall of an apple. The movement of nature is never dialectical; the first part of any event does not logically imply the last part of it. Physics is descriptive, historical, reporting after the fact what are found to be the habits of matter. But if these habits are constant and calculable we call the vitality of them mechanical. Thus the larger processes of nature, no matter how vital they may be and whatever consciousness may accompany them, will always be mechanical if they can be calculated and predicted, being a combination of the more minute and widespread processes which they contain. The only question therefore is: Do processes such as nutrition and reproduction arise by a combination of such events as the fall of apples? Or are they irreducible events, and units of mechanism by themselves? That is the dilemma as it appears in science. Both possibilities will always remain open, because however far mechanical analysis may go, many phenomena, as human apprehension presents them, will always remain irreducible to any common denominator with the rest; and on the other hand, wherever the actual reduction of the habits of animals to those of matter may have stopped, we can never know that a further education is impossible.

The balance of reasonable presumption, however, is not even. The most inclusive movements known to us in nature, the astronomical, are calculable, and so are the most minute and pervasive processes, the chemical. These are also, if evolution is to be accepted, the earliest processes upon which all others have supervened and out of which, as it were, they have grown. Apart from miraculous intervention, therefore, the assumption seems to be inevitable that the intermediate processes are calculable too, and compounded out of the others. The appearance to the contrary presented in animal and social life is easily explicable on psychological grounds. We read inevitably in terms of our passions those things which affect them or are analogous to what involves passion in ourselves; and when the mechanism of them is hidden from us, as is that of our bodies, we suppose that these passions which we find on the surface in ourselves, or read into other creatures, are the substantial and only forces that carry on our part of the world. Penetrating this illusion, dispassionate observers in all ages have received the general impression that nature is one and mechanical. This was, and still remains, a general impression only; but I suspect no one who walks the earth with his eyes open would be concerned to resist it, were it not for certain fond human conceits which such a view would rebuke and, if accepted, would tend to obliterate. The psychological illusion that our ideas and purposes are original facts and forces (instead of expressions in consciousness of facts and forces which are material) and the practical and optical illusion that everything wheels about us in this world—these are the primitive persuasions which the enemies of naturalism have always been concerned to protect.

One might indeed be a vitalist in biology, out of pure caution and conscientiousness, without sharing those prejudices; and many a speculative philosopher has been free from them who has been a vitalist in metaphysics. Schopenhauer, for instance, observed that the cannon-ball which, if self-conscious, would think it moved freely, would be quite right in thinking so. The 'Will' was as evident to him in mechanism as in animal life. M. Bergson, in the more hidden reaches of his thought, seems to be a universal vitalist; apparently an *élan vital* must have existed once to deposit in inorganic matter the energy stored there, and to set mechanism going. But he relies on biology alone to prove the present existence of an independent effort to live; this is needed to do what mechanism, as he thinks, could never do; it is not needed to do, as in Schopenhauer, what mechanism does. M. Bergson thus introduces his metaphysical force as a peculiar requirement of biology; he breaks the continuity of nature; he loses the poetic justification of a metaphysical vitalism; he asks us to believe that life is not a natural expression of material being, but an alien and ghostly madness descending into it—I say a ghostly madness, for why should disembodied life wish that the body should live? This vitalism is not a kind of biology more prudent and literal than the mechanical kind (as a scientific vitalism would be), but far less legitimately speculative. Nor is it a frank and thorough mythology, such as the total spectacle of the universe might suggest to an imaginative genius. It is rather a popular animism, insisting on a sympathetic interpretation of nature where human sympathy is quick and easy, and turning this sympathy into a revelation of the Absolute, but leaving the rest of nature cold, because to sympathize with its movement there is harder for anxious, self-centred mortals, and requires a disinterested mind. M. Bergson would have us believe that mankind is what nature has set her heart on and the best she can do, for whose sake she has been long making very special efforts. We are fortunate that at least her darling is all mankind and not merely Israel.

In spite, then, of M. Bergson's learning as a naturalist and his eye for the facts—things Aristotle also possessed—he is, like Aristotle, profoundly out of sympathy with nature. Aristotle was alienated from nature and any penetrating study of it by the fact that he was a disciple of Socrates, and therefore essentially a moralist and a logician. M. Bergson is alienated from nature by something quite different; he is the

adept of a very modern, very subtle, and very arbitrary art,
that of literary psychology. In this art the imagination is
invited to conceive things as if they were all centres of passion
and sensation. Literary psychology is not a science; it is
practised by novelists and poets; yet if it is to be brilliantly
executed it demands a minute and extended observation of
life. Unless your psychological novelist had crammed his
memory with pictures of the ways and aspects of men he would
have no starting-point for his psychological fictions; he would
not be able to render them circumstantial and convincing. Just
so M. Bergson's achievements in psychological fiction, to be
so brilliantly executed as they are, required all his learning.
The history of philosophy, mathematics, and physics, and
above all natural history, had to supply him first with sug-
gestions; and if he is not really a master in any of those fields,
that is not to be wondered at. His heart is elsewhere. To write
a universal biological romance, such as he has sketched for us
in his system, he would ideally have required all scientific
knowledge, but only as Homer required the knowledge of
seamanship, generalship, statecraft, augury, and charioteer-
ing, in order to turn the aspects of them into poetry, and not
with that technical solidity which Plato unjustly blames him
for not possessing. Just so M. Bergson's proper achievement
begins where his science ends, and his philosophy lies entirely
beyond the horizon of possible discoveries or empirical
probabilities. In essence, it is myth or fable; but in the texture
and degree of its fabulousness it differs notably from the
performances of previous metaphysicians. Primitive poets,
even ancient philosophers, were not psychologists; their fables
were compacted out of elements found in practical life, and
they reckoned in the units in which language and passion
reckon—wooing, feasting, fighting, vice, virtue, happiness,
justice. Above all, they talked about persons or about ideals;
this man, this woman, this typical thought or sentiment was
what fixed their attention and seemed to them the ultimate
thing. Not so M. Bergson: he is a microscopic psychologist,
and even in man what he studies by preference is not some

integrated passion or idea, but something far more recondite; the minute texture of sensation, memory, or impulse. Sharp analysis is required to distinguish or arrest these elements, yet these are the predestined elements of his fable; and so his anthropomorphism is far less obvious than that of most poets and theologians, though no less real.

This peculiarity in the terms of the myth carries with it a notable extension in its propriety. The social and moral phenomena of human life cannot be used in interpreting life elsewhere without a certain conscious humour. This makes the charm of avowed writers of fable; their playful travesty and dislocation of things human, which would be puerile if they meant to be naturalists, render them piquant moralists; for they are not really interpreting animals, but under the mask of animals maliciously painting men. Such fables are morally interesting and plausible just because they are psychologically false. If Aesop could have reported what lions and lambs, ants and donkeys, really think and feel, his poems would have been perfect riddles to the public; and they would have had no human value except that of illustrating, to the truly speculative philosopher, the irresponsible variety of animal consciousness and its incommensurable types. Now M. Bergson's psychological fictions, being drawn from what is rudimentary in man, have a better chance of being literally true beyond man. Indeed what he asks us to do, and wishes to do himself, is simply to absorb so completely the aspect and habit of things that the soul of them may take possession of us: that we may know by intuition the *élan vital* that the smile of Francesca expressed.

The correctness of such an intuition, however, rests on a circumstance which M. Bergson does not notice, because his psychology is literary and not scientific. It rests on the possibility of imitation. When the organism observed and that of the observer have a similar structure and can imitate one another, the idea produced in the observer by intent contemplation is like the experience present to the person contemplated. But where this contagion of attitude, and therefore of feeling, is impossible, our intuition of our neighbours' souls remains subjective and has no value as a revelation. Psychological novelists, when they describe people such as they themselves are or might have been, may describe them truly; but beyond that limit their personages are merely plausible, that is, such as might be conceived by an equally ignorant reader in the presence of the same external indications. So, for instance, the judgment which a superficial traveller passes on foreign manners or religions is plausible to him and to his compatriots just because it represents the feeling that such manifestations awaken in strangers and does not attempt to convey the very different feeling really involved for the natives; had the latter been discovered and expressed, the traveller's book would have found little understanding and no sale in his own country. This plausibility to the ignorant is present in all spontaneous myth. Nothing more need be demanded of irresponsible fiction, which makes no pretensions to be a human document, but is merely a human entertainment.

Now, a human psychology, even of the finest grain, when it is applied to the interpretation of the soul of matter, or of the soul of the whole universe, obviously yields a view of the irresponsible and subjective sort; for it is not based on any close similarity between the observed and the observer: man and the ether, man and cosmic evolution, cannot mimic one another, to discover mutually how they feel. But just because merely human, such an interpretation may remain always plausible to man; and it would be an admirable entertainment if there were no danger that it should be taken seriously. The idea Paul has of Peter, Spinoza observes, expresses the nature of Peter less than it betrays that of Paul; and so an idea framed by a man of the consciousness of things in general reveals the mind of that man rather than the mind of the universe; but the mind of the man too may be worth knowing, and the illusive hope of discovering everything may lead him truly to disclose himself. Such a disclosure of the lower depths of man by himself is M. Bergson's psychology; and the psychological romance, purporting to describe the inward nature of the universe, which he has built out of that introspection, is his metaphysics.

Many a point in this metaphysics may seem strange, fantastic, and obscure; and so it really is, when dislocated and projected metaphysically; but not one will be found to be arbitrary; not one but is based on attentive introspection and perception of the immediate. Take, for example, what is M. Bergson's starting-point, his somewhat dazzling doctrine that to be is to last, or rather to feel oneself endure. This is a hypostasis of 'true' (i.e. immediately felt) duration. In a sensuous day-dream past feelings survive in the present, images of the long ago are shuffled together with present sensations, the roving imagination leaves a bright wake behind it like a comet, and pushes a rising wave before it, like the bow of a ship; all is fluidity, continuity without identity, novelty without surprise. Hence, too, the doctrine of freedom: the images that appear in such a day-dream are often congruous in character with those that preceded, and mere prolongations of them; but this prolongation itself modifies them, and what develops is in no way deducible or predictable out of what exists. This situation is perfectly explicable scientifically. The movement of consciousness will be self-congruous and sustained when it rests on continuous processes in the same tissues, and yet quite unpredictable from within, because the direct sensuous report of bodily processes (in nausea, for instance, or in hunger) contains no picture of their actual mechanism. Even wholly new features, due to little crises in bodily life, may appear in a dream to flow out of what already exists, yet freely develop it; because in dreams comparison, the attempt to be consistent, is wholly in abeyance, and also because the new feature will come imbedded in others which are not new, but have dramatic relevance in the story. So immediate consciousness yields the two factors of Bergsonian freedom, continuity and indetermination.

Again, take the somewhat disconcerting assertion that movement exists when there is nothing that moves, and no space that it moves through. In vision, perhaps, it is not easy to imagine a consciousness of motion without some presentation of a field, and of a distinguishable something in it; but if we descend to somatic feelings (and the more we descend, with M. Bergson, the closer we are to reality), in shooting pains or the sense of intestinal movements, the feeling of a change and of a motion is certainly given in the absence of all idea of a *mobile* or of distinct points (or even of a separate field) through which it moves; consciousness begins with the sense of change, and the terms of the felt process are only qualitative limits, bred out of the felt process itself. Even a more paradoxical tenet of our philosopher finds its justification here. He says that the units of motion are indivisible, that they are acts; so that to solve the riddle about Achilles and the tortoise we need no mathematics of the infinitesimal, but only to ask Achilles how he accomplishes the feat. Achilles would reply that in so many strides he would do it; and we may be surprised to learn that these strides are indivisible, so that, apparently, Achilles could not have stumbled in the middle of one, and taken only half of it. Of course, in nature, in what non-Bergsonians call reality, he could: but not in his immediate feeling, for if he had stumbled, the real stride, that which he was aware of taking, would have been complete at the stumbling-point. It is certain that consciousness comes in stretches, in breaths: all its data are aesthetic wholes, like visions or snatches of melody; and we should never be aware of anything were we not aware of something all at once.

When a man has taught himself—and it is a difficult art—to revert in this way to rudimentary consciousness and to watch himself live, he will be able, if he likes, to add a plausible chapter to speculative psychology. He has unearthed in himself the animal sensibility which has thickened, budded, and crystallized into his present somewhat intellectual image of the world. He has touched again the vegetative stupor, the multiple disconnected landscapes, the 'blooming buzzing confusion' which his reason has partly set in order. May he not have in all this a key to the consciousness of other creatures? Animal psychology, and sympathy with the general life of

nature, are vitiated both for naturalists and for poets by the
human terms they must use, terms which presuppose distinctions which non-human beings probably have not made. These
distinctions correct the illusions of immediate appearance in
ways which only a long and special experience has imposed
upon us, and they should not be imported into other souls.
We are old men trying to sing the loves of children; we are
wingless bipeds trying to understand the gods. But the data
of the immediate are hardly human; it is probable that at that
level all sentience is much alike. From that common ground
our imagination can perhaps start safely, and follow such
hints as observation furnishes, until we learn to live and feel
as other living things do, or as nature may live and feel as a
whole. Instinct, for instance, need not be, as our human
prejudice suggests, a rudimentary intelligence; it may be a
parallel sort of sensibility, an imageless awareness of the
presence and character of other things, with a superhuman
ability to change oneself so as to meet them. Do we not feel
something of this sort ourselves in love, in art, in religion?
M. Bergson is a most delicate and charming poet on this
theme, and a plausible psychologist; his method of accumu-
lating and varying his metaphors, and leaving our intuition
to itself under that artful stimulus, is the only judicious and
persuasive method he could have employed, and his knack at it
is wonderful. We recover, as we read, the innocence of the
mind. It seems no longer impossible that we might, like the
wise men in the story-books, learn the language of birds; we
share for the moment the siestas of plants; and we catch the
quick consciousness of the waves of light, vibrating at inconceivable rates, each throb forgotten as the next follows upon
it; and we may be tempted to play on Shakespeare and say:

> Like as the waves make towards the pebbled shore,
> So do *their spirits* hasten to their end.

Some reader of M. Bergson might say to himself: All this
is ingenious introspection and divination; grant that it is true,
and how does that lead to a new theory of the universe? You

have been studying surface appearances and the texture of primitive consciousness; that is a part of the internal rumble of this great engine of the world. How should it loosen or dissolve that engine, as your philosophy evidently professes that it must? That nature exists we perceive whenever we resume our intellectual and practical life, interrupted for a moment by this interesting reversion to the immediate. The consciousness which in introspection we treat as an object is, in operation, a cognitive activity: it demonstrates the world. You would never yourself have conceived the minds of ethereal vibrations, or of birds, or of ants, or of men suspending their intelligence, if you had known of no men, ants, birds, or ether. It is the material objects that suggest to you their souls, and teach you how to conceive them. How then should the souls be substituted for the bodies, and abolish them?

Poor guileless reader! If philosophers were straightforward men of science, adding each his mite to the general store of knowledge, they would all substantially agree, and while they might make interesting discoveries, they would not herald each his new transformation of the whole universe. But philosophers are either revolutionists or apologists, and some of them, like M. Bergson, are revolutionists in the interests of apologetics. Their art is to create some surprising inversion of things, some system of the universe contrary to common apprehension, or to defend some such inverted system, propounded by poets long ago, and perhaps consecrated by religion. It would not require a great man to say calmly: Men, birds, even ether-waves, if you will, feel after this and this fashion. The greatness and the excitement begin when he says: Your common sense, your practical intellect, your boasted science have entirely deceived you; see what the real truth is instead! So M. Bergson is bent on telling us that the immediate, as he describes it, is the sole reality: all else is unreal, artificial, and a more or less convenient symbol in discourse— discourse itself being taken, of course, for a movement in immediate sensibility, which is what it is existentially, but never for an excursion into an independent logical realm, which is what it is spiritually and in intent. So we must revise all our psychological observations, and turn them into metaphysical dogmas. It would be nothing to say simply: *For immediate feeling* the past is contained in the present, movement is prior to that which moves, spaces are many, disconnected, and incommensurable, events are indivisible wholes, perception is in its object and identical with it, the future is unpredictable, the complex is bred out of the simple, and evolution is creative, its course being obedient to a general tendency or groping impulse, not to any exact law. No, we must say instead: *In the universe at large* the whole past is preserved bodily in the present, duration is real and space is only imagined; all is motion, and there is nothing substantial that moves; times are incommensurable; men, birds, and waves are nothing but the images of them (our perceptions, like their spirits, being some compendium of these images); chance intervenes in the flux, but evolution is due to an absolute Effort which exists *in vacuo* and is simplicity itself; and this Effort, without having an idea of what it pursues, nevertheless produces it out of nothing.

The accuracy or the hollowness of M. Bergson's doctrine, according as we take it for literary psychology or for natural philosophy, will appear clearly in the following instance:

Anyone who has ever practised literary composition knows very well that, after he has devoted long study to the subject, collected all the documents, and taken all his notes, one thing more is needful before he can actually embark on the work of composition; namely, an effort, often a very painful one, to plant himself all at once in the very heart of the subject, and to fetch from as profound a depth as possible the momentum by which he need simply let himself be borne along in the sequel. This momentum, as soon as it is acquired, carries the mind forward along a path where it recovers all the facts it had gathered together, and a thousand other details besides. The momentum develops and breaks up of itself into particulars that might be retailed *ad infinitum*. The more he advances the more he finds; he will never have exhausted the subject; and nevertheless if he turns round suddenly to face the momentum he feels at his back and see what it is, it eludes him; for it is not a thing but a direction of movement, and though capable of being extended indefinitely, it is simplicity itself.*

This is evidently well observed: heighten the tone a little, and you might have a poem on those joyful pangs of gestation and parturition which are not denied to a male animal. It is a description of the *sensation* of literary composition, of the *immediate experience* of a writer as words and images rise into his mind. He cannot summon his memories explicitly, for he would first have to remember them to do so; his consciousness of inspiration, of literary creation, is nothing but a consciousness of pregnancy and of a certain 'direction of movement', as if he were being wafted in a balloon; and just in its moments of highest tension his mind is filled with mere expectancy and mere excitement, without images, plans, or motives; and what guides it is inwardly, as M. Bergson says, simplicity itself. Yet excellent as such a description is psychologically, it is a literary confession rather than a piece of science; for scientific psychology is a part of natural history, and when in nature we come upon such a notable phenomenon as this, that some men write and write eloquently, we should at once study the antecedents and the conditions under which this occurs; we should try, by experiment if possible, to see what variations in the result follow upon variations in the situation. At once we should begin to perceive how casual and superficial are those data of introspection which M. Bergson's account reproduces. Does that painful effort, for instance, occur always? Is it the moral source, as he seems to suggest, of the good and miraculous fruits that follow? Not at all: such an effort is required only when the writer is overworked, or driven to express himself under pressure; in the spontaneous talker or singer, in the orator surpassing himself and overflowing with eloquence, there is no effort at all; only facility, and joyous undirected abundance. We should further ask whether *all* the facts previously gathered are recovered, and

* 'Introduction à la Métaphysique', *Revue de Métaphysique et de Morale* (janvier 1903).

all correctly, and what relation the 'thousand other details' have to them; and we should find that everything was controlled and supplied by the sensuous endowment of the literary man, his moral complexion, and his general circumstances. And we should perceive at the same time that the momentum which to introspection was so mysterious was in fact the discharge of many automatisms long imprinted on the system, a system (as growth and disease show) that has its internal vegetation and crises of maturity, to which facility and error in the recovery of the past, and creation also, are closely attached. Thus we should utterly refuse to say that this momentum was capable of being extended indefinitely or was simplicity itself. It may be a good piece of literary psychology to say that simplicity precedes complexity, for it precedes complexity in consciousness. Consciousness dwindles and flares up most irresponsibly, so long as its own flow alone is regarded, and it continually arises out of nothing, which indeed is simplicity itself. But it does not arise without real conditions outside, which cannot be discovered by introspection, nor divined by that literary psychology which proceeds by imagining what introspection might yield in others.

There is a deeper mystification still in this passage, where a writer is said to 'plant himself in the very heart of the subject'. The general tenor of M. Bergson's philosophy warrants us in taking this quite literally to mean that the field from which inspiration draws its materials is not the man's present memory nor even his past experience, but the subject itself which that experience and this memory regard: in other words, what we write about and our latent knowledge are the same thing. When Shakespeare was composing his *Antony and Cleopatra*, for instance, he planted himself in the very heart of Rome and of Egypt, and in the very heart of the Queen of Egypt herself; what he had gathered from Plutarch and from elsewhere was, according to M. Bergson's view, a sort of glimpse of the remote reality itself, as if by telepathy he had been made to witness some part of it; or rather as if the scope of his consciousness had been suddenly extended in one direction, so as to embrace and contain bodily a bit of that outlying experience. Thus when the poet sifts his facts and sets his imagination to work at unifying and completing them, what he does is to pierce to Egypt, Rome, and the inner consciousness of Cleopatra, to fetch *thence* the profound momentum which is to guide him in composition; and it is there, not in the adventitious later parts of his own mind, that he should find the thousand other details which he may add to the picture.

Here again, in an exaggerated form, we have a transcript of the immediate, a piece of really wonderful introspection, spoiled by being projected into a theory of nature, which it spoils in its turn. Doubtless Shakespeare, in the heat of dramatic vision, lived his characters, transported himself to their environment, and felt the passion of each, as we do in a dream, dictating their unpremeditated words. But all this is in imagination; it is true only within the framework of our dream. In reality, of course, Shakespeare never pierced to Rome nor to Egypt; his elaborations of his data are drawn from his own feelings and circumstances, not from those of Cleopatra. This transporting oneself into the heart of a subject is a loose metaphor: the best one can do is to transplant the subject into one's own heart and draw *from oneself* impulses as profound as possible with which to vivify tradition and make it over in one's own image. Yet I fear that to speak so is rationalism, and would be found to involve, to the horror of our philosopher, that life is cognitive and spiritual, but dependent, discontinuous, and unsubstantial. What he conceives instead is that consciousness is a stuff out of which things are made, and has all the attributes, even the most material, of its several objects; and that there is no possibility of knowing, save by becoming what one is trying to know. So perception, for him, lies where its object does, and is some part of it; memory is the past experience itself, somehow shining through into the present; and Shakespeare's Cleopatra, I should infer, would have to be some part of Cleopatra herself—in those moments when she spoke English.

It is hard to be a just critic of mysticism because mysticism can never do itself justice in words. To conceive of an external actual Cleopatra and an external actual mind of Shakespeare is to betray the cause of pure immediacy; and I suspect that if M. Bergson heard of such criticisms as I am making, he would brush them aside as utterly blind and scholastic. As the mystics have always said that God was not far from them, but dwelt in their hearts, meaning this pretty literally: so this mystical philosophy of the immediate, which talks sometimes so scientifically of things and with such intimacy of knowledge, feels that these things are not far from it, but dwell literally in its heart. The revelation and the sentiment of them, if it be thorough, is just what the things are. The total aspects to be discerned in a body *are* that body; and the movement of those aspects, when you enact it, *is* the spirit of that body, and at the same time a part of your own spirit. To suppose that a man's consciousness (either one's own or other people's) is a separate fact over and above the shuffling of the things he feels, or that these things are anything over and above the feeling of them which exists more or less everywhere in diffusion—that, for the mystic, is to be once for all hopelessly intellectual, dualistic, and diabolical. If you cannot shed the husk of those dead categories—space, matter, mind, truth, person—life is shut out of your heart. And the mystic, who always speaks out of experience, is certainly right in this, that a certain sort of life is shut out by reason, the sort that reason calls dreaming or madness; but he forgets that reason too is a kind of life, and that of all the kinds—mystical, passionate, practical, aesthetic, intellectual—with their various degrees of light and heat, the life of reason is that which some people may prefer. I confess I am one of these, and I am not inclined, even if I were able, to reproduce M. Bergson's sentiments as he feels them. He is his own perfect expositor. All a critic can aim at is to understand these sentiments as existing facts, and to give them the place that belongs to them in the moral world. To understand, in most cases, is intimacy enough.

Herbert Spencer says somewhere that the yolk of an egg is homogeneous, the highly heterogeneous bird being differentiated in it by the law of evolution. I cannot think what assured Spencer of this homogeneity in the egg, except the fact that perhaps it all tasted alike, which might seem good proof to a pure empiricist. Leibniz, on the contrary, maintained that the organization of nature was infinitely deep, every part consisting of an endless number of discrete elements. Here we may observe the difference between good philosophy and bad. The idea of Leibniz is speculative and far outruns the evidence, but it is speculative in a well-advised, penetrating, humble, and noble fashion; while the idea of Spencer is foolishly dogmatic, it is a piece of ignorant self-sufficiency, like that insular empiricism that would deny that Chinamen were real until it had actually seen them. Nature is richer than experience and wider than divination; and it is far rasher and more arrogant to declare that any part of nature is simple than to suggest the sort of complexity that perhaps it might have. M. Bergson, however, is on the side of Spencer. After studiously examining the egg on every side—for he would do more than taste it—and considering the source and destiny of it, he would summon his intuition to penetrate to the very heart of it, to its spirit, and then he would declare that this spirit was a vital momentum without parts and without ideas, and was simplicity itself. He would add that it was the free and original creator of the bird, because it is of the essence of spirit to bestow more than it possesses and to build better than it knows. Undoubtedly actual spirit is simple and does not know how it builds; but for that very reason actual spirit does not really create or build anything, but merely watches, now with sympathetic, now with shocked attention, what is being created and built for it. Doubtless new things are always arising, new islands, new persons, new philosophies; but that the real cause of them should be simpler than they, that their Creator, if I may use this language, should be ignorant and give more than he has, who can stomach that?

Let us grant, however, since the thing is not abstractly

inconceivable, that eggs really have no structure. To what, then, shall we attribute the formation of birds? Will it follow that evolution, or differentiation, or the law of the passage from the homogeneous to the heterogeneous, or the dialectic of the concept of pure being, or the impulse towards life, or the vocation of spirit is what actually hatches them? Alas, these words are but pedantic and rhetorical cloaks for our ignorance, and to project them behind the facts and regard them as presiding from thence over the course of nature is a piece of the most deplorable scholasticism. If eggs are really without structure, the true causes of the formation of birds are the last conditions, whatever they may be, that introduce that phenomenon and determine its character—the type of the parents, the act of fertilization, the temperature, or whatever else observation might find regularly to precede and qualify that new birth in nature. These facts, if they were the ultimate and deepest facts in the case, would be the ultimate and only possible terms in which to explain it. They would constitute the mechanism of reproduction; and if nature were no finer than that in its structure, science could not go deeper than that in its discoveries. And although it is frivolous to suppose that nature ends in this way at the limits of our casual apprehension, and has no hidden roots, yet philosophically that would be as good a stopping place as any other. Ultimately we should have to be satisfied with some factual conjunction and method in events. If atoms and their collisions, by any chance, were the ultimate and inmost facts discoverable, they would supply the explanation of everything, in the only sense in which anything existent can be explained at all. If somebody then came to us enthusiastically and added that the Will of the atoms so to be and move was the true cause, or the Will of God that they should move so, he would not be reputed, I suppose, to have thrown a bright light on the subject.

Yet this is what M. Bergson does in his whole defence of metaphysical vitalism, and especially in the instance of the evolution of eyes by two different methods, which is his palmary argument. Since in some molluscs and in vertebrates organs that coincide in being organs of vision are reached by distinct paths, it cannot have been the propulsion of mechanism in each case, he says, that guided the developments, which, being divergent, would never have led to coincident results, but the double development must have been guided by a common *tendency towards vision.* Suppose (what some young man in a laboratory may by this time have shown to be false) that M. Bergson's observations have sounded the facts to the bottom; it would then be of the ultimate nature of things that, given light and the other conditions, the two methods of development will end in eyes; just as, for a peasant, it is of the ultimate nature of things that puddles can be formed in two quite opposite ways, by rain falling from heaven and by springs issuing from the earth; but as the peasant would not have reached a profound insight into nature if he had proclaimed the presence in her of a *tendency to puddles,* to be formed in inexplicably different ways; so the philosopher attains to no profound insight when he proclaims in her a *tendency to vision.* If those words express more than ignorance, they express the love of it. Even if the vitalists were right in despairing of further scientific discoveries, they would be wrong in offering their verbiage as a substitute. Nature may possibly have only a very loose, hazy constitution, to be watched and understood as sailors watch and understand the weather; but Neptune and Aeolus are not thereby proved to be the authors of storms. Yet M. Bergson thinks if life could only be safely shown to arise unaccountably, that would prove the invisible efficacy of a mighty tendency to life. But would the ultimate contexture and miracle of things be made less arbitrary, and less a matter of brute fact, by the presence behind them of an actual and arbitrary effort that such should be their nature? If this word 'effort' is not a mere figure of rhetoric, a name for a movement in things of which the end happens to interest us more than the beginning, if it is meant to be an effort actually and consciously existing, then we must proceed to ask: Why did this effort exist? Why did it choose that particular end to strive for? How did it reach the con-

ception of that end, which had never been realized before, and
which no existent nature demanded for its fulfilment? How
did the effort, once made specific, select the particular matter
it was to transform? Why did this matter respond to the
disembodied effort that it should change its habits? Not one
of these questions is easier to answer than the question why
nature is living or animals have eyes. Yet without seeking to
solve the only real problem, namely, how nature is actually
constituted, this introduction of metaphysical powers raises
all the others, artificially and without occasion. This side of
M. Bergson's philosophy illustrates the worst and most
familiar vices of metaphysics. It marvels at some appearance,
not to investigate it, but to give it an unctuous name. Then it
turns this name into a power, that by its operation creates the
appearance. This is simply verbal mythology or the hypostasis
of words, and there would be some excuse for a rude person
who should call it rubbish.

The metaphysical abuse of psychology is as extraordinary
in modern Europe as that of fancy ever was in India or of
rhetoric in Greece. We find, for instance, Mr Bradley mur-
muring, as a matter almost too obvious to mention, that the
existence of anything not sentient is unmeaning to him; or,
if I may put this evident principle in other words, that nothing
is able to exist unless something else is able to discover it.
Yet even if discovered the poor candidate for existence would
be foiled, for it would turn out to be nothing but a modifica-
tion of the mind falsely said to discover it. Existence and
discovery are conceptions which the malicious criticism of
knowledge (which is the psychology of knowledge abused)
pretends to have discarded and outgrown altogether; the conception of immediacy has taken their place. This malicious
criticism of knowledge is based on the silent assumption that
knowledge is impossible. Whenever you mention anything,
it baffles you by talking instead about your idea of what you
mention; and if ever you describe the origin of anything, it
substitutes, as a counter-theory, its theory of the origin of
your description. This, however, would not be a counter-

theory at all if the criticism of knowledge had not been corrupted into a negative dogma, maintaining that ideas of things
are the only things possible and that therefore only ideas and
not things can have an origin. Nothing could better illustrate
how deep this cognitive impotence has got into people's bones
than the manner in which, in the latest schools of philosophy,
it is being disavowed; for unblushing idealism is distinctly
out of fashion. M. Bergson tells us he has solved a difficulty
that seemed hopeless by avoiding a fallacy common to idealism
and realism. The difficulty was that if you started with self-
existent matter you could never arrive at mind, and if you
started with self-existent mind you could never arrive at
matter. The fallacy was that both schools innocently supposed
there was an existing world to discover, and each thought it
possible that its view should describe that world as it really
was. What now is M. Bergson's solution? That no articulated
world, either material or psychical, exists at all, but only a
tendency or enduring effort to evolve images of both sorts;
or rather to evolve images which in their finer texture and
vibration are images of matter, but which grouped and fore-
shortened in various ways are images of minds. The idea of
nature and the idea of consciousness are two apperceptions or
syntheses of the same stuff of experience. The two worlds
thus become substantially identical, continuous, and super-
posable; each can merge insensibly into the other. 'To perceive all the influences of all the points of all bodies would be
to sink to the condition of a material object.'* To perceive
some of these influences, by having created organs that shut
out the others, is to be a mind.

This solution is obtained by substituting, as usual, the ideas
of things for the things themselves and cheating the honest
man who was talking about objects by answering him as if he
were talking about himself. Certainly, if we could limit ourselves to feeling life flow and the whole world vibrate, we
should not raise the question debated between realists and
idealists; but not to raise a question is one thing and to have

* *Matière et Mémoire* [Paris, 1896], p. 38.

solved it is another. What has really been done is to offer us a history, *on the assumption of idealism*, of the idea of mind and the idea of matter. This history may be correct enough psychologically, and such as a student of the life of reason might possibly come to; but it is a mere evasion of the original question concerning the relation of this mental evolution to the world it occurs in. In truth, an enveloping world is assumed by these hereditary idealists not to exist; they rule it out *a priori*, and the life of reason is supposed by them to constitute the whole universe. To be sure, they say they transcend idealism no less than realism, because they mark the point where, by contrast or selection from other objects, the mind has come to be distinguished: but the subterfuge is vain, because by 'mind' they mean simply the idea of mind, and they give no name, except perhaps experience, to the mind that forms that idea. Matter and mind, for these transcendentalists posing as realists, merge and flow so easily together only because both are images or groups of images in an original mind presupposed but never honestly posited. It is in this forgotten mind, also, as the professed idealists urge, that the relations of proximity and simultaneity between various lives can alone subsist, if to subsist is to be experienced.

There is, however, one point of real difference, at least initially, between the idealism of M. Bergson and that of his predecessors. The universal mind, for M. Bergson, is in process of actual transformation. It is not an omniscient God but a cosmic sensibility. In this sensibility matter, with all its vibrations felt in detail, forms one moving panorama together with all minds, which are patterns visible at will from various points of view in that same woof of matter; and so the great experiment crawls and shoots on, the dream of a giant without a body, mindful of the past, uncertain of the future, shuffling his images, and threading his painful way through a labyrinth of cross-purposes.

Such at least is the notion which the reader gathers from the prevailing character of M. Bergson's words; but I am not sure that it would be his ultimate conclusion. Perhaps it is to be out of sympathy with his spirit to speak of an ultimate conclusion at all; nothing comes to a conclusion and nothing is ultimate. Many dilemmas, however, are inevitable, and if the master does not make a choice himself, his pupils will divide and trace the alternative consequences for themselves in each direction. If they care most for a real fluidity, as William James did, they will stick to something like what I have just described; but if they care most for immediacy, as we may suspect that M. Bergson does, they will transform that view into something far more orthodox. For a real fluidity and an absolute immediacy are not compatible. To believe in real change you must put some trust in representation, and if you posit a real past and a real future you posit independent objects. In absolute immediacy, on the contrary, instead of change taken realistically, you can have only a feeling of change. The flux becomes an idea in the absolute, like the image of a moving spiral, always flowing outwards or inwards but with its centre and its circumference always immovable. Duration, we must remember, is simply the sense of lasting; no time is real that is not lived through. Therefore various lives cannot be dated in a common time, but have no temporal relations to one another. Thus, if we insist on immediacy, the vaunted novelty of the future and the inestimable freedom of life threaten to become (like all else) the given *feeling* of novelty or freedom, in passing from a given image of the past to a given image of the future—all these terms being contained in the present; and we have reverted to the familiar conception of absolute immutability in absolute life. M. Bergson has studied Plotinus and Spinoza; I suspect he has not studied them in vain.

Nor is this the only point at which this philosophy, when we live a while with it, suddenly drops its mask of novelty and shows us a familiar face. It would seem, for instance, that beneath the drama of creative evolution there was a deeper nature of things. For apparently creative evolution (apart from the obstacle of matter, which may be explained away idealistically) has to submit to the following conditions: first, to create in sequence, not all at once; second, to create some particular sequence only, not all possible sequences side by side; and third, to continue the one sequence chosen, since if the additions of every new moment were irrelevant to the past, no sequence, no vital persistence or progress would be secured, and all effort would be wasted. These are compulsions; but it may also, I suppose, be thought a *duty* on the part of the vital impulse to be true to its initial direction and not to halt, as it well might, like the self-reversing Will of Schopenhauer, on perceiving the result of its spontaneous efforts. Necessity would thus appear behind liberty and duty before it. This summons to life to go on, and these conditions imposed upon it, might then very plausibly be attributed to a Deity existing beyond the world, as is done in religious tradition; and such a doctrine, if M. Bergson should happen to be holding it in reserve, would perhaps help to explain some obscurities in his system, such, for instance, as the power of potentiality to actualize itself, of equipoise to become suddenly emphasis on one particular part, and of spirit to pursue an end chosen before it is conceived, and when there is no nature to predetermine it.

It has been said that M. Bergson's system precludes ethics: I cannot think that observation just. Apart from the moral inspiration which appears throughout his philosophy, which is indeed a passionate attempt to exalt (or debase) values into powers, it offers, I should say, two starting-points for ethics. In the first place, the *élan vital* ought not to falter, although it can do so: therefore, to persevere, labour, experiment, propagate, must be duties, and the opposite must be sins. In the second place, freedom, in adding uncaused increments to life, ought to do so in continuation of the whole past, though it might do so frivolously: therefore it is a duty to be studious, consecutive, loyal; you may move in any direction but you must carry the whole past with you. I will not say this suggests a sound system of ethics, because it would be extracted from dogmas which are physical and incidentally incredible; nor would it represent a mature and disillusioned morality, because it would look to the future and not to the eternal; nevertheless it would be deeply ethical, expressing the feelings that have always inspired Hebraic morality.

A good way of testing the calibre of a philosophy is to ask what it thinks of death. Philosophy, said Plato, is a meditation on death, or rather, if we would do justice to his thought, an aspiration to live disembodied; and Schopenhauer said that the spectacle of death was the first provocation to philosophy. M. Bergson has not yet treated of this subject; but we may perhaps perceive for ourselves the place that it might occupy in his system.* Life, according to him, is the original and absolute force. In the beginning, however, it was only a potentiality or tendency. To become specific lives, life had to emphasize and bring exclusively to consciousness, here and there, special possibilities of living; and where these special lives have their chosen boundary (if this way of putting it is not too Fichtean) they posit or create a material environment. Matter is the view each life takes of what for it are rejected or abandoned possibilities of living. This might show how the absolute will to live, if it was to be carried out, would have to begin by evoking a sense of dead or material things about it; it would not show how death could ever overtake the will itself. If matter were merely the periphery which life has to draw round itself, in order to be a definite life, matter could never abolish any life; as the ring of a circus or the sand of the arena can never abolish the show for which they have been prepared. Life would then be fed and defined by matter, as an artist is served by the matter he needs to carry on his art.

Yet in actual life there is undeniably such a thing as danger and failure. M. Bergson even thinks that the facing of in-

---

* M. Bergson has shown at considerable length that the idea of non-existence is more complex, psychologically, than the idea of existence, and posterior to it. He evidently thinks this disposes of the reality of non-existence also: for it is the reality that he wishes to exorcize by his words. If, however, non-existence and the idea of non-existence were identical, it would have been impossible for me not to exist before I was born: my non-existence then would be more complex than my existence now, and posterior to it. The initiated would not recoil from this consequence, but it might open the eyes of some catechumens. It is a good test of the malicious theory of knowledge.

creased dangers is one proof that vital force is an absolute thing; for if life were an equilibrium, it would not displace itself and run new risks of death, by making itself more complex and ticklish, as it does in the higher organisms and the finer arts.* Yet if life is the only substance, how is such a risk of death possible at all? I suppose the special life that arises about a given nucleus of feeling, by emphasizing some of the relations which that feeling has in the world, might be abolished if a greater emphasis were laid on another set of its relations, starting from some other nucleus. We must remember that these selections, according to M. Bergson, are not apperceptions merely. They are creative efforts. The future constitution of the flux will vary in response to them. Each mind sucks the world, so far as it can, into its own vortex. A cross-apperception will then amount to a contrary force. Two souls will not be able to dominate the same matter in peace and friendship. Being forces, they will pull that matter in different ways. Each soul will tend to devour and to direct exclusively the movement influenced by the other soul. The one that succeeds in ruling that movement will live on; the other, I suppose, will die, although M. Bergson may not like that painful word. He says the lower organisms store energy for the higher organisms to use; but when a sheep appropriates the energy stored up in grass, or a man that stored up in mutton, it looks as if the grass and the sheep had perished. Their *élan vital* is no longer theirs, for in this rough world to live is to kill. Nothing arises in nature, Lucretius says, save helped by the death of some other thing. Of course, this is no defeat for the *élan vital* in general; for according to our philosopher the whole universe from the beginning has been making for just that supreme sort of consciousness which

* This argument against mechanism is a good instance of the difficulties which mythological habits of mind import unnecessarily into science. An equilibrium would not displace itself! But an equilibrium is a natural result, not a magical entity. It is continually displaced, as its constituents are modified by internal movements or external agencies; and while many a time the equilibrium is thereby destroyed altogether, sometimes it is replaced by a more elaborate and perilous equilibrium; as glaciers carry many rocks down, but leave some, here and there, piled in the most unlikely pinnacles and pagodas.

man, who eats the mutton, now possesses. The sheep and the grass were only things by the way and scaffolding for our precious humanity. But would it not be better if some being should arise nobler than man, not requiring abstract intellect nor artificial weapons, but endowed with instinct and intuition and, let us say, the power of killing by radiating electricity? And might not men then turn out to have been mere explosives, in which energy was stored for convenient digestion by that superior creature? A shocking thought, no doubt, like the thought of death, and more distressing to our vital feelings than is the pleasing assimilation of grass and mutton in our bellies. Yet I can see no ground, except a desire to flatter oneself, for not crediting the *élan vital* with some such digestive intention. M. Bergson's system would hardly be more speculative if it entertained this possibility, and it would seem more honest.

The vital impulse is certainly immortal; for if we take it in the naturalistic exoteric sense, for a force discovered in biology, it is an independent agent coming down into matter, organizing it against its will, and stirring it like the angel the pool of Bethesda. Though the ripples die down, the angel is not affected. He has merely flown away. And if we take the vital impulse mystically and esoterically, as the *only* primal force, creating matter in order to play with it, the immortality of life is even more obvious; for there is then nothing else in being that could possibly abolish it. But when we come to immortality for the individual, all grows obscure and ambiguous. The original tendency of life was certainly cosmic and not distinguished into persons: we are told it was like a wireless message sent at the creation which is being read off at last by the humanity of today. In the naturalistic view, the diversity of persons would seem to be due to the different material conditions under which one and the same spiritual purpose must fight its way towards realization in different times and places. It is quite conceivable, however, that in the mystical view the very sense of the original message should comport this variety of interpretations, and that the purpose should always have been to produce diverse individuals.

The first view, as usual, is the one which M. Bergson has prevailingly in mind, and communicates most plausibly; while he holds to it he is still talking about the natural world, and so we still know what he is talking about. On this view, however, personal immortality would be impossible; it would be, if it were aimed at, a self-contradiction in the aim of life; for the diversity of persons would be due to impediments only, and souls would differ simply in so far as they mutilated the message which they were all alike trying to repeat. They would necessarily, when the spirit was victorious, be re-absorbed and identified in the universal spirit. This view also seems most consonant with M. Bergson's theory of primitive reality, as a flux of fused images, or a mind lost in matter; to this view, too, is attributable his hostility to intelligence, in that it arrests the flux, divides the fused images, and thereby murders and devitalizes reality. Of course the destiny of spirit would not be to revert to that diffused materiality; for the original mind lost in matter had a very short memory; it was a sort of cosmic trepidation only, whereas the ultimate mind would remember all that, in its efforts after freedom, it had ever superadded to that trepidation or made it turn into. Even the abstract views of things taken by the practical intellect would, I fear, have to burden the universal memory to the end. We should be remembered, even if we could no longer exist.

On the other more profound view, however, might not personal immortality be secured? Suppose the original message said: Translate me into a thousand tongues! In fulfilling its duty, the universe would then continue to divide its dream into phantom individuals; as it had to insulate its parts in the beginning in order to dominate and transform them freely, so it would always continue to insulate them, so as not to lose its cross-vistas and its mobility. There is no reason, then, why individuals should not live for ever. But a condition seems to be involved which may well make belief stagger. It would be impossible for the universe to divide its images into particular minds unless it preserved the images of their particular bodies also. Particular minds arise, according to this philosophy, in the interests of practice: which means, biologically, to secure a better adjustment of the body to its environment, so that it may survive. Mystically, too, the fundamental force is a half-conscious purpose that practice, or freedom, should come to be; or rather, that an apparition or experience of practice and freedom should arise; for in this philosophy appearance is all. To secure this desirable apparition of practice special tasks are set to various nuclei in felt space (such, for instance, as the task to *see*), and the image of a body (in this case that of an eye) is gradually formed, in order to execute that task; for evidently the Absolute can see only if it looks, and to look it must first choose a point of view and an optical method. This point of view and this method posit the individual; they fix him in time and space, and determine the quality and range of his passive experience: they are his body. If the Absolute, then, wishes to retain the individual not merely as one of its memories but as one of its organs of practical life, it must begin by retaining the image of his body. His body must continue to figure in that landscape of nature which the absolute life, as it pulses, keeps always composing and recomposing. Otherwise a personal mind, a sketch of things made from the point of view and in the interests of that body, cannot be preserved.

M. Bergson, accordingly, should either tell us that our bodies are going to rise again, or he should not tell us, or give us to understand, that our minds are going to endure. I suppose he cannot venture to preach the resurrection of the body to this weak-kneed generation; he is too modern and plausible for that. Yet he is too amiable to deny to our dilated nostrils some voluptuous whiffs of immortality. He asks if we are not 'led to suppose' that consciousness passes through matter to be tempered like steel, to constitute distinct personalities, and prepare them for a higher existence. Other animal minds are but human minds arrested; men at last (what men, I wonder?) are 'capable of remembering all and willing all and controlling their past and their future', so that 'we shall have no repugnance in admitting that in man, though perhaps in man alone, consciousness pursues its path beyond this earthly life.' Elsewhere he says, in a phrase already much quoted and perhaps destined to be famous, that in man the spirit can 'spurn every kind of resistance and break through many an obstacle, perhaps even death'. Here the tenor has ended on the inevitable high note, and the gallery is delighted. But was that the note set down for him in the music? And has he not sung it in falsetto?

The immediate knows nothing about death; it takes intelligence to conceive it; and that perhaps is why M. Bergson says so little about it, and that little so far from serious. But he talks a great deal about life, he feels he has penetrated deeply into its nature; and yet death, together with birth, is the natural analysis of what life is. What is this creative purpose, that must wait for sun and rain to set it in motion? What is this life, that in any individual can be suddenly extinguished by a bullet? What is this *élan vital*, that a little fall in temperature would banish altogether from the universe? The study of death may be out of fashion, but it is never out of season. The omission of this, which is almost the omission of wisdom from philosophy, warns us that in M. Bergson's thought we have something occasional and partial, the work of an astute apologist, a party man, driven to desperate speculation by a timid attachment to prejudice. Like other terrified idealisms, the system of M. Bergson has neither good sense, nor rigour, nor candour, nor solidity. It is a brilliant attempt to confuse the lessons of experience by refining upon its texture, an attempt to make us halt, for the love of primitive illusions, in the path of discipline and reason. It is likely to prove a successful attempt, because it flatters the weaknesses of the moment, expresses them with emotion, and covers them with a feint at scientific speculation. It is not, however, a powerful system, like that of Hegel, capable of bewildering and obsessing many who have no natural love for shams. M. Bergson will hardly bewilder; his style is too clear, the field where his just observations lie—the immediate—is too well defined, and the mythology which results from projecting the terms of the immediate into the absolute, and turning them into powers, is too obviously verbal. He will not long impose on any save those who enjoy being imposed upon; but for a long time he may increase their number. His doctrine is indeed alluring. Instead of telling us, as a stern and contrite philosophy would, that the truth is remote, difficult, and almost undiscoverable by human efforts, that the universe is vast and unfathomable, yet that the knowledge of its ways is precious to our better selves, if we would not live befooled, this philosophy rather tells us that nothing is truer or more precious than our rudimentary consciousness, with its vague instincts and premonitions, that everything ideal is fictitious, and that the universe, at heart, is as palpitating and irrational as ourselves. Why then strain the inquiry? Why seek to dominate passion by understanding it? Rather live on; work, it matters little at what, and grow, it matters nothing in what direction. Exert your instinctive powers of vegetation and emotion; let your philosophy itself be a frank expression of this flux, the roar of the ocean in your little sea-shell, a momentary posture of your living soul, not a stark adoration of things reputed eternal.

So the intellectual faithlessness and the material servility of the age are flattered together and taught to justify themselves theoretically. They cry joyfully, *non peccavi*, which is the modern formula for confession. M. Bergson's philosophy itself is a confession of a certain mystical rebellion and atavism in the contemporary mind. It will remain a beautiful monument to the passing moment, a capital film for the cinematograph of history, full of psychological truth and of a kind of restrained sentimental piety. His thought has all the charm that can go without strength and all the competence that can go without mastery. This is not an age of mastery; it is confused with too much business; it has not brave simplicity. The mind has forgotten its proper function, which is to crown life by quickening it into intelligence, and thinks if it could only prove that it accelerated life, that might perhaps justify its existence; like a philosopher at sea who, to make himself useful, should blow into the sail.

THE PHILOSOPHY OF
MR BERTRAND RUSSELL

HYPOSTATIC ETHICS

If Mr Russell, in his essay on 'The Elements of Ethics', had wished to propitiate the unregenerate naturalist, before trying to convert him, he could not have chosen a more skilful procedure; for he begins by telling us that 'what is called good conduct is conduct which is a means to other things which are good on their own account; and hence...the study of what is good or bad on its own account must be included in ethics'. Two consequences are involved in this: first, that ethics is concerned with the economy of all values, and not with 'moral' goods only, or with duty; and second, that values may and do inhere in a great variety of things and relations, all of which it is the part of wisdom to respect, and if possible to establish. In this matter, according to our author, the general philosopher is prone to one error and the professed moralist to another:

The philosopher, bent on the construction of a system, is inclined to simplify the facts unduly...and to twist them into a form in which they can all be deduced from one or two general principles. The moralist, on the other hand, being primarily concerned with conduct, tends to become absorbed in means, to value the actions men ought to perform more than the ends which such actions serve... Hence most of what they value in this world would have to be omitted by many moralists from any imagined heaven, because there such things as self-denial and effort and courage and pity could find no place...Kant has the bad eminence of combining both errors in the highest possible degree, since he holds that there is nothing good except the virtuous will—a view which simplifies the good as much as any philosopher could wish, and mistakes means for ends as completely as any moralist could enjoin.

Those of us who are what Mr Russell would call ethical sceptics will be delighted at this way of clearing the ground; it opens before us the prospect of a moral philosophy that

161

should estimate the various values of things known and of things imaginable, showing what combinations of goods are possible in any one rational system, and (if fancy could stretch so far) what different rational systems would be possible in places and times remote enough from one another not to come into physical conflict. Such ethics, since it would express in reflection the dumb but actual interests of men, might have both influence and authority over them; two things which an alien and dogmatic ethics necessarily lacks. The joy of the ethical sceptic in Mr Russell is destined, however, to be short-lived. Before proceeding to the expression of concrete ideals, he thinks it necessary to ask a preliminary and quite abstract question, to which his essay is chiefly devoted; namely, what is the right definition of the predicate 'good', which we hope to apply in the sequel to such a variety of things? And he answers at once: the predicate 'good' is indefinable. This answer he shows to be unavoidable, and so evidently unavoidable that we might perhaps have been absolved from asking the question; for, as he says, the so-called definitions of 'good'—that it is pleasure, the desired, and so forth—are not definitions of the predicate 'good', but designations of the things to which this predicate is applied by different persons. Pleasure, and its rivals, are not synonyms for the abstract quality 'good', but names for classes of concrete facts that are supposed to possess that quality. From this correct, if somewhat trifling, observation, however, Mr Russell, like Mr Moore before him, evokes a portentous dogma. Not being able to define good, he hypostasizes it. 'Good and bad', he says, 'are qualities which belong to objects independently of our opinions, just as much as round and square do; and when two people differ as to whether a thing is good, only one of them can be right, though it may be very hard to know which is right.' 'We cannot maintain that for me a thing ought to exist on its own account, while for you it ought not; that would merely mean that one of us is mistaken, since in fact everything either ought to exist, or ought not.' Thus we are asked to believe that good attaches to things for no reason or cause, and according to no principles of distribution; that it must be found there by a sort of receptive exploration in each separate case; in other words, that it is an absolute, not a relative thing, a primary and not a secondary quality.

That the quality 'good' is indefinable is one assertion, and obvious; but that the presence of this quality is unconditioned is another, and astonishing. My logic, I am well aware, is not very accurate or subtle; and I wish Mr Russell had not left it to me to discover the connection between these two propositions. Green is an indefinable predicate, and the specific quality of it can be given only in intuition; but it is a quality that things acquire under certain conditions, so much so that the same bit of grass, at the same moment, may have it from one point of view and not from another. Right and left are indefinable; the difference could not be explained without being invoked in the explanation; yet everything that is to the right is not to the right on no condition, but obviously on the condition that someone is looking in a certain direction; and if someone else at the same time is looking in the opposite direction, what is truly to the right will be truly to the left also. If Mr Russell thinks this is a contradiction, I understand why the universe does not please him. The contradiction would be real, undoubtedly, if we suggested that the *idea* of good was at any time or in any relation the *idea* of evil, or the *intuition* of right that of left, or the *quality* of green that of yellow; these disembodied essences are fixed by the intent that selects them, and in that ideal realm they can never have any relations except the dialectical ones implied in their nature, and these relations they must always retain. But the contradiction disappears when, instead of considering the qualities in themselves, we consider the things of which those qualities are aspects; for the qualities of things are not compacted by implication, but are conjoined irrationally by nature, as she will; and the same thing may be, and is at once yellow and green, to the left and to the right, good and evil, many and one, large and small; and whatever verbal paradox there

may be in this way of speaking (for from the point of view of nature it is natural enough) had been thoroughly explained and talked out by the time of Plato, who complained that people should still raise a difficulty so trite and exploded.*
Indeed, while square is always square, and round round, a thing that is round may actually be square also, if we allow it to have a little body, and to be a cylinder.

But perhaps what suggests this hypostasis of good is rather the fact that what others find good, or what we ourselves have found good in moods with which we retain no sympathy, is sometimes pronounced by us to be bad; and far from inferring from this diversity of experience that the present good, like the others, corresponds to a particular attitude or interest of ours, and is dependent upon it, Mr Russell and Mr Moore infer instead that the presence of the good must be independent of all interests, attitudes and opinions. They imagine that the truth of a proposition attributing a certain relative quality to an object contradicts the truth of another proposition, attributing to the same object an opposite relative quality. Thus if a man here and another man at the antipodes

---

* Plato, *Philebus*, 14 D. The dialectical element in this dialogue is evidently the basis of Mr Russell's, as of Mr Moore's, ethics; but they have not adopted the other elements in it, I mean the political and the theological. As to the political element, Plato everywhere conceives the good as the eligible in life, and refers it to human nature and to the pursuit of happiness—that happiness which Mr Russell, in a rash moment, says is but a name which some people prefer to give to pleasure. Thus in the *Philebus* (11 D) the good looked for is declared to be 'some state and disposition of the soul which has the property of making all men happy'; and later (66 D) the conclusion is that insight is better than pleasure 'as an element in human life'. As to the theological element, Plato, in hypostasizing the good, does not hypostasize it as good, but as cause or power, which is, it seems to me, the sole category that justifies hypostasis, and logically involves it; for if things have a ground at all, that ground must exist before them and beyond them. Hence the whole Platonic and Christian scheme, in making the good independent of private will and opinion, by no means makes it independent of the direction of nature in general and of human nature in particular; for all things have been created with an innate predisposition towards the creative good, and are capable of finding happiness in nothing else. Obligation, in this system, remains internal and vital. Plato attributes a single vital direction and a single moral source to the cosmos. This is what determines and narrows the scope of the true good; for the true good is that relevant to nature. Plato would not have been a dogmatic moralist, had he not been a theist.

call opposite directions up, 'only one of them can be right, though it may be very hard to know which is right'.

To protect the belated innocence of this state of mind, Mr Russell, so far as I can see, has only one argument, and one analogy. The argument is that 'if this were not the case, we could not reason with a man as to what is right'. 'We do in fact hold that when one man approves of a certain act, while another disapproves, one of them is mistaken, which would not be the case with a mere emotion. If one man likes oysters and another dislikes them, we do not say that either of them is mistaken.' In other words, we are to maintain our prejudices, however absurd, lest it should become unnecessary to quarrel about them! Truly the debating society has its idols, no less than the cave and the theatre. The analogy that comes to buttress somewhat this singular argument is the analogy between ethical propriety and physical or logical truth. An ethical proposition may be correct or incorrect, in a sense justifying argument, when it touches what is good as a means, that is, when it is not intrinsically ethical, but deals with causes and effects, or with matters of fact or necessity. But to speak of the truth of an ultimate good would be a false collocation of terms; an ultimate good is chosen, found, or aimed at; it is not opined. The ultimate intuitions on which ethics rests are not debatable, for they are not opinions we hazard but preferences we feel; and it can be neither correct nor incorrect to feel them. We may assert these preferences fiercely or with sweet reasonableness, and we may be more or less incapable of sympathizing with the different preferences of others; about oysters we may be tolerant, like Mr Russell, and about character intolerant; but that is already a great advance in enlightenment, since the majority of mankind have regarded as hateful in the highest degree anyone who indulged in pork, or beans, or frogs' legs, or who had a weakness for anything called 'unnatural'; for it is the things that offend their animal instincts that intense natures have always found to be, intrinsically and *par excellence*, abominations.

I am not sure whether Mr Russell thinks he has disposed

of this view where he discusses the proposition that the good is the desired and refutes it on the ground that 'it is commonly admitted that there are bad desires; and when people speak of bad desires, they seem to mean desires for what is bad'. Most people undoubtedly call desires bad when they are generically contrary to their own desires, and call objects that disgust them bad, even when other people covet them. This human weakness is not, however, a very high authority for a logician to appeal to, being too like the attitude of the German lady who said that Englishmen called a certain object *bread*, and Frenchmen called it *pain*, but that it really was *Brod*. Scholastic philosophy is inclined to this way of asserting itself; and Mr Russell, though he candidly admits that there are ultimate differences of opinion about good and evil, would gladly minimize these differences, and thinks he triumphs when he feels that the prejudices of his readers will agree with his own; as if the constitutional unanimity of all human animals, supposing it existed, could tend to show that the good they agreed to recognize was independent of their constitution.

In a somewhat worthier sense, however, we may admit that there are desires for what is bad, since desire and will, in the proper psychological sense of these words, are incidental phases of consciousness, expressing but not constituting those natural relations that make one thing good for another. At the same time the words desire and will are often used, in a mythical or transcendental sense, for those material dispositions and instincts by which vital and moral units are constituted. It is in reference to such constitutional interests that things are 'really' good or bad; interests which may not be fairly represented by any incidental conscious desire. No doubt any desire, however capricious, represents some momentary and partial interest, which lends to its objects a certain real and inalienable value; yet when we consider, as we do in human society, the interests of men, whom reflection and settled purposes have raised more or less to the ideal dignity of individuals, then passing fancies and passions may indeed have bad objects, and be bad themselves, in that they thwart the more comprehensive interests of the soul that entertains them. Food and poison are such only relatively, and in view of particular bodies, and the same material thing may be food and poison at once; the child, and even the doctor, may easily mistake one for the other. For the human system whisky is truly more intoxicating than coffee, and the contrary opinion would be an error; but what a strange way of vindicating this real, though relative, distinction, to insist that whisky is more intoxicating in itself, without reference to any animal; that it is pervaded, as it were, by an inherent intoxication, and stands dead drunk in its bottle! Yet just in this way Mr Russell and Mr Moore conceive things to be dead good and dead bad. It is such a view, rather than the naturalistic one, that renders reasoning and self-criticism impossible in morals; for wrong desires, and false opinions as to value, are conceivable only because a point of reference or criterion is available to prove them such. If no point of reference and no criterion were admitted to be relevant, nothing but physical stress could give to one assertion of value greater force than to another. The shouting moralist no doubt has his place, but not in philosophy.

That good is not an intrinsic or primary quality, but relative and adventitious, is clearly betrayed by Mr Russell's own way of arguing, whenever he approaches some concrete ethical question. For instance, to show that the good is not pleasure, he can avowedly do nothing but appeal 'to ethical judgments with which almost everyone would agree'. He repeats, in effect, Plato's argument about the life of the oyster, having pleasure with no knowledge. Imagine such mindless pleasure, as intense and prolonged as you please, and would you choose it? Is it your good? Here the British reader, like the blushing Greek youth, is expected to answer instinctively, No! It is an *argumentum ad hominem* (and there can be no other kind of argument in ethics); but the man who gives the required answer does so not because the answer is self-evident, which it is not, but because he is the required sort of man. He is shocked at the idea of resembling an oyster. Yet changeless pleasure, without memory or reflection, without the wearisome intermixture of arbitrary images, is just what the mystic, the voluptuary, and perhaps the oyster find to be good. Ideas, in their origin, are probably signals of alarm; and the distress which they marked in the beginning always clings to them in some measure, and causes many a soul, far more profound than that of the young Protarchus or of the British reader, to long for them to cease altogether. Such a radical hedonism is indeed inhuman; it undermines all conventional ambitions, and is not a possible foundation for political or artistic life. But that is all we can say against it. Our humanity cannot annul the incommensurable sorts of good that may be pursued in the world, though it cannot itself pursue them. The impossibility which people labour under of being satisfied with pure pleasure as a goal is due to their want of imagination, or rather to their being dominated by an imagination which is exclusively human.

The author's estrangement from reality reappears in his treatment of egoism, and most of all in his 'Free Man's Religion'. Egoism, he thinks, is untenable because 'if I am right in thinking that my good is the only good, then every one else is mistaken unless he admits that my good, not his, is the only good'. 'Most people...would admit that it is better two people's desires should be satisfied than only one person's...Then what is good is not good *for me* or *for you*, but is simply good.' 'It is, indeed, so evident that it is better to secure a greater good for *A* than a lesser good for *B*, that it is hard to find any still more evident principle by which to prove this. And if *A* happens to be someone else, and *B* to be myself, that cannot affect the question, since it is irrelevant to the general question who *A* and *B* may be.' To the question, as the logician states it after transforming men into letters, it is certainly irrelevant; but it is not irrelevant to the case as it arises in nature.[1] If two goods are somehow rightly pro-

---

[1] Cf. Santayana's letter of 10 November 1913 to a former colleague at Harvard, Professor B. A. G. Fuller: 'His [Bertrand Russell's] theory of the natural world...is, in comparison with the reality of nature and even of experience, what the report of a battle might be in the mind of a telegraph wire through which a full description of it had been sent. There would be a perfectly

nounced to be equally good, no circumstance can render one
better than the other. And if the locus in which the good is to
arise is somehow pronounced to be indifferent, it will certainly
be indifferent whether that good arises in me or in you. But
how shall these two pronouncements be made? In practice,
values vannot be compared save as represented or enacted in
the private imagination of somebody: for we could not conceive that an alien good *was* a good (as Mr Russell cannot
conceive that the life of an ecstatic oyster is a good) unless we
could sympathize with it in some way in our own persons;
and on the warmth which we felt in so representing the alien
good would hang our conviction that it was truly valuable,
and had worth in comparison with our own good. The voice
of reason, bidding us prefer the greater good, no matter who
is to enjoy it, is also nothing but the force of sympathy, bringing a remote existence before us vividly *sub specie boni*. Capacity
for such sympathy measures the capacity to recognize duty
and therefore, in a moral sense, to have it. Doubtless it is
conceivable that all wills should become co-operative, and
that nature should be ruled magically by an exact and universal sympathy; but this situation must be actually attained
in part before it can be conceived or judged to be an authoritative ideal. The tigers cannot regard it as such, for it would
suppress the tragic good called ferocity, which makes, in their
eyes, the chief glory of the universe. Therefore the inertia of
nature, the ferocity of beasts, the optimism of mystics, and
the selfishness of men and nations must all be accepted as conditions for the peculiar goods, essentially incommensurable,
which they can generate severally. It is misplaced vehemence
to call them intrinsically detestable, because they do not (as
they cannot) generate or recognize the goods we prize.

In the real world, persons are not abstract egos, like *A* and
B, so that to benefit one is clearly as good as to benefit another.
Indeed, abstract egos could not be benefited, for they could

adequate representation of everything in dots, dashes, and pauses, but no
blood, no passions, no drama, no heroes, and no poor devils. On the other hand,
Russell's lectures on logic (one or two of which he has shown me) are very
clear and enlightening...'

not be modified at all, even if somehow they could be distinguished. It would be the qualities or objects distributed among them that would carry, wherever they went, each its inalienable cargo of value, like ships sailing from sea to sea. But it is quite vain and artificial to imagine different goods charged with such absolute and comparable weights; and actual egoism is not the thin and refutable thing that Mr Russell makes of it. What it really holds is that a given man, oneself, and those akin to him, are qualitatively better than other beings; that the things they prize are intrinsically better than the things prized by others; and that therefore there is no injustice in treating these chosen interests as supreme. The injustice, it is felt, would lie rather in not treating things so unequal unequally. This feeling may, in many cases, amuse the impartial observer, or make him indignant; yet it may, in every case, according to Mr Russell, be absolutely just. The refutation he gives of egoism would not dissuade any fanatic from exterminating all his enemies with a good conscience; it would merely encourage him to assert that what he was ruthlessly establishing was the absolute good. Doubtless such conscientious tyrants would be wretched themselves, and compelled to make sacrifices which would cost them dear; but that would only extend, as it were, the pernicious egoism of that part of their being which they had allowed to usurp a universal empire. The twang of intolerance and of self-mutilation is not absent from the ethics of Mr Russell and Mr Moore, even as it stands; and one trembles to think what it may become in the mouths of their disciples. Intolerance itself is a form of egoism, and to condemn egoism intolerantly is to share it.

I cannot help thinking that a consciousness of the relativity of values, if it became prevalent, would tend to render people more truly social than would a belief that things have intrinsic and unchangeable values, no matter what the attitude of anyone to them may be. If we said that goods, including the right distribution of goods, are relative to specific natures, moral warfare would continue, but not with poisoned arrows. Our private sense of justice itself would be acknowledged to have but a relative authority, and while we could not have a higher duty than to follow it, we should seek to meet those whose aims were incompatible with it as we meet things physically inconvenient, without insulting them as if they were morally vile or logically contemptible. Real unselfishness consists in sharing the interests of others. Beyond the pale of actual unanimity the only possible unselfishness is chivalry—a recognition of the inward right and justification of our enemies fighting against us. This chivalry has long been practised on the battlefield without abolishing the causes of war; and it might conceivably be extended to all the conflicts of men with one another, and of the warring elements within each breast. Policy, hypnotization, and even surgery may be practised without exorcisms or anathemas. When a man has decided on a course of action, it is a vain indulgence in expletives to declare that he is sure that course is absolutely right. His moral dogma expresses its natural origin all the more clearly the more hotly it is proclaimed; and ethical absolutism, being a mental grimace of passion, refutes what it says by what it is...[1]

[1] The two essays by Russell referred to in this critique—'The Elements of Ethics' and 'The Free Man's Religion'—are to be found in his *Philosophical Essays* (London, 1910), pp. 1–58 and 59–70.

EGOTISM IN GERMAN
PHILOSOPHY

THE PROTESTANT HERITAGE

...German philosophy has inherited from Protestantism its earnestness and pious intention; also a tendency to retain, for whatever changed views it may put forward, the names of former beliefs. God, freedom, and immortality, for instance, may eventually be transformed into their opposites, since the oracle of faith is internal; but their names may be kept, together with a feeling that what will now bear those names is much more satisfying than what they originally stood for. If it should seem that God came nearest to us, and dwelt within us, in the form of vital energy, if freedom should turn out really to mean personality, if immortality, in the end, should prove identical with the endlessness of human progress, and if these new thoughts should satisfy and encourage us as the evanescent ideas of God, freedom, and immortality satisfied and encouraged our fathers, why should we not use these consecrated names for our new conceptions, and thus indicate the continuity of religion amid the flux of science? This expedient is not always hypocritical. It was quite candid in men like Spinoza and Emerson, whose attachment to positive religion had insensibly given way to a half-mystical, half-intellectual satisfaction with the natural world, as their eloquent imagination conceived it. But whether candid or disingenuous, this habit has the advantage of oiling the wheels of progress with a sacred unction. In facilitating change it blurs the consciousness of change, and leads people to associate with their new opinions sentiments which are logically incompatible with them. The attachment of many tender-minded people to German philosophy is due to this circumstance, for German philosophy is not tender.

The beauty and the torment of Protestantism is that it

opens the door so wide to what lies beyond it. This progressive quality it has fully transmitted to all the systems of German philosophy. Not that each of them, like the earlier Protestant sects, does not think itself true and final; but in spite of itself it suggests some next thing. We must expect, therefore, that the more conservative elements in each system should provoke protests in the next generation; and it is hard to say whether such inconstancy is a weakness, or is simply loyalty to the principle of progress. Kant was a Puritan; he revered the rule of right as something immutable and holy, perhaps never obeyed in the world. Fichte was somewhat freer in his Calvinism; the rule of right was the moving power in all life and nature, though it might have been betrayed by a doomed and self-seeking generation. Hegel was a very free and superior Lutheran; he saw that the divine will was necessarily and continuously realized in this world, though we might not recognize the fact in our petty moral judgments. Schopenhauer, speaking again for this human judgment, revolted against that cruel optimism, and was an indignant atheist; and finally, in Nietzsche, this atheism became exultant; he thought it the part of a man to abet the movement of things, however calamitous, in order to appropriate its wild force and be for a moment the very crest of its wave.

Protestantism was not a reformation by accident, because it happened to find the Church corrupt; it is a reformation essentially, in that every individual must reinterpret the Bible and the practices of the Church in his own spirit. If he accepted them without renewing them in the light of his personal religious experience, he would never have what Protestantism thinks living religion. German philosophy has inherited this characteristic; it is not a cumulative science that can be transmitted ready-made. It is essentially a reform, a revision of traditional knowledge, which each neophyte must make for himself, under pain of rendering only lip-service to transcendental truth, and remaining at heart unregenerate. His chief business is to be converted; he must refute for himself the natural views with which he and all other men have begun life. And still these views—like the temptations of Satan—inevitably form themselves afresh in each generation, and even in the philosopher, between one spell of introspective thought and another, so that he always has to recapitulate his saving arguments from the beginning. Each new idealist in each of his books, often in every lecture and every chapter, must run back to refute again the same lonely opponents—materialism, naturalism, dualism, or whatever he may call them. Dead as each day he declares these foes to be, he has to fight them again in his own soul on the morrow. Hence his continual preoccupation lest he fall away, or lest the world should forget him. To preserve his freedom and his idealism he must daily conquer them anew. This philosophy is secondary, critical, sophistical; it has a perennial quarrel with inevitable opinions.

Protestantism, in spite of its personal status, wished to revert to primitive Christianity. In this desire it was guided partly by a conventional faith in the Scriptures, and partly by a deep sympathy with experimental religion. German religion and philosophy are homesick: they wish to be quite primitive once more. And they actually remain primitive in spirit, spontaneous and tentative, even in the midst of the most cumbrous erudition, as a composition of Dürer's, where flesh, fish, and fowl crowd every corner, still remains primitive, puzzled, and oppressed. Such a naïve but overloaded mind is lost in admiration of its own depth and richness; yet, in fact, it is rather helpless and immature; it has not learned to select what suffices, or to be satisfied with what is best.

Faith for the Germans must be a primitive and groundless assurance, not knowledge credibly transmitted by others whose experience may have been greater than our own. Even philosophy is not conceived as a reasonable adjustment to what may have been discovered to be the constitution of the world; it is in the first instance a criticism, to dissolve that reputed knowledge, and then, when primitive innocence is happily restored, it is a wager or demand made beyond all evidence, and in contempt of all evidence, in obedience to an innate impulse. Of course, it is usual, as a concession to the weaker brethren, to assume that experience, in the end, will seem to satisfy these demands, and that we shall win our bets and our wars; but the point of principle, borrowed by German philosophy from Protestantism, is that the authority of faith is intrinsic and absolute, while any external corroboration of it is problematical and not essential to the rightness of the assumptions that faith makes. In this we have a fundamental characteristic of the school. Carried (as it seldom is) to its logical conclusion, it leads to the ultra-romantic and ultra-idealistic doctrine that the very notion of truth or fact is a fiction of the will, invented to satisfy our desire for some fixed point of reference in thought. In this doctrine we may see the culmination of the Protestant rebellion against mediation in religion, against external authority, and against dogma.

The Protestant precept to search the Scriptures, and the sense that every man must settle the highest questions for himself, have contributed to the zeal with which science and scholarship have been pursued in Germany. In no other country has so large, so industrious, and (amid its rude polemics) so co-operative a set of professors devoted itself to all sorts of learning. But as the original motive was to save one's soul, an apologetic and scholastic manner has often survived: the issue is prejudged and egotism has appeared even in science. For favourable as Protestantism is to investigation and learning, it is almost incompatible with clearness of thought and fundamental freedom of attitude. If the controlling purpose is not political or religious, it is at least 'philosophical', that is to say, arbitrary.

We must remember that the greater part of the 'facts' on which theories are based are reported or inferred facts—*all* in the historical sciences, since the documents and sources must first be pronounced genuine or spurious by the philosophical critic. Here presumptions and private methods of inference determine what shall be admitted for a fact, to say nothing of the interpretation to be given to it. Hence a piece of Biblical or Homeric criticism, a history of Rome or of Germany often becomes a little system of egotistical philosophy, posited and defended with all the parental zeal and all the increasing conviction with which a prophet defends his supernatural inspirations.

The distinction between Mary and Martha is not a German distinction: in Germany the rapt idealist is busy about many things, so that his action is apt to be heady and his contemplation perturbed. Only the principle is expected to be spiritual, the illustrations must all be material and mundane. There is no paradox in German idealism turning to material science, commerce, and war for a fresh field of operation. No degeneracy is implied in such an extension of its vocation, especially when the other ideals of the state—pure learning, art, social organization—are pursued at the same time with an equal ardour. The test of a genuine German idealist is that he should forget and sink his private happiness in whatever service the state may set him to do.

In view of this political fidelity the changing opinions of men are all indifferent to true religion. It is not a question of *correctness* in opinion or conduct, since for the idealist there can be no external standard of truth, existence, or excellence on which such correctness could depend. Ideas are so much real experience and have no further subject-matter. Thought is simply more or less rich, elaborate, or vehement, like a musical composition, and more or less consistent with itself. It is all a question of depth and fullness of experience, obtained by hacking one's way through this visionary and bewitched existence, the secret purpose of which is to serve the self in its development. In this philosophy imagination that is sustained is called knowledge, illusion that is coherent is called truth, and will that is systematic is called virtue. . .

It has never been my good fortune to see wild beasts in the jungle, but I have sometimes watched a wild bull in the ring, and I can imagine no more striking, simple, and heroic example of animal faith; especially when the bull is what is technically called noble, that is, when he follows the lure

again and again with eternal singleness of thought, eternal
courage, and no suspicion of a hidden agency that is mocking
him. What the red rag is to this brave creature, their passions,
inclinations, and chance notions are to the heathen. What they
will they will; and they would deem it weakness and dis-
loyalty to ask whether it is worth willing or whether it is
attainable. The bull, magnificently sniffing the air, surveys
the arena with the cool contempt and disbelief of the idealist,
as if he said: 'You seem, you are a seeming; I do not quarrel
with you, I do not fear you. I am real, you are nothing.' Then
suddenly, when his eye is caught by some bright cloak displayed before him, his whole soul changes. His will awakes and
he seems to say: 'You are my destiny; I want you, I hate you,
you shall be mine, you shall not stand in my path. I will gore
you. I will disprove you. I will pass beyond you. I shall be,
you shall not have been.' Later, when sorely wounded and
near his end, he grows blind to all these excitements. He
smells the moist earth, and turns to the dungeon where an
hour ago he was at peace. He remembers the herd, the pasture
beyond, and he dreams: 'I shall not die, for I love life. I shall
be young again, young always, for I love youth. All this out-
cry is nought to me, this strange suffering is nought. I will go
to the fields again, to graze, to roam, to love.'

So exactly, with not one least concession to the unsuspected
reality, the heathen soul stands bravely before a painted world,
covets some bauble, and defies death. Heathenism is the
religion of will, the faith which life has in itself because it is
life, and in its aims because it is pursuing them...

Let us admire the sincerity of this searching confession.
Virtue itself, if it relied on self-consciousness for its philosophy, could not justify itself on other grounds. If the difference between virtue and vice is hereby obliterated, that only
proves that the difference is not founded on self-consciousness
but on the circumstances and powers under which we live.
What self-consciousness can disclose is not the basis of anything. All will is the expression of some animal body, frail and
mortal, but teachable and rich in resource. The environment

in which this will finds itself controls and rewards its various movements, and establishes within it the difference between virtue and vice, wisdom and folly... In this sense the Greeks were the least heathen of men. They were singularly docile to political experiment, to law, to methodical art, to the proved limitations and resources of mortal life. This life they found closely hedged about by sky, earth, and sea, by war, madness, and conscience with their indwelling deities, by oracles and local genii with their accustomed cults, by a pervasive fate, and the jealousy of invisible gods. Yet they saw that these divine forces were constant, and that they exercised their pressure and bounty with so much method that a prudent art and religion could be built up in their midst...

The whole transcendental philosophy, if made ultimate, is false, and nothing but a private perspective. The will is absolute neither in the individual nor in humanity. Nature is not a product of the mind, but on the contrary there is an external world, ages prior to any idea of it, which the mind recognizes and feeds upon. There is a steady human nature within us, which our moods and passions may wrong but cannot annul. There is no categorical imperative but only the operation of instincts and interests more or less subject to discipline and mutual adjustment. Our whole life is a compromise, an incipient loose harmony between the passions of the soul and the forces of nature, forces which likewise generate and protect the souls of other creatures, endowing them with powers of expression and self-assertion comparable with our own, and with aims no less sweet and worthy in their own eyes; so that the quick and honest mind cannot but practise courtesy in the universe, exercising its will without vehemence or forced assurance, judging with serenity, and in everything discarding the word absolute as the most false and the most odious of words. As Montaigne observes, 'He who sets before him, as in a picture, this vast image of our mother Nature in her entire majesty; who reads in her aspect such universal and continual variety; who discerns himself therein, and not himself only but a whole kingdom, to be but a most delicate dot—he alone esteems things according to the just measure of their greatness.'

HEGEL AND THE EGOTISM OF IDEAS

When we are discussing egotism need we speak of Hegel? The tone of this philosopher, especially in his later writings, was full of contempt for everything subjective: the point of view of the individual, his opinions and wishes, were treated as of no account unless they had been brought into line with the providential march of events and ideas in the great world. This realism, pronounced and even acrid as it was, was still idealistic in the sense that the substance of the world was conceived not to be material but conceptual—a law or logic which animated phenomena and was the secret of their movement. The world was like a riddle or confused oracle; and the solution to the puzzle lay in the romantic instability or self-contradiction inherent in every finite form of being, which compelled it to pass into something different. The direction of this movement we might understand sympathetically in virtue of a sort of vital dialectic or dramatic necessity in our own reflection. Hegel was a solemn sophist: he made discourse the key to reality.

This technical realism in Hegel was reinforced by his historical imagination, which continually produces an impression of detachment, objectivity, and impersonal intelligence; he often seems to be lost in the events of his story and to be plucking the very heart out of the world. Again, he adored the state, by which in his view the individual should be entirely subjugated, not for the benefit of other individuals (that would be a sort of vicarious selfishness no less barren than private profit), but in the rapt service of common impersonal ends.

The family was a first natural group in which the individual should be happy to lose himself, the trade guild was another, and the state was the highest and most comprehensive of all;

there was nothing worthy or real in a man except his functions in society.

Nevertheless this denial of egotism is apparent only. It is a play within the play. On the smaller stage the individual—save for his lapses and stammerings—is nothing but the instrument and vehicle of divine decrees; in fact he is a puppet, and the only reality of him is the space he fills in the total spectacle. But that little stage is framed in by another, often overlooked, but ever present; and on this larger and nearer stage the ego struts alone. It is I that pull the strings, enjoy the drama, supply its plot and moral, and possess the freedom and actuality which my puppets lack. On the little stage the soul of a man is only one of God's ideas, and his whole worth lies in helping out the pantomime; on the big stage, God is simply my idea of God and the purpose of the play is to express my mind. The spectacle in which every individual dances automatically to the divine tune is only my dream.

The philosophy of Hegel is accordingly subjective and all its realism is but a pose and a tone wilfully assumed. That this is the truth of the matter might be inferred, apart from many continual hints and implications, from the fact that the system is transcendental and founded on Kant. Objectivity can, therefore, be only a show, a matter of make-believe, something imputed to things and persons by the mind, whose poetic energies it manifests. Everything must be set down as a creation of mind, simply because it is an object of thought or knowledge.

This underlying subjectivism also explains the singular satisfaction of Hegel, whose glance was comprehensive enough, with so strangely limited a world as he describes to us. He described what he knew best or had heard of most, and felt he had described the universe. This illusion was inevitable, because his principle was that the universe was created by description and resided in it. The mission of Hegel, as he himself conceived it, was not to discover the real world or any part of it: in theory he retracted all belief in a real world and set in its place his conception or knowledge of it—therefore quite adequate to its object. If China was the oldest country he had heard of, the world began with China, and if Prussia was the youngest and he (as he had to be) its latest philosopher, the world ended with Prussia and with himself. This seems a monstrous egotism, but it is not arbitrary; in one sense it was the least pretentious of attitudes, since it was limited to the description of a current view, not of a separate or prior object. The value of a philosophy could lie only in the fullness and fidelity with which it might focus the conceptions of the age in which it arose. Hegel hoped to do this for his own times; he did not covet truth to anything further.

The same attitude explains the servility of his moral philosophy, which is simply an apology for the established order of things and for the prejudices of his time and country. His deepest conviction was that no system of ethics could be more, and if it tried to be more would be less, because it would be merely personal. When, for instance, he condemned harshly the Roman *patria potestas* it was because it offended the individualism of the Protestant and modern conscience; and if in the next breath he condemned even more harshly the sentimentalists who made tender feeling and good intentions the test of virtue, it was because these individual consciences absolved themselves from conformity to the established Church and state. To inquire whether in itself or in respect to human economy generally, the morality of Buddha, or Socrates, or Rousseau was the best would have seemed to him absurd: the question could only be what approaches or contributions each of these made to the morality approved by the Lutheran community and by the Prussian ministry of education and public worship. The truth, then as now, was whatever every good German believed. This pious wish of Hegel's to interpret the orthodoxy of his generation was successful, and the modest hopes of his philosophy were fulfilled. Never perhaps was a system so true to its date and so false to its subject.

The egotism of Hegel appears also in his treatment of mathematical and physical questions. The infinite he called the false infinite, so as to avoid the dilemmas which it placed him in, such as why the evolution of the Idea began six thousand years ago, or less; what more could happen now that in his self-consciousness that evolution was complete; why it should have gone on in this planet only, or if it had gone on elsewhere also, why the Idea evolving there might not have been a different Idea. But all such questions are excluded when one understands that this philosophy is only a point of view: the world it describes is a vista not separable from the egotistical perspectives that frame it in. The extent of the world need not be discussed, because that extent is an appearance only; in reality the world has no extent, because it is only my present idea.

The infinite thus lost its application; but the word was too idealistic to be discarded. Accordingly the title of true infinite was bestowed on the eventual illusion of completeness, on an alleged system of relations out of relation to anything beyond. That nothing existent, unless it was the bad infinite, could be absolute in this manner did not ruffle Hegel, for the existent did not really concern him but only 'knowledge', that is, a circle of present and objectless ideas. Knowledge, however limited in fact, always has the completeness in question for the egotist, whose objects are not credited with existing beyond himself. Egotism could hardly receive a more radical expression than this: to declare the ego infinite because it can never find anything that is beyond its range.

The favourite tenet of Hegel that everything involves its opposite is also a piece of egotism; for it is equivalent to making things conform to words, not words to things; and the ego, particularly in philosophers, is a nebula of words. In defining things, if you insist on defining them, you are constrained to define them by their relation to other things, or even exclusion of them. If, therefore, things are formed by your definitions of them, these relations and exclusions will be the essence of things. The notion of such intrinsic relativity in things is a sophism even in logic, since elementary terms can never be defined, yet may be perfectly well understood and

arrested in intuition; but what here concerns us is rather the
egotistical motive behind that sophism: namely, that the most
verbal and subjective accidents to which the names of things
are subject in human discourse should be deputed to be the
groundwork of the things and their inmost being.

Egotistical, too, was Hegel's tireless hatred of what he
called the abstract understanding. In his criticisms of this
faculty and the opinions it forms there is much keenness and
some justice. People often reason in the abstract, floating on
words as on bladders: in their knowingness they miss the
complexity and volume of real things. But the errors or
abuses into which verbal intelligence may fall would never
produce that implacable zeal with which Hegel persecutes it.
What obsesses him is the fear that, in spite of its frivolity, the
understanding may some day understand: that it may correct
its inadequacies, trace the real movement of things, and seeing
their mechanism, lose that *effet d'ensemble*, that dramatic illusion, which he calls reason. . .

When we have understood all this, those traits of Hegel's
which at first sight seem least egotistical—his historical insight and his enthusiasm for organized society—take on a new
colour. That historical insight is not really sympathetic; it is
imperious, external, contemptuous, feigned. If you are a
modern reading the Greeks, especially if you read them in the
romantic spirit of Goethe's classicism, and know of them just
what Hegel knew, you will think his description wonderfully
penetrating, masterly and complete: but would Aeschylus or
Plato have thought it so? They would have laughed, or rather
they would not have understood that such a description referred to them at all. It is the legend of the Greeks, not the
life of the Greeks, that is analysed by him. So his account of
medieval religion represents the Protestant legend, not the
Catholic experience. What we know little or nothing about
seems to us in Hegel admirably characterized: what we know
intimately seems to us painted with the eye of a pedantic,
remote, and insolent foreigner. It is but an idea of his own
that he is foisting upon us, calling it our soul. He is creating

a world in his head which might be admirable, if God had made it.

Everyone is subject to such illusions of perspective and to the pathos of distance, now favourable, now unfavourable to what he studies; but Hegel, thinking he had the key to the divine design, fancied himself deeply sympathetic because he saw in everything some fragment of himself. But no part of the world was that; every part had its own inalienable superiority, which to transcend was to lose for ever. To the omniscient egotist every heart is closed. The past will never give away its secret except to some self-forgetful and humble lover who by nature has a kindred destiny. The egotist who thinks to grasp it, so as to serve it up at his philosophic banquet, or exhibit it in his museum of antiquities, grasps only himself; and in that sense, to his confusion, his egotism turns out true.

The egotism that appears in this lordly way of treating the past is egotism of the imagination, the same that was expressed in the romantic love of nature, which was really a very subtle, very studious, very obstinate love of self, intent on finding some reference and deference to oneself in everything. But there is also an egotism of passion, which in Hegel appears in his worship of the state. 'The passions' is the old and fit name for what the Germans call ideals. The passions are not selfish in the sense in which the German moralists denounce selfishness; they are not contrived by him who harbours them for his ulterior profit. They are ideal, dangerous, often fatal. Even carnal passions are not selfish, if by the self we understand the whole man: they are an obsession to which he sacrifices himself. But the transcendental philosophy with its migratory ego can turn any single passion, or any complex of passions, into a reputed centre of will, into a moral personage. As the passion usurps more and more of the man's nature it becomes a fierce egotist in his place; it becomes fanaticism or even madness.

This substitution of a passion for a man, when nobody thought the ego migratory, seemed a disease. What folly, we said to the human soul, to sacrifice your natural life to this partial, transitory, visionary passion! But the German idealist recognizes no natural life, no natural individual. His ego can migrate into any political body or any synthetic idea. Therefore, his passions, far from seeming follies to him, seem divine inspirations, calls to sacrifice, fidelities to the ideal.

I am far from wishing to say that a German idealist is commonly just to all the passions and raises them in turn to be his highest and absolute will. His passions are generally few and mental. Accidents of training or limitations of temperament keep him respectable; but he is never safe. Dazzle him with a sophism, such, for instance, as that 'the more evil the more good', or hypnotize him with a superstition, such as that 'organization is an end in itself', and nothing more is needed to turn him into a romantic criminal.

Even the Absolute requires an enemy to whet its edge upon, and the state, which according to Hegel is morally absolute, requires rival states in order that its separate individuality may not seem to vanish, and with it the occasion for blessed and wholesome wars. Hegel rejects the notion that nations have any duties to one another because, as he asserts, there is no moral authority or tribunal higher than the state, to which its government could be subject. This assertion is evidently false, since in the first place there is God or, if the phrase be preferred, there is the highest good of mankind, hedging in very narrowly the path that states should follow between opposite vices; and in the second place there is the individual, whose natural allegiance to his family, friends, and religion, to truth and to art, is deeper and holier than his allegiance to the state, which for the soul of man is a historical and geographical accident. No doubt at the present stage of civilization there is more to be gained than lost by co-operating loyally with the governments under which we happen to live, not because any state is divine, but because as yet no less cumbrous machinery is available for carrying on the economy of life with some approach to decency and security. For Hegel, however, the life of the state was the moral substance, and the souls of men but the accidents; and as to the judgment of God he asserted that it was none other than the course of history. This is a characteristic saying, in which he seems to proclaim the moral government of the world, when in truth he is sanctifying a brutal law of success and succession. The best government, of course, succumbs in time like the worst, and sooner; the dark ages followed upon the Roman Empire and lasted twice as long. But Hegel's God was simply the world, or a formula supposed to describe the world. He despised every ideal not destined to be realized on earth, he respected legality more than justice, and extant institutions more than moral ideals; and he wished to flatter a government in whose policy war and even crime were recognized weapons.

This reign of official passion is not, let me repeat, egotism in the natural man who is subject to it; it is the sacrifice of the natural man and of all men to an abstract obsession, called an ideal. The vice of absoluteness and egotism is transferred to that visionary agent. The man may be docile and gentle enough, but the demon he listens to is ruthless and deaf. It forbids him to ask, 'At what price do I pursue this ideal? How much harm must I do to attain this good?' No; this imperative is categorical. The die is cast, the war against human nature and happiness is declared, and an idol that feeds on blood, the Absolute state, is set up in the heart and over the city.

The Life of Reason

REASON IN COMMON SENSE

FIRST STEPS AND FIRST
FLUCTUATIONS

...If consciousness could ever have the function of guiding conduct better than instinct can, in the beginning it would be most incompetent for that office. Only the routine and equilibrium which healthy instinct involves keep thought and will at all within the limits of sanity. The predetermined interests we have as animals fortunately focus our attention on practical things, pulling it back, like a ball with an elastic cord, within the radius of pertinent matters. Instinct alone compels us to neglect and seldom to recall the irrelevant infinity of ideas. Philosophers have sometimes said that all ideas come from experience; they never could have been poets and must have forgotten that they were ever children. The great difficulty in education is to get experience out of ideas. Shame, conscience, and reason continually disallow and ignore what consciousness presents; and what are they but habit and latent instinct asserting themselves and forcing us to disregard our midsummer madness? Idiocy and lunacy are merely reversions to a condition in which present consciousness is in the ascendant and has escaped the control of unconscious forces. We speak of people being 'out of their senses', when they have in fact fallen back into them; or of those who have 'lost their mind', when they have lost merely that habitual control over consciousness which prevented it from flaring into all sorts of obsessions and agonies. Their bodies having become deranged, their minds, far from correcting that derangement, instantly share and betray it. A dream is always simmering below the conventional surface of speech and reflection. Even in the highest reaches and serenest meditations of science it sometimes breaks through. Even there we are seldom constant enough to conceive a truly natural world; somewhere

189

passionate, fanciful, or magic elements will slip into the scheme and baffle rational ambition.

A body seriously out of equilibrium, either with itself or with its environment, perishes outright. Not so a mind. Madness and suffering can set themselves no limit; they lapse only when the corporeal frame that sustains them yields to circumstances and changes its habit. If they are unstable at all, it is because they ordinarily correspond to strains and conjunctions which a vigorous body overcomes, or which dissolve the body altogether. A pain not incidental to the play of practical instincts may easily be recurrent, and it might be perpetual if even the worst habits were not intermittent and the most useless agitations exhausting. Some respite will therefore ensue upon pain, but no magic cure. Madness, in like manner, if pronounced, is precarious, but when speculative enough to be harmless or not strong enough to be debilitating, it too may last for ever.

An imaginative life may therefore exist parasitically in a man, hardly touching his action or environment. There is no possibility of exorcizing these apparitions by their own power. A nightmare does not dispel itself; it endures until the organic strain which caused it is relaxed either by natural exhaustion or by some external influence. Therefore human ideas are still for the most part sensuous and trivial, shifting with the chance currents of the brain, and representing nothing, so to speak, but personal temperature. Personal temperature, moreover, is sometimes tropical. There are brains like a South American jungle, as there are others like an Arabian desert, strewn with nothing but bones. While a passionate sultriness prevails in the mind, there is no end to its luxuriance. Languages intricately articulate, flaming mythologies, metaphysical perspectives lost in infinity, arise in remarkable profusion. In time, however, there comes a change of climate and the whole forest disappears.

It is easy, from the standpoint of acquired practical competence, to deride a merely imaginative life. Derision, however, is not interpretation, and the better method of overcoming erratic ideas is to trace them out dialectically and see if they will not recognize their own fatuity. The most irresponsible vision has certain principles of order and valuation by which it estimates itself; and in these principles the Life of Reason is already broached, however halting may be its development. We should lead ourselves out of our dream, as the Israelites were led out of Egypt, by the promise and eloquence of that dream itself. Otherwise we might kill the goose that lays the golden egg, and by proscribing imagination abolish science.

Visionary experience has a first value in its possible pleasantness. Why any form of feeling should be delightful is not to be explained transcendentally: a physiological law may, after the fact, render every instance predictable; but no logical affinity between the formal quality of an experience and the impulse to welcome it will thereby be disclosed. We find, however, that pleasure suffuses certain states of mind and pain others; which is another way of saying that, for no reason, we love the first and detest the second. The polemic which certain moralists have waged against pleasure and in favour of pain is intelligible when we remember that their chief interest is edification, and that ability to resist pleasure and pain alike is a valuable virtue in a world where action and renunciation are the twin keys to happiness. But to deny that pleasure is a good and pain an evil is a grotesque affectation: it amounts to giving 'good' and 'evil' artificial definitions and thereby reducing ethics to arbitrary verbiage. Not only is good that adherence of the will to experience of which pleasure is the basal example, and evil the corresponding rejection which is the very essence of pain, but when we pass from good and evil in sense to their highest embodiments, pleasure remains eligible and pain something which it is a duty to prevent. A man who without necessity deprived any person of a pleasure or imposed on him a pain, would be a contemptible knave, and the person so injured would be the first to declare it, nor could the highest celestial tribunal, if it was just, reverse that sentence. For it suffices that one being, however weak, loves or abhors anything, no matter how slightly, for that thing to acquire a proportionate value which no chorus of contradiction ringing through all the spheres can ever wholly abolish. An experience good or bad in itself remains so for ever, and its inclusion in a more general order of things can only change that totality proportionately to the ingredient absorbed, which will infect the mass, so far as it goes, with its own colour. The more pleasure a universe can yield, other things being equal, the more beneficent and generous is its general nature; the more pains its constitution involves, the darker and more malign is its total temper. To deny this would seem impossible, yet it is done daily; for there is nothing people will not maintain when they are slaves to superstition; and candour and a sense of justice are, in such a case, the first things lost.

Pleasures differ sensibly in intensity; but the intensest pleasures are often the blindest, and it is hard to recall or estimate a feeling with which no definite and complex object is conjoined. The first step in making pleasure intelligible and capable of being pursued is to make it pleasure in something. The object it suffuses acquires a value, and gives the pleasure itself a place in rational life. The pleasure can now be named, its variations studied in reference to changes in its object, and its comings and goings foreseen in the order of events. The more articulate the world that produces emotion the more controllable and recoverable is the emotion itself. Therefore diversity and order in ideas make the life of pleasure richer and easier to lead. A voluminous dumb pleasure might indeed outweigh the pleasure spread thin over a multitude of tame perceptions, if we could only weigh the two in one scale; but to do so is impossible, and in memory and prospect, if not in experience, diversified pleasure must needs carry the day...

When consciousness begins to add diversity to its intensity, its value is no longer absolute and inexpressible. The felt variations in its tone are attached to the observed movement of its objects; in these objects its values are imbedded. A world loaded with dramatic values may thus arise in imagination;

terrible and delightful presences may chase one another across the void; life will be a kind of music made by all the senses together. Many animals probably have this form of experience; they are not wholly submerged in a vegetative stupor; they can discern what they love or fear. Yet all this is still a disordered apparition that reels itself off amid sporadic movements, efforts, and agonies. Now gorgeous, now exciting, now indifferent, the landscape brightens and fades with the day. If a dog, while sniffing about contentedly, sees afar off his master arriving after long absence, the change in the animal's feeling is not merely in the quantity of pure pleasure; a new circle of sensations appears, with a new principle governing interest and desire; instead of waywardness subjection, instead of freedom love. But the poor brute asks for no reason why his master went, why he has come again, why he should be loved, or why presently while lying at his feet you forget him and begin to grunt and dream of the chase—all that is an utter mystery, utterly unconsidered. Such experience has variety, scenery, and a certain vital rhythm; its story might be told in dithyrambic verse. It moves wholly by inspiration; every event is providential, every act unpremeditated. Absolute freedom and absolute helplessness have met together: you depend wholly on divine favour, yet that unfathomable agency is not distinguishable from your own life. This is the condition to which some forms of piety invite men to return; and it lies in truth not far beneath the level of ordinary human consciousness.

The story which such animal experience contains, however, needs only to be better articulated in order to disclose its underlying machinery. The figures even of that disordered drama have their exits and their entrances; and their cues can be gradually discovered by a being capable of fixing his attention and retaining the order of events. Thereupon a third step is made in imaginative experience. As pleasures and pains were formerly distributed among objects, so objects are now marshalled into a world. *Felix qui potuit rerum cognoscere causas*, said a poet who stood near enough to fundamental

human needs and to the great answer which art and civilization can make to them, to value the Life of Reason and think
it sublime. To discern causes is to turn vision into knowledge
and motion into action. It is to fix the associates of things,
so that their respective transformations are collated, and they
become significant of one another. In proportion as such
understanding advances, each moment of experience becomes
consequential and prophetic of the rest. The calm places in
life are filled with power and its spasms with resource. No
emotion can overwhelm the mind, for of none is the basis or
issue wholly hidden; no event can disconcert it altogether,
because it sees beyond. Means can be looked for to escape
from the worst predicament; and whereas each moment had
been formerly filled with nothing but its own adventure and
surprised emotion, each now makes room for the lesson of
what went before and surmises what may be the plot of the
whole.

At the threshold of reason there is a kind of choice. Not all
impressions contribute equally to the new growth; many, in
fact, which were formerly equal in rank to the best, now grow
obscure. Attention ignores them, in its haste to arrive at what
is significant of something more. Nor are the principles of
synthesis, by which the aristocratic few establish their oli-
garchy, themselves unequivocal. The first principles of logic
are like the senses, few but arbitrary. They might have been
quite different and yet produced, by a now unthinkable
method, a language no less significant than the one we speak.
Twenty-six letters may suffice for a language, but they are a
wretched minority among all possible sounds. So the forms
of perception and the categories of thought, which a gram-
marian's philosophy might think primordial necessities, are
no less casual than words or their syntactical order. Why, we
may ask, did these forms assert themselves here? What principles of selection guide mental growth?

To give a logical ground for such a selection is evidently
impossible, since it is logic itself that is to be accounted for.
A natural ground is, in strictness, also irrelevant, since natural

connections, where thought has not reduced them to a sort of equivalence and necessity, are mere data and juxtapositions. Yet it is not necessary to leave the question altogether unanswered. By using our senses we may discover, not indeed why each sense has its specific quality or exists at all, but what are its organs and occasions. In like manner we may, by developing the Life of Reason, come to understand its conditions. When consciousness awakes, the body has, as we long afterward discover, a definite organization. Without guidance from reflection bodily processes have been going on, and most precise affinities and reactions have been set up between its organs and the surrounding objects.

On these affinities and reactions sense and intellect are grafted. The plants are of different nature, yet growing together they bear excellent fruit. It is as the organs receive appropriate stimulations that attention is riveted on definite sensations. It is as the system exercises its natural activities that passion, will, and meditation possess the mind. No syllogism is needed to persuade us to eat, no prophecy of happiness to teach us to love. On the contrary, the living organism, caught in the act, informs us how to reason and what to enjoy. The soul adopts the body's aims; from the body and from its instincts she draws a first hint of the right means to those accepted purposes. Thus reason enters into partnership with the world and begins to be respected there; which it would never be if it were not expressive of the same mechanical forces that are to preside over events and render them fortunate or unfortunate for human interests. Reason is significant in action only because it has begun by taking, so to speak, the body's side; that sympathetic bias enables her to distinguish events pertinent to the chosen interests, to compare impulse with satisfaction, and, by representing a new and circular current in the system, to preside over the formation of better habits, habits expressing more instincts at once and responding to more opportunities.

THE DISCOVERY OF NATURAL OBJECTS

...We talk of recurrent perceptions, but materially considered no perception recurs. Each recurrence is one of a finite series and holds for ever its place and number in that series. Yet human attention, while it can survey several simultaneous impressions and find them similar, cannot keep them distinct if they grow too numerous. The mind has a native bias and inveterate preference for form and identification. Water does not run downhill more persistently than attention turns experience into constant terms. The several repetitions of one essence given in consciousness will tend at once to be neglected, and only the essence itself—the character shared by those sundry perceptions—will stand and become a term in mental discourse. After a few strokes of the clock, the reiterated impressions merge and cover one another; we lose count and perceive the quality and rhythm but not the number of the sounds. If this is true of so abstract and mathematical a perception as is counting, how emphatically true must it be of continuous and infinitely varied perceptions flowing in from the whole spatial world. Glimpses of the environment follow one another in quick succession, like a regiment of soldiers in uniform; only now and then does the stream take a new turn, catch a new ray of sunlight, or arrest our attention at some break.

The senses in their natural play revert constantly to familiar objects, gaining impressions which differ but slightly from one another. These slight differences are submerged in apperception, so that sensation comes to be not so much an addition of new items to consciousness as a reburnishing there of some imbedded device. Its character and relations are only slightly modified at each fresh rejuvenation. To catch the passing phenomenon in all its novelty and idiosyncrasy is a work of artifice and curiosity. Such an exercise does violence to intellectual instinct and involves an aesthetic power of diving bodily into the stream of sensation, having thrown overboard all rational ballast and escaped at once the inertia and the momentum of practical life. Normally every datum of sense is at once devoured by a hungry intellect and digested for the sake of its vital juices. The result is that what ordinarily remains in memory is no representative of particular moments or shocks—though sensation, as in dreams, may be incidentally recreated from within —but rather a logical possession, a sense of acquaintance with a certain field of reality, in a word, a consciousness of *knowledge*.

But what, we may ask, is this reality, which we boast to know? May not the sceptic justly contend that nothing is so unknown and indeed unknowable as this pretended object of knowledge? The sensations which reason treats so cavalierly were at least something actual while they lasted and made good their momentary claim to our interest; but what is this new ideal figment, unseizable yet ever present, invisible but indispensable, unknowable yet alone interesting or important? Strange that the only possible object or theme of our knowledge should be something we cannot know.

An answer to these doubts will perhaps appear if we ask ourselves what sort of contact with reality would satisfy us, and in what terms we expect or desire to possess the subject-matter of our thoughts. Is it simply corroboration that we look for? Is it a verification of truth in sense? It would be unreasonable, in that case, after all the evidence we demand has been gathered, to complain that the ideal term thus concurrently suggested, the supersensible substance, reality, or independent object, does not itself descend into the arena of immediate sensuous presentation. Knowledge is not eating, and we cannot expect to devour and possess *what we mean*. Knowledge is recognition of something absent; it is a salutation, not an embrace. It is an advance on sensation precisely because it is representative. The terms or goals of thought have for their function to subtend long tracts of sensuous experience, to be ideal links between fact and fact, invisible wires behind the scenes, threads along which inference may run in making phenomena intelligible and controllable. An idea that should become an image would cease to be ideal;

a principle that is to remain a principle can never become a fact. A God that you could see with the eyes of the body, a heaven you might climb into by a ladder planted at Bethel, would be parts of this created and interpretable world, not terms in its interpretation nor objects in a spiritual sphere. Now external objects are thought to be principles and sources of experience; they are accordingly conceived realities on an ideal plane. We may look for all the evidence we choose before we declare our inference to be warranted; but we must not ask for something more than evidence, nor expect to know realities without inferring them anew. They are revealed only to understanding. We cannot cease to think and still continue to know.

It may be said, however, that principles and external objects are interesting only because they symbolize further sensations, that thought is an expedient of finite minds, and that representation is a ghostly process which we crave to materialize into bodily possession. We may grow sick of inferring truth and long rather to become reality. Intelligence is after all no compulsory possession; and while some of us would gladly have more of it, others find that they already have too much. The tension of thought distresses them and to represent what they cannot be and would not be is not a natural function of their spirit. To such minds experience that should merely corroborate ideas would prolong dissatisfaction. The ideas must be realized; they must pass into immediacy. If reality (a word employed generally in a eulogistic sense) is to mean this desired immediacy, no ideal of thought can be real. All intelligible objects and the whole universe of mental discourse would then be an unreal and conventional structure, impinging ultimately on sense, from which it would derive its sole validity.

There would be no need of quarrelling with such a philosophy, were not its use of words rather misleading. Call experience in its existential and immediate aspect, if you will, the sole reality; that will not prevent reality from having an ideal dimension. The intellectual world will continue to give beauty, meaning and scope to those bubbles of consciousness on which it is painted. Reality would not be, in that case, what thought aspires to reach. Consciousness is the least ideal of things when reason is taken out of it. Reality would then need thought to give it all those human values of which, in its substance, it would have been wholly deprived; and the ideal would still be what lent music to throbs and significance to being.

The equivocation favoured by such language at once begins to appear. Is not thought with all its products a part of experience? Must not sense, if it be the only reality, be sentient sometimes of the ideal? What the site is to a city, that is immediate experience to the universe of discourse. The latter is all held materially within the limits defined by the former; but if immediate experience be the seat of the moral world, the moral world is the only interesting possession of immediate experience. When a waste is built on, however, it is a violent paradox to call it still a waste; and an immediate experience that represents the rest of sentience, with all manner of ideal harmonies read into the whole in the act of representing it, is an immediate experience raised to its highest power: it is the Life of Reason. In vain, then, will a philosophy of intellectual abstention limit so Platonic a term as reality to the immediate aspect of existence, when it is the ideal aspect that endows existence with character and value, together with representative scope and a certain lien upon eternity...

FLUX AND CONSTANCY IN
HUMAN NATURE

...Reason is a human function. Though the name of reason has been applied to various alleged principles of cosmic life, vital or dialectical, these principles all lack the essence of rationality, in that they are not conscious movements toward satisfaction, not, in other words, moral and beneficent principles at all. Be the instability of human nature what it may, therefore, the instability of reason is not less, since reason is but a function of human nature. However relative and subordinate, in a physical sense, human ideals may be, these ideals remain the only possible moral standards for man, the only tests which he can apply for value or authority in any other quarter. And among unstable and relative ideals none is more relative and unstable than that which transports all value to a universal law, itself indifferent to good and evil, and worships it as a deity. Such an idolatry would indeed be impossible if it were not partial and veiled, arrived at in following out some human interest and clung to by force of moral inertia and the ambiguity of words. In truth mystics do not practise so entire a renunciation of reason as they preach: eternal validity and the capacity to deal with absolute reality are still assumed by them to belong to thought or at least to feeling. Only they overlook in their description of human nature just that faculty which they exercise in their speculation; their map leaves out the ground on which they stand. The rest, which they are not identified with for the moment, they proceed to regard *de haut en bas* and to discredit as a momentary manifestation of universal laws, physical or divine. They forget that this faith in law, this absorption in the blank reality, this enthusiasm for the ultimate thought, are mere human passions like the rest; that they endure them as they might a fever and that the animal instincts are patent on which those spiritual yearnings repose.

This last fact would be nothing against the feelings in question, if they were not made vehicles for absolute revelations. On the contrary, such a relativity in instincts is the source of their importance. In virtue of this relativity they have some basis and function in the world; for did they not repose on human nature they could never express or transform it. Religion and philosophy are not always beneficent or important, but when they are it is precisely because they help to develop human faculty and to enrich human life. To imagine that by means of them we can escape from human nature and survey it from without is an ostrich-like illusion obvious to all but to the victim of it. Such a pretension may cause admiration in the schools, where self-hypnotization is easy, but in the world it makes its professors ridiculous. For in their eagerness to empty their mind of human prejudices they reduce its rational burden to a minimum, and if they still continue to dogmatize, it is sport for the satirist to observe what forgotten accident of language or training has survived the crash of the universe and made the one demonstrable path to Absolute Truth.

Neither the path of abstraction followed by the mystics, nor that of direct and, as it avers, unbiased observation followed by the naturalists, can lead beyond that region of common experience, traditional feeling, and conventional thought which all minds enter at birth and can elude only at the risk of inward collapse and extinction. The fact that observation involves the senses, and the senses their organs, is one which a naturalist can hardly overlook; and when we add that logical habits, sanctioned by utility, are needed to interpret the data of sense, the humanity of science and all its constructions becomes clearer than day. Superstition itself could not be more human. The path of unbiased observation is not a path away from conventional life; it is a progress in conventions. It improves human belief by increasing the proportion of two of its ingredients, attentive perception and practical calculus. The whole resulting vision, as it is sustained from moment to moment by present experience and instinct, has no value apart from actual ideals. And if it proves human nature to be unstable, it can build that proof on nothing more stable than human faculty as at the moment it happens to be.

Nor is abstraction a less human process, as if by becoming very abstruse indeed we could hope to become divine. Is it not a commonplace of the schools that to form abstract ideas is the prerogative of man's reason? Is not abstraction a method by which mortal intelligence makes haste? Is it not the makeshift of a mind overloaded with its experience, the trick of an eye that cannot master a profuse and ever-changing world? Shall these diagrams drawn in fancy, this system of signals in thought, be the Absolute Truth dwelling within us? Do we attain reality by making a silhouette of our dreams? If the scientific world be a product of human faculties, the metaphysical world must be doubly so; for the material there given to human understanding is here worked over again by human art. This constitutes the dignity and value of dialectic, that in spite of appearances it is so human; it bears to experience a relation similar to that which the arts bear to the same, where sensible images, selected by the artist's genius and already coloured by his aesthetic bias, are redyed in the process of reproduction whenever he has a great style, and saturated anew with his mind.

There can be no question, then, of eluding human nature or of conceiving it and its environment in such a way as to stop its operation. We may take up our position in one region of experience or in another; we may, in unconsciousness of the interests and assumptions that support us, criticize the truth or value of results obtained elsewhere. Our criticism will be solid in proportion to the solidity of the unnamed convictions that inspire it, that is, in proportion to the deep roots and fruitful ramifications which those convictions may have in human life. Ultimate truth and ultimate value will be reasonably attributed to those ideas and possessions which can give human nature, as it is, the highest satisfaction. We may admit that human nature is variable; but that admission, if justified, will be justified by the satisfaction which it gives human nature to make it. We might even admit that human ideals are vain but only if they were nothing worth for the attainment of the veritable human ideal . . .

The error, however, would be profound and the contradiction hopeless if we should deny the ideal authority of human nature because we had discovered its origin and conditions. Nature and evolution, let us say, have brought life to the present form; but this life lives, these organs have determinate functions, and human nature, here and now, in relation to the ideal energies it unfolds, is a fundamental essence, a collection of activities with determinate limits, relations, and ideals. The integration and determinateness of these faculties is the condition for any synthetic operation of reason. As the structure of the steam-engine has varied greatly since its first invention, and its attributions have increased, so the structure of human nature has undoubtedly varied since man first appeared upon the earth; but as in each steam-engine at each moment there must be a limit of mobility, a unity of function and a clear determination of parts and tensions, so in human nature, as found at any time in any man, there is a definite scope by virtue of which alone he can have a reliable memory, a recognizable character, a faculty of connected thought and speech, a social utility, and a moral ideal. On man's given structure, on his activity hovering about fixed objects, depends the possibility of conceiving or testing any truth or making any progress in happiness...

REASON IN SOCIETY

FREE SOCIETY

...Comradeship is a form of friendship still akin to general sociability and gregariousness. When men are 'in the same boat together', when a common anxiety, occupation, or sport unites them, they feel their human kinship in an intensified form without any greater personal affinity subsisting between them. The same effect is produced by a common estrangement from the rest of society. For this reason comradeship lasts no longer than the circumstances that bring it about. Its constancy is proportionate to the monotony of people's lives and minds. There is a lasting bond among schoolfellows because no one can become a boy again and have a new set of playmates. There is a persistent comradeship with one's countrymen, especially abroad, because seldom is a man pliable and polyglot enough to be at home among foreigners, or really to understand them. There is an inevitable comradeship with men of the same breeding or profession, however bad these may be, because habits soon monopolize the man. Nevertheless a greater buoyancy, a longer youth, a richer experience, would break down all these limits of fellowship. Such clingings to the familiar are three parts dread of the unfamiliar and want of resource in its presence, for one part in them of genuine loyalty. Plasticity loves new moulds because it can fill them, but for a man of sluggish mind and bad manners there is decidedly no place like home.

Though comradeship is an accidental bond, it is the condition of ideal friendship, for the ideal, in all spheres, is nothing but the accidental confirming itself and generating its own standard. Men must meet to love, and many other accidents besides conjunction must conspire to make a true friendship possible. In order that friendship may fulfil the conditions even of comradeship, it is requisite that the friends have the same social status, so that they may live at ease together and have congenial tastes. They must further have enough community of occupation and gifts to give each an appreciation of the other's faculty; for qualities are not complementary unless they are qualities of the same substance. Nothing must be actual in either friend that is not potential in the other.

For this reason, among others, friends are generally of the same sex, for when men and women agree, it is only in their conclusions; their reasons are always different. So that while intellectual harmony between men and women is easily possible, its delightful and magic quality lies precisely in the fact that it does not arise from mutual understanding, but is a conspiracy of alien essences and a kissing, as it were, in the dark. As man's body differs from woman's in sex and strength, so his mind differs from hers in quality and function: they can co-operate but can never fuse. . .

Friends, moreover, should have been young together. Much difference in age defeats equality and forbids frankness on many a fundamental subject; it confronts two minds of unlike focus: one near-sighted and without perspective, the other seeing only the background of present things. While comparisons in these respects may be interesting and borrowings sometimes possible, lending the older mind life and the younger mind wisdom, such intercourse has hardly the value of spontaneous sympathy, in which the spark of mutual intelligence flies, as it should, almost without words. Contagion is the only source of valid mind-reading: you must imitate to understand, and where the plasticity of two minds is not similar their mutual interpretations are necessarily false. They idealize in their friends whatever they do not invent or ignore, and the friendship which should have lived on energies conspiring spontaneously together dies into conscious appreciation.

All these are merely permissive conditions for friendship; its positive essence is yet to find. How, we may ask, does the vision of the general *socius*, humanity, become specific in the vision of a particular friend without losing its ideality or reverting to practical values? Of course, individuals might be singled out for the special benefits they may have conferred; but a friend's only gift is himself, and friendship is not friendship, it is not a form of free or liberal society, if it does not terminate in an ideal possession, in an object loved for its own sake. Such objects can be ideas only, not forces, for forces are subterranean and instrumental things, having only such value as they borrow from their ulterior effects and manifestations. To praise the utility of friendship, as the ancients so often did, and to regard it as a political institution justified, like victory or government, by its material results, is to lose one's moral bearings. The value of victory or good government is rather to be found in the fact that, among other things, it might render friendship possible. We are not to look now for what makes friendship useful, but for whatever may be found in friendship that may lend utility to life.

The first note that gives sociability a personal quality and raises the comrade into an incipient friend is doubtless sensuous affinity. Whatever reaction we may eventually make on an impression, after it has had time to soak in and to merge in some practical or intellectual habit, its first assault is always on the senses, and no sense is an indifferent organ. Each has, so to speak, its congenial rate of vibration and gives its stimuli a varying welcome. Little as we may attend to these instinctive hospitalities of sense, they betray themselves in unjustified likes and dislikes felt for casual persons and things, in the *je ne sais quoi* that makes instinctive sympathy. Voice, manner, aspect, hints of congenial tastes and judgments, a jest in the right key, a gesture marking the right aversions, all these trifles leave behind a pervasive impression. We reject a vision we find indigestible and without congruity to our inner dream; we accept and incorporate another into our private pantheon, where it becomes a legitimate figure, however dumb and subsidiary it may remain.

In a refined nature these sensuous premonitions of sympathy are seldom misleading. Liking cannot, of course, grow into friendship overnight as it might into love; the pleasing impression, even if retained, will lie perfectly passive and harmless in the mind, until new and different impressions follow to deepen the interest at first evoked and to remove its centre of gravity altogether from the senses. In love, if the field is clear, a single glimpse may, like Tristan's potion, produce a violent and irresistible passion; but in friendship the result remains more proportionate to the incidental causes, discrimination is preserved, jealousy and exclusiveness are avoided. That vigilant, besetting, insatiable affection, so full of doubts and torments, with which the lover follows his object, is out of place here; for the friend has no property in his friend's body or leisure or residual ties; he accepts what is offered and what is acceptable, and the rest he leaves in peace. He is distinctly not his brother's keeper, for the society of friends is free.

Friendship may indeed come to exist without sensuous liking or comradeship to pave the way; but unless intellectual sympathy and moral appreciation are powerful enough to react on natural instinct and to produce in the end the personal affection which at first was wanting, friendship does not arise. Recognition given to a man's talent or virtue is not properly friendship. Friends must desire to live as much as possible together and to share their work, thoughts, and pleasures. Good-fellowship and sensuous affinity are indispensable to give spiritual communion a personal accent; otherwise men would be indifferent vehicles for such thoughts and powers as emanated from them, and attention would not be in any way arrested or refracted by the human medium through which it beheld the good.

No natural vehicle, however, is indifferent; no natural organ is or should be transparent. Transparency is a virtue only in artificial instruments, organs in which no blood flows and whose intrinsic operation is not itself a portion of human life. In looking through a field-glass I do not wish to perceive the lenses nor to see rainbows about their rim; yet I should not wish the eye itself to lose its pigments and add no dyes to the bulks it discerns. The sense for colour is a vital endowment and an ingredient in human happiness; but no vitality is added by the intervention of further media which are not themselves living organs.

A man is sometimes a coloured and sometimes a clear medium for the energies he exerts. When a thought conveyed or a work done enters alone into the observer's experience, no friendship is possible. This is always the case when the master is dead; for if his reconstructed personality retains any charm, it is only as an explanation or conceived nexus for the work he performed. In a philosopher or artist, too, personality is merely instrumental, for, although in a sense pervasive, a creative personality evaporates into its expression, and whatever part of it may not have been translated into ideas is completely negligible from the public point of view. That portion of a man's soul which he has not alienated and objectified is open only to those who know him otherwise than by his works and do not estimate him by his public attributions Such persons are his friends. Into their lives he has entered not merely through an idea with which his name may be associated, not through the fame of some feat he may have performed, but by awakening an inexpressible animal sympathy, by the contagion of emotions felt before the same objects. Estimation has been partly arrested at its medium and personal relations have added their homely accent to universal discourse. Friendship might thus be called ideal sympathy refracted by a human medium, or comradeship and sensuous affinity colouring a spiritual light.

If we approach friendship from above and compare it with more ideal loyalties, its characteristic is its animal warmth and its basis in chance conjunctions; if we approach it from below and contrast it with mere comradeship or liking, its essence seems to be the presence of common ideal interests. That is a silly and effeminate friendship in which the parties are always thinking of the friendship itself and of how each stands in the other's eyes; a sentimental fancy of that sort, in which nothing tangible or ulterior brings people together, is rather a feeble form of love than properly a friendship. In extreme youth such a weakness may perhaps indicate capacity for friendship of a nobler type, because when taste and know-ledge have not yet taken shape, the only way, often, in which ideal interests can herald themselves is in the guise of some imagined union from which it is vaguely felt they might be developed, just as in love sexual and social instincts mask themselves in an unreasoning· obsession, or as for mystic devotion every ideal masks itself in God. All these senti-mental feelings are at any rate mere preludes, but preludes in fortunate cases to more discriminating and solid interests, which such a tremulous overture may possibly pitch on a higher key.

The necessity of backing personal attachment with ideal interests is what makes true friendship so rare. It is found chiefly in youth, for youth best unites the two requisite con-ditions—affectionate comradeship and ardour in pursuing such liberal aims as may be pursued in common. Life in camp or college is favourable to friendship, for there generous activi-ties are carried on in unison and yet leave leisure for playful expansion and opportunity for a choice in friends. The ancients, so long as they were free, spent their whole life in forum and palaestra, camp, theatre, and temple, and in consequence could live by friendship even in their maturer years; but modern life is unfavourable to its continuance. What with business cares, with political bonds remote and invisible, with the prior claims of family, and with individualities both of mind and habit growing daily more erratic, early friends find themselves very soon parted by unbridgeable chasms. For friendship to flourish personal life would have to become more public and social life more simple and humane...

IDEAL SOCIETY

...Similar beings herding together in the same places are naturally subject to simultaneous reactions, and the sense of this common reaction makes possible the conception of many minds having a common experience. The elements of this experience they express to one another by signs. For when spontaneous reactions occur together in many animals, each,

knowing well his own emotion, will inevitably take the perceived attitude and gesture of his fellows for its expression—
for his own attitude and gesture he knows nothing of; and he
will thus possess, without further instruction, the outward sign
for his inner experience.

It is easy to see how a moral world can grow out of these
primary intuitions. Knowing, for instance, the expression of
anger, a man may come to find anger directed against himself; together with physical fear in the presence of attack, he
will feel the contagion of his enemy's passion, especially if his
enemy be the whole group whose reactions he is wont to
share, and something in him will strive to be angry together
with the rest of the world. He will perfectly understand that
indignation against himself which in fact he instinctively
shares. This self-condemning emotion will be his sense of
shame and his conscience. Words soon come to give definition
to such a feeling, which without expression in language would
have but little stability. For when a man is attracted to an act,
even if it be condemned by others, he views it as delightful
and eligible in itself; but when he is forced, by the conventional
use of words, to attach to that act an opprobrious epithet, an
epithet which he himself has always applied with scorn, he finds
himself unable to suppress the emotion connoted by the word;
he cannot defend his rebellious intuition against the tyranny
of language; he is inwardly confused and divided against himself, and out of his own mouth convicted of wickedness.

A proof of the notable influence that language has on these
emotions may be found in their transformations. The con-
nivance of a very few persons is sufficient to establish among
them a new application of eulogistic terms; it will suffice to
suppress all qualms in the pursuance of their common impulse
and to consecrate a new ideal of character. It is accordingly
no paradox that there should be honour among thieves, kindness among harlots, and probity among fanatics. They have
not lost their conscience; they have merely introduced a
flattering heresy into the conventional code, to make room for
the particular passion indulged in their little world.

Ideal Society

Sympathy with the general mind may also take other forms. Public opinion, in a vivacious and clear-headed community, may be felt to be the casual and irresponsible thing which in truth it is. Homer, for instance, has no more solemn vehicle for it than the indefinite and unaccentable τις. 'So', he tells us, 'somebody or anybody said.' In the Greek tragedians this unauthoritative entity was replaced by the chorus, an assemblage of conventional persons, incapable of any original perception, but possessing a fund of traditional lore, a just if somewhat encumbered conscience, and the gift of song. This chorus was therefore much like the Christian Church and like that celestial choir of which the Church wishes to be the earthly echo. Like the Church, the tragic chorus had authority, because it represented a wide, if ill-digested, experience; and it had solemnity, because it spoke in archaic tropes, emotional and obscure symbols of prehistoric conflicts. These sacramental forms retained their power to move in spite of their little pertinence to living issues, partly on account of the mystery which enshrouded their forgotten passion and partly on account of the fantastic interpretations which that pregnant obscurity allowed.

Far more powerful, however, are those embodiments of the general conscience which religion furnishes in its first and spontaneous phase, as when the Hebrew prophets dared to cry, 'So saith the Lord.' Such faith in one's own inspiration is a more pliable oracle than tradition or a tragic chorus, and more responsive to the needs and changes of the hour. Occidental philosophers, in their less simple and less eloquent manner, have often repeated that arrogant Hebraic cry: they have told us in their systems what God thinks about the world. Such pretensions would be surprising did we not remind ourselves of the obvious truth that what men attribute to God is nothing but the ideal they value and grope for in themselves, and that the commandments, mythically said to come from the Most High, flow in fact from common reason and local experience...

REASON IN RELIGION

THE CHRISTIAN EPIC

Revolutions are ambiguous things. Their success is generally proportionate to their power of adaptation and to the re-absorption within them of what they rebelled against. A thousand reforms have left the world as corrupt as ever, for each successful reform has founded a new institution, and this institution has bred its new and congenial abuses. What is capable of truly purifying the world is not the mere agitation of its elements, but their organization into a natural body that shall exude what redounds and absorb or generate what is lacking to the perfect expression of its soul.

Whence fetch this seminal force and creative ideal? It must evidently lie already in the matter it is to organize; otherwise it would have no affinity to that matter, no power over it, and no ideality or value in respect to the existences whose standard and goal it was to be. There can be no goods antecedent to the natures they benefit, no ideals prior to the wills they define. A revolution must find its strength and legitimacy not in the reformer's conscience and dream but in the temper of that society which he would transform; for no transformation is either permanent or desirable which does not forward the spontaneous life of the world, advancing those issues toward which it is already inwardly directed. How should a gospel bring glad tidings, save by announcing what was from the beginning native to the heart?

No judgment could well be shallower, therefore, than that which condemns a great religion for not being faithful to that local and partial impulse which may first have launched it into the world. A great religion has something better to consider: the conscience and imagination of those it ministers to. The prophet who announced it first was a prophet only because he had a keener sense and clearer premonition than other men

212

of their common necessities; and he loses his function and is a prophet no longer when the public need begins to outrun his intuitions. Could Hebraism spread over the Roman Empire and take the name of Christianity without adding anything to its native inspiration? Is it to be lamented that we are not all Jews? Yet what makes the difference is not the teaching of Jesus—which is pure Hebraism reduced to its spiritual essence —but the worship of Christ—something perfectly Greek. Christianity would have remained a Jewish sect had it not been made at once speculative, universal, and ideal by the infusion of Greek thought, and at the same time plastic and devotional by the adoption of pagan habits. The incarnation of God in man, and the divinization of man in God are pagan conceptions, expressions of pagan religious sentiment and philosophy. Yet what would Christianity be without them? It would have lost not only its theology, which might be spared, but its spiritual aspiration, its artistic affinities, and the secret of its metaphysical charity and joy. It would have remained unconscious, as the Gospel is, that the hand or the mind of man can ever construct anything. Among the Jews there were no liberal interests for the ideal to express. They had only elementary human experience—the perpetual Oriental round of piety and servitude in the bosom of a scorched, exhausted country. A disillusioned eye, surveying such a world, could find nothing there to detain it; religion, when wholly spiritual, could do nothing but succour the afflicted, understand and forgive the sinful, and pass through the sad pageant of life unspotted and resigned. Its pity for human ills would go hand in hand with a mystic plebeian insensibility to natural excellence. It would breathe what Tacitus, thinking of the liberal life, could call *odium generis humani*; it would be inimical to human genius.

There were, we may say, two things in Apostolic teaching which rendered it capable of converting the world. One was the later Jewish morality and mysticism, beautifully expressed in Christ's parables and maxims, and illustrated by his miracles, those cures and absolutions which he was ready to dispense, whatever their sins, to such as called upon his name. This democratic and untrammelled charity could powerfully appeal to an age disenchanted with the world, and especially to those lower classes which pagan polity had covered with scorn and condemned to hopeless misery. The other point of contact which early Christianity had with the public need was the theme it offered to contemplation, the philosophy of history which it introduced into the western world, and the delicious unfathomable mysteries into which it launched the fancy. Here, too, the figure of Christ was the centre for all eyes. Its lowliness, its simplicity, its humanity were indeed, for a while, obstacles to its acceptance; they did not really lend themselves to the metaphysical interpretation which was required. Yet even Greek fable was not without its Apollo tending flocks and its Demeter mourning for her lost child and serving in meek disguise the child of another. Feeling was ripe for a mythology loaded with pathos. The humble life, the homilies, the sufferings of Jesus could be felt in all their incomparable beauty, all the more when the tenderness and tragedy of them, otherwise too poignant, were relieved by the story of his miraculous birth, his glorious resurrection, and his restored divinity.

The Gospel, thus grown acceptable to the pagan mind, was, however, but a grain of mustard-seed destined to branch and flower in its new soil in a miraculous manner. Not only was the Greek and Roman to refresh himself under its shade, but birds of other climates were to build their nests, at least for a season, in its branches. Hebraism, when thus expanded and paganized, shows many new characteristics native to the minds which had now adopted and transformed it. The Jews, for instance, like other Orientals, had a figurative way of speaking and thinking; their poetry and religion were full of the most violent metaphors. Now to the classic mind violent and improper metaphors were abhorrent. Uniting, as it did, clear reason with lively fancy, it could not conceive one thing to *be* another, nor relish the figure of speech that so described it, hoping by that unthinkable phrase to suggest its affinities.

But the classic mind could well conceive transformation, of which indeed nature is full; and in Greek fables anything might change its form, become something else, and display its plasticity, not by imperfectly being many things at once, but by being the perfection of many things in succession. While metaphor was thus unintelligible and confusing to the Greek, metamorphosis was perfectly familiar to him. Wherever Hebrew tradition, accordingly, used violent metaphors, puzzling to the Greek Christian, he rationalized them by imagining a metamorphosis instead; thus, for instance, the metaphor of the Last Supper, so harmless and vaguely satisfying to an Oriental audience, became the doctrine of transubstantiation—a doctrine where images are indeed lacking to illustrate the concepts, but where the concepts themselves are not confused. For that bread should *become* flesh and wine blood is not impossible, seeing that the change occurs daily in digestion; what the assertion in this case contradicts is merely the evidence of sense.

Thus at many a turn in Christian tradition a metaphysical mystery takes the place of a poetic figure; the former now expressing by a little miraculous drama the emotion which the latter expressed by a tentative phrase. And the emotion is thereby immensely clarified and strengthened; it is, in fact, for the first time really expressed. For the idea that Christ stands upon the altar and mingles still with our human flesh is an explicit assertion that his influence and love are perpetual; whereas the original parable revealed at most the wish and aspiration, contrary to fact, that they might have been so. By substituting embodiment for allegory, the Greek mind thus achieved something very congenial to its habits: it imagined the full and adequate expression, not in words but in existences, of the emotion to be conveyed. The Eucharist is to the Last Supper what a centaur is to a horseman or a tragedy to a song. Similarly a Dantesque conception of hell and paradise embodies in living detail the innocent apologue in the Gospel about a separation of the sheep from the goats. The result is a chimerical metaphysics, containing much which, in reference to existing facts, is absurd, but that meta-physics, when taken for what it truly is, a new mythology, utters the subtler secrets of the new religion not less in-geniously and poetically than pagan mythology reflected the daily shifts in nature and in human life.

Metaphysics became not only a substitute for allegory but at the same time a background for history. Neo-Platonism had enlarged, in a way suited to the speculative demands of the time, the cosmos conceived by Greek science. In an in-telligible region, unknown to cosmography and peopled at first by the Platonic ideas and afterward by Aristotle's solitary God, there was now the Absolute One, too exalted for any predicates, but manifesting its essence in the first place in a supreme Intelligence, the second hypostasis of a Trinity; and in the second place in the Soul of the World, the third hypo-stasis, already relative to natural existence. Now the Platonists conceived these entities to be permanent and immutable; the physical world itself had a meaning and an expressive value, like a statue, but no significant history. When the Jewish notion of creation and divine government of the world pre-sented itself to the Greeks, they hastened to assimilate it to their familiar notions of imitation, expression, finality, and significance. And when the Christians spoke of Christ as the Son of God, who now sat at his right hand in the heavens, their Platonic disciples immediately thought of the Nous or Logos, the divine Intelligence, incarnate as they had always believed in the whole world, and yet truly the substance and essence of divinity. To say that this incarnation had taken place pre-eminently, or even exclusively, in Christ was not an impossible concession to make to pious enthusiasm, at least if the philosophy involved in the old conception could be retained and embodied in the new orthodoxy. Sacred history could thus be interpreted as a temporal execution of eternal decrees, and the plan of salvation as an ideal necessity. Cosmic scope and metaphysical meaning were given to Hebrew tenets, so un-speculative in their original intention, and it became possible even for a Platonic philosopher to declare himself a Christian.

The eclectic Christian philosophy thus engendered constitutes one of the most complete, elaborate, and impressive products of the human mind. The ruins of more than one civilization and of more than one philosophy were ransacked to furnish materials for this heavenly Byzantium. It was a myth circumstantial and sober enough in tone to pass for an account of facts, and yet loaded with enough miracle, poetry, and submerged wisdom to take the place of a moral philosophy and present what seemed at the time an adequate ideal to the heart. Many a mortal, in all subsequent ages, perplexed and abandoned in this ungovernable world, has set sail resolutely for that enchanted island and found there a semblance of happiness; its narrow limits give so much room for the soul and its penitential soil breeds so many consolations. True, the brief time and narrow argument into which Christian imagination squeezes the world must seem to a speculative pantheist childish and poor, involving, as it does, a fatuous perversion of nature and history and a ridiculous emphasis laid on local events and partial interests. Yet just this violent reduction of things to a human stature, this half-innocent, half-arrogant assumption that what is important for a man must control the whole universe, is what made Christian philosophy originally appealing[1] and what still arouses, in certain quarters, enthusiastic belief in its beneficence and finality...

Let the reader fill out this outline for himself with its thousand details; let him remember the endless mysteries, arguments, martyrdoms, consecrations that carried out the sense and made vital the beauty of the whole. Let him pause before the phenomenon; he can ill afford, if he wishes to

---

[1] For an exacting corollary to this, see Santayana's magnificent essay in *Winds of Doctrine*, 'Modernism and Christianity': '...it is not those [Christians] who accept the deluge, the resurrection, and the sacraments only as symbols that are the vital party, but those who accept them literally; for only these have anything to say to the poor, or to the rich, that can refresh them. In a frank supernaturalism, in a tight clericalism, not in a pleasant secularization, lies the sole hope of the Church. Its sole dignity also lies there...As to modernism, it is suicide...It concedes everything; for it concedes that everything in Christianity, as Christians hold it, is an illusion.'

understand history or the human mind, to let the apparition float by unchallenged without delivering up its secret. What shall we say of this Christian dream?

Those who are still troubled by the fact that this dream is by many taken for a reality, and who are consequently obliged to defend themselves against it, as against some dangerous error in science or in philosophy, may be allowed to marshal arguments in its disproof. Such, however, is not my intention. Do we marshal arguments against the miraculous birth of Buddha, or the story of Cronos devouring his children? We seek rather to honour the piety and to understand the poetry embodied in those fables. If it be said that those fables are believed by no one, I reply that those fables are or have been believed just as unhesitatingly as the Christian theology, and by men no less reasonable or learned than the unhappy apologists of our own ancestral creeds. Matters of religion should never be matters of controversy. We neither argue with a lover about his taste, nor condemn him, if we are just, for knowing so human a passion. That he harbours it is no indication of a want of sanity on his part in other matters. But while we acquiesce in his experience, and are glad he has it, we need no arguments to dissuade us from sharing it. Each man may have his own loves, but the object in each case is different. And so it is, or should be, in religion. Before the rise of those strange and fraudulent Hebraic pretensions there was no question among men about the national, personal, and poetic character of religious allegiance. It could never have been a duty to adopt a religion not one's own any more than a language, a coinage, or a costume not current in one's own country. The idea that religion contains a literal, not a symbolic, representation of truth and life is simply an impossible idea. Whoever entertains it has not come within the region of profitable philosophizing on that subject. His science is not wide enough to cover all existence. He has not discovered that there can be no moral allegiance except to the ideal. His certitude and his arguments are no more pertinent to the religious question than would be the insults, blows, and murders to which, if he could, he would appeal in the next instance. Philosophy may describe unreason, as it may describe force; it cannot hope to refute them.

THE BELIEF IN A FUTURE LIFE

At no point are the two ingredients of religion, superstition and moral truth, more often confused than in the doctrine of immortality, yet in none are they more clearly distinguishable. Ideal immortality is a principle revealed to insight; it is seen by observing the eternal quality of ideas and validities, and the affinity to them native to reason or the cognitive energy of mind. A future life, on the contrary, is a matter for faith or presumption; it is a prophetic hypothesis regarding occult existences. This latter question is scientific and empirical, and should be treated as such. A man is, forensically speaking, the same man after the nightly break in his consciousness. After many changes in his body and after long oblivion, parcels of his youth may be revived and may come to figure again among the factors in his action. Similarly, if evidence to that effect were available, we might establish the resurrection of a given soul in new bodies or its activity in remote places and times. Evidence of this sort has in fact always been offered copiously by rumour and superstition. The operation of departed spirits, like that of the gods, has been recognized in many a dream, or message, or opportune succour. The Dioscuri and Saint James the Apostle have appeared— preferably on white horses—in sundry battles. Spirits duly invoked have repeated forgotten gossip and revealed the places where crimes had been committed or treasure buried. More often, perhaps, ghosts have walked the night without any ostensible or useful purpose, apparently in obedience to some ghastly compulsion that crept over them in death, as if a hesitating sickle had left them still hanging to life by one attenuated fibre.

The mass of this evidence, ancient and modern, traditional and statistical, is beneath consideration; the palpitating mood

in which it is gathered and received, even when ostensibly
scientific, is such that gullibility and fiction play a very large
part in the report; for it is not to be assumed that a man,
because he speaks in the first person and addresses a learned
society, has lost the primordial faculty of lying. When due
allowance has been made, however, for legend and fraud,
there remains a certain residuum of clairvoyance and telepathy, and an occasional abnormal obedience of matter to
mind which might pass for magic. There are unmistakable
indications that in these regions we touch lower and more
rudimentary faculties. There seems to be, as is quite natural,
a sub-human sensibility in man, wherein ideas are connected
together by bonds so irrational and tenacious that they seem
miraculous to a mind already trained in practical and relevant
thinking. This sub-human sense, far from representing important truths more clearly than ordinary apprehension can,
reduces consciousness again to a tangle of trivial impressions,
shots of uncertain range, as if a skin had not yet formed over
the body. It emerges in tense and disorganized moments. Its
reports are the more trifling the more startlingly literal their
veracity. It seems to represent a stratum of life beneath moral
or intellectual functions, and beneath all personality. When
proof has been found that a ghost has actually been seen, proof
is required that the phantom has been rightly recognized and
named; and this imputed identity is never demonstrable and
in most cases impossible. So in the magic cures which from
time immemorial have been recorded at shrines of all
religions, and which have been attributed to wonder-workers
of every sect: the one thing certain about them is that they
prove neither the truth of whatever myth is capriciously associated with them, nor the goodness or voluntary power of the
miracle-worker himself. Healer and medium are alike vehicles
for some elemental energy they cannot control, and which as
often as not misses fire; at best they feel a power going out
of them which they themselves undergo, and which radiates
from them like electricity, to work, as chance will have it,
good or evil in the world. The whole operation lies, in so far

as it really takes place at all, on the lowest levels of un-intelligence, in a region closely allied to madness in conscious-ness and to sporadic impulses in the physical sphere.

Among the blind, the retina having lost its function, the rest of the skin is said to recover its primordial sensitiveness to distance and light, so that the sightless have a clearer premonition of objects about them than seeing people could have in the dark. So when reason and the ordinary processes of sense are in abeyance a certain universal sensibility seems to return to the soul; influences at other times not appreciable make then a sensible impression, and automatic reactions may be run through in response to a stimulus normally quite in-sufficient. Now the complexity of nature is prodigious; every-thing that happens leaves, like buried cities, almost indelible traces which an eye, by chance attentive and duly prepared, can manage to read, recovering for a moment the image of an extinct life. Symbols, illegible to reason, can thus sometimes read themselves out in trance and madness. Faint vestiges may be found in matter of forms which it once wore, or which, like a perfume, impregnated and got lodgment within it. Slight echoes may suddenly reconstitute themselves in the mind's silence; and a half-stunned consciousness may catch brief glimpses of long-lost and irrelevant things. Real ghosts are such reverberations of the past, exceeding ordinary imagination and discernment both in vividness and in fidelity; they may not be explicable without appealing to material influences subtler than those ordinarily recognized, as they are obviously not discoverable without some derangement and hypertrophy of the senses.

That such subtler influences should exist is entirely conso-nant with reason and experience; but only a hankering tender-ness for superstition, a failure to appreciate the function both of religion and of science, can lead to reverence for such oracular gibberish as these influences provoke. The world is weary of experimenting with magic. In utter seriousness and with immense solemnity whole races have given themselves up to exploiting these shabby mysteries; and while a new survey of the facts, in the light of natural science and psychology, is certainly not superfluous, it can be expected to lead to nothing but a more detailed and conscientious description of natural processes. The thought of employing such investigations to save at the last moment religious doctrines founded on moral ideas is a pathetic blunder; the obscene supernatural has nothing to do with rational religion. If it were discovered that wretched echoes of a past life could be actually heard by putting one's ear long enough to a tomb, and if (*per impossibile*) those echoes could be legitimately attributed to another mind, and to the very mind, indeed, whose former body was interred there, a melancholy chapter would indeed be added to man's earthly fortunes, since it would appear that even after death he retained, under certain conditions, a fatal attachment to his dead body and to the other material instruments of his earthly life. Obviously such a discovery would teach us more about dying than about immortality; the truths disclosed, since they would be disclosed by experiment and observation, would be psycho-physical truths, implying nothing about what a truly disembodied life might be, if one were attainable; for a disembodied life could by no possibility betray itself in spectres, rumblings, and spasms. Actual thunders from Sinai and an actual discovery of two stone tables would have been utterly irrelevant to the moral authority of the ten commandments or to the existence of a truly supreme being. No less irrelevant to a supramundane immortality is the length of time during which human spirits may be condemned to operate on earth after their bodies are quiet. In other words, spectral survivals would at most enlarge our conception of the soul's physical basis, spreading out the area of its manifestations; they could not possibly, seeing the survivals are physical, reveal the disembodied existence of the soul.

Such a disembodied existence, removed by its nature from the sphere of empirical evidence, might nevertheless be actual, and grounds of a moral or metaphysical type might be sought for postulating its reality. Life and the will to live are at bottom identical. Experience itself is transitive and can hardly arise apart from a forward effort and prophetic apprehension by which adjustments are made to a future unmistakably foreseen. This premonition, by which action seeks to justify and explain itself to reflection, may be analysed into a group of memories and sensations of movement, generating ideal expectations which might easily be disappointed; but scepticism about the future can hardly be maintained in the heat of action. A postulate acted on is an act of genuine and dogmatic faith. I not only postulate a morrow when I prepare for it, but ingenuously and heartily believe that the morrow will come. This faith does not amount to certitude; I may confess, if challenged, that before tomorrow I and the world and time itself might conceivably come to an end together; but that idle possibility, so long as it does not slacken action, will not disturb belief. Every moment of life accordingly trusts in life's continuance; and this prophetic interpretation of action, so long as action lasts, amounts to continual faith in futurity.

A sophist might easily transform this psychological necessity into a dazzling proof of immortality. To believe anything he might say, is to be active; but action involves faith in a future and in the fruits of action; and as no living moment can be without this confidence, belief in extinction would be self-contradictory and at no moment a possible belief. The question, however, is not whether every given moment has or has not a specious future before it to which it looks forward, but whether the realization of such foresight, a realization which during waking life is roughly usual, is incapable of failing. Now expectation, never without its requisite antecedents and natural necessity, often lacks fulfilment, and never finds its fulfilment entire; so that the necessity of a postulate gives no warrant for its verification. Expectation and action are constantly suspended together; and what happens whenever thought loses itself or stumbles, what happens whenever in its shifts it forgets its former objects, might well happen at crucial times to that train of intentions which we call a particular life or the life of humanity. The prophecy involved in action is not insignificant, but it is notoriously fallible and depends for its fulfilment on external conditions. The question accordingly really is whether a man expecting to live for ever or one expecting to die in his time has the more representative and trustworthy notion of the future. The question, so stated, cannot be solved by an appeal to evidence, which is necessarily all on one side, but only by criticizing the value of evidence as against instinct and hope, and by ascertaining the relative status which assumption and observation have in experience.

The transcendental compulsion under which action labours of envisaging a future, and the animal instinct that clings to life and flees from death as the most dreadful of evils, are the real grounds why immortality seems initially natural and good. Confidence in living for ever is anterior to the discovery that all men are mortal and to the discovery that the thinker is himself a man. These discoveries flatly contradict that confidence, in the form in which it originally presents itself, and all doctrines of immortality which adult philosophy can entertain are more or less subterfuges and afterthoughts by which the observed fact of mortality and the native inconceivability of death are more or less clumsily reconciled.

The most lordly and genuine fashion of asserting immortality would be to proclaim one's self an exception to the animal race and to point out that the analogy between one's singular self and others is altogether lame and purely conventional. Any proud barbarian, with a tincture of transcendental philosophy, might adopt this tone. 'Creatures that perish', he might say, 'are and can be nothing but puppets and painted shadows in my mind. My conscious will forbids its own extinction; it scorns to level itself with its own objects and instruments. The world, which I have never known to exist without me, exists by my co-operation and consent; it can never extinguish what lends it being. The death prophetically accepted by weaklings, with such small insight and courage, I mock and altogether defy: it can never touch me.'

Such solipsistic boasts may not have been heard in historic times from the lips of men speaking in their own persons. Language has an irresistible tendency to make thought communistic and ideally transferable to others. It forbids a man to say of himself what it would be ridiculous to hear from another. Now solipsism in another man is a comic thing: and a mind, prompted perhaps by hell and heaven to speak solipsistically, is stopped by the laughable echo of its own words, when it remembers its bold sayings. Language, being social, resists a virgin egotism and forbids it to express itself publicly, no matter how well grounded it may be in transcendental logic and in animal instinct. Social convention is necessarily materialistic, since the beginning of all moral reasonableness consists in taming the transcendental conceit native to a living mind, in attaching it to its body, and bringing the will that thought itself absolute down to the rank of animals and men. Otherwise no man would acknowledge another's rights or even conceive his existence.

Primeval solipsism—the philosophy of untamed animal will—has accordingly taken to the usual by-paths and expressed itself openly only in myth or by a speculative abstraction in which the transcendental spirit, for which all the solipsistic privileges were still claimed, was distinguished from the human individual. The gods, it was said, were immortal; and although on earth spirit must submit to the yoke and service of matter, on whose occasions it must wait, yet there existed in the ether other creatures more normally and gloriously compounded, since their forms served and expressed their minds, which ruled also over the elements and feared no assault from time. With the advent of this mythology experience and presumption divided their realms; experience was allowed to shape men's notions of vulgar reality, but presumption, which could not be silenced, was allowed to suggest a second sphere, thinly and momentarily veiled to mortal sense, in which the will's premonitions were abundantly realized.

This expedient had the advantage of endowing the world with creatures that really satisfied human aspirations, such as at any moment they might be. The gods possessed longevity, beauty, magic celerity of movement, leisure, splendour of life, indefinite strength, and practical omniscience. When the gods were also expressions for natural forces, this function somewhat prejudiced their ideality, and they failed to correspond perfectly to what their worshippers would have most esteemed; but religious reformers tended to expunge naturalism from theology and to represent the gods as entirely admirable. The Greek gods, to be sure, always continued to have genealogies, and the fact of having been born is a bad augury for immortality; but other religions, and finally the Greek philosophers themselves, conceived unbegotten gods, in whom the human rebellion against mutability was expressed absolutely.

Thus a place was found in nature for the constant and perpetual element which crude experience seems to contain or at least to suggest. Unfortunately the immortal and the human were in this mythology wholly divorced, so that while immortality was vindicated for something in the universe it was emphatically denied to man and to his works. Contemplation, to be satisfied with this situation, had to be heroically unselfish and resigned; the gods' greatness and glory had to furnish sufficient solace for all mortal defeats. At the same time all criticism had to be deprecated, for reflection would at once have pointed out that the divine life in question was either a personification of natural processes and thus really in flux and full of oblivion and imperfection, or else a hypostasis of certain mental functions and ideals, which could not really be conceived apart from the natural human life which they informed and from which they had been violently abstracted.

Another expedient was accordingly found, especially by mystics and philosophers, for uniting the mortal and immortal in existence while still distinguishing them in essence. *Cur Deus Homo* might be said to be the theme of all such speculations. Plato had already found the eternal in the form which the temporal puts on, or, if the phrase be preferred, had seen in the temporal and existential nothing but an individuated case of the ideal. The soul was immortal, unbegotten, impassible; the bodies it successively inhabited and the experience it gathered served merely to bring out its nature with greater or less completeness. To somewhat the same effect the German transcendentalists identified and distinguished the private and the universal spirit. What lived in each man and in each moment was the Absolute—for nothing else could really exist—and the expression which the Absolute there took on was but a transitional phase of its total self-expression, which, could it be grasped in its totality, would no longer seem subject to contradiction and flux. An immortal agent therefore went through an infinite series of acts, each transitory and relative to the others, but all possessed of inalienable reality and eternal significance. In such formulations the divorce was avoided between the intellectual and the sensuous factor in experience—a divorce which the myth about immortal gods and mortal men had introduced. On the other hand existential immortality was abandoned; only an ideal permanence, only significance, was allowed to any finite being, and the better or future world of which ancient poets had dreamt, Olympus, and every other heaven, was altogether abolished. There was an eternal universe where everything was transitory and a single immortal spirit at no two moments the same. The world of idealism realized no particular ideal, and least of all the ideal of a natural and personal immunity from death.

First, then, a man may refuse to admit that he must die at all; then, abashed at the arrogance of that assertion, he may consider the immortal life of other creatures, like the earth and stars, which seem subject to no extinction, and he may ascribe to these a perpetual consciousness and personality. Finally, confessing the fabulous character of those deities, he may distinguish an immortal agent or principle within himself, identify it with the inner principle of all other beings, and contrast it with its varying and conditioned expressions. But scarcely is this abstraction attained when he must perceive its worthlessness, since the natural life, the concrete aims, and the personal career which immortality was intended to save from dissolution are wholly alien to a nominal entity which endures through all change, however fundamental, and cohabits with every nature, however hostile and odious to humanity. If immortality is to be genuine, what is immortal must be something definite, and if this immortality is to concern life and not mere significance or ideal definition, that which endures must be an individual creature with a fixed nucleus of habits and demands, so that its persistence may contain progress and achievement.

Herewith we may dismiss the more direct attempts to conceive and assert a future life. Their failure drives us to a consideration of indirect attempts to establish an unobservable but real immortality through revelation and dogma. Such an immortality would follow on transmigration or resurrection, and would be assigned to a supernatural sphere, a second empirical world present to the soul after death, where her fortunes would not be really conceivable without a reconstituted body and a new material environment.

Many a man dies too soon and some are born in the wrong age or station. Could these persons drink at the fountain of youth at least once more they might do themselves fuller justice and cut a better figure at last in the universe. Most people think they have stuff in them for greater things than time suffers them to perform. To imagine a second career is a pleasing antidote for ill fortune; the poor soul wants another chance. But how should a future life be constituted if it is to satisfy this demand, and how long need it last? It would evidently have to go on in an environment closely analogous to earth; I could not, for instance, write in another world the epics which the necessity of earning my living may have stifled here, did that other world contain no time, no heroic struggles, or no metrical language. Nor is it clear that my epics, to be perfect, would need to be quite endless. If what is foiled in me is really poetic genius and not simply a tendency toward perpetual motion, it would not help me if in heaven, in lieu of my dreamt-of epics, I were allowed to beget several robust children. In a word, if hereafter I am to be the same man improved I must find myself in the same world corrected. Were I transformed into a cherub or transported into a timeless ecstasy, it is hard to see in what sense I should continue to exist. Those results might be interesting in themselves and might enrich the universe; they would not prolong my life nor retrieve my disasters.

For this reason a future life is after all best represented by those frankly material ideals which most Christians—being Platonists—are wont to despise. It would be genuine happiness for a Jew to rise again in the flesh and live for ever in Ezekiel's New Jerusalem, with its ceremonial glories and civic order. It would be truly agreeable for any man to sit in well-watered gardens with Mohammed, clad in green silks, drinking delicious sherbets, and transfixed by the gazelle-like glance of some young girl, all innocence and fire. Amid such scenes a man might remain himself and might fulfil hopes that he had actually cherished on earth. He might also find his friends again, which in somewhat generous minds is perhaps the thought that chiefly sustains interest in a posthumous existence. But to recognize his friends a man must find them in their bodies, with their familiar habits, voices, and interests; for it is surely an insult to affection to say that he could find them in an eternal formula expressing their idiosyncrasy. When, however, it is clearly seen that another life, to supplement this one, must closely resemble it, does not the magic of immortality altogether vanish? Is such a reduplication of earthly society at all credible? And the prospect of awakening again among houses and trees, among children and dotards, among wars and rumours of wars, still fettered to one personality and one accidental past, still uncertain of the future, is not this prospect wearisome and deeply repulsive? Having passed through these things once and bequeathed them to posterity, is it not time for each soul to rest? The universe doubtless contains all sorts of experiences, better and worse than the human; but it is idle to attribute to a particular man a life divorced from his circumstances and from his body.

Dogmas about such a posthumous experience find some shadowy support in various illusions and superstitions that surround death, but they are developed into articulate prophecies chiefly by certain moral demands. One of these requires rewards and punishments more emphatic and sure than those which conduct meets with in this world. Another requires merely a more favourable and complete opportunity for the soul's development. Considerations like these are pertinent to moral philosophy. It touches the notion of duty whether an exact hedonistic retribution is to be demanded for what is termed merit and guilt: so that without such supernatural remuneration virtue, perhaps, would be discredited and deprived of a motive. It likewise touches the ideality and nobleness of life whether human aims can be realized satisfactorily only in the agent's singular person, so that the fruits of effort would be forthwith missed if the labourer himself should disappear.

To establish justice in the world and furnish an adequate incentive to virtue was once thought the chief business of a future life. The Hebraic religions somewhat overreached themselves on these points: for the grotesque alternative between hell and heaven in the end only aggravated the injustice it was meant to remedy. Life is unjust in that it subordinates individuals to a general mechanical law, and the deeper and longer hold fate has on the soul, the greater that injustice. A perpetual life would be a perpetual subjection to arbitrary power, while a last judgment would be but a last fatality. That hell may have frightened a few villains into omitting a crime is perhaps credible; but the embarrassed silence which the churches, in a more sensitive age, prefer to maintain on that wholesome doctrine—once, as they taught, the only rational basis for virtue—shows how their teaching has to follow the independent progress of morals. Nevertheless, persons are not wanting, apparently free from ecclesiastical constraint, who still maintain that the value of life depends on its indefinite prolongation. By an artifice of reflection they substitute vanity for reason, and selfish for ingenuous instincts in man. Being apparently interested in nothing but their own careers, they forget that a man may remember how little he counts in the world and suffer that rational knowledge to inspire his purposes. Intense morality has always envisaged earthly goods and evils, and even when a future life has been accepted vaguely, it has never given direction to human will or aims, which at best it could only proclaim more emphatically. It may indeed be said that no man of any depth of soul has made his prolonged existence the touchstone of his enthusiasms. Such an instinct is carnal, and if immortality is to add a higher inspiration to life it must not be an immortality of selfishness. What a despicable creature must a man be, and how sunk below the level of the most barbaric virtue, if he cannot bear to live for his children, for his art, or for country!

To turn these moral questions, however, into arguments for a physical speculation, like that about human longevity, resurrection, or metempsychosis, a hybrid principle is required: thus, even if we have answered those moral questions in the conventional way and satisfied ourselves that personal immortality is a postulate of ethics, we cannot infer that immortality therefore exists unless we import into the argument a tremendous optimistic postulate, to the effect that what is requisite for moral rationality must in every instance be realized in experience.

Such an optimistic postulate, however, as the reader must have repeatedly observed, is made not only despite all experience but in ignorance of the conditions under which alone ideals are framed and retain their significance. Every ideal expresses individual and specific tendencies, proper at some moment to some natural creature; every ideal therefore has for its basis a part only of the dynamic world, so that its fulfilment is problematical and altogether adventitious to its existence and authority. To decide whether an ideal can be or will be fulfilled we must examine the physical relation between such organic forces as the ideal expresses and the environment in which those forces operate; we may then perceive how far a realization of the given aims is possible, how far it must fail, and how far the aims in question, by a shift in their natural basis, will lapse and yield to others, possibly more capable of execution and more stable in the world. The question of success is a question of physics. To say that an ideal will be inevitably fulfilled simply because it is an ideal is to say something gratuitous and foolish. Pretence cannot in the end avail against experience.

Nevertheless, it is important to define ideals even before their realization is known to be possible, because they constitute one of the two factors whose interaction and adjustment is moral life, factors which are complementary and diverse in function and may be independently ascertained. The value of existences is wholly borrowed from their ideality, without direct consideration of their fate, while the existence of ideals is wholly determined by natural forces, without direct relation to their fulfilment. Existence and ideal value can therefore be initially felt and observed apart, although of course a complete description would lay bare physical necessity in the ideals entertained and inevitable ideal harmonies among the facts discovered. Human life, lying as it does in the midst of a larger process, will surely not be without some congruity with the universe. Every creature lends potential values to a world in which it can satisfy some at least of its demands and learn, perhaps, to modify the others. Happiness is always a natural and an essentially possible thing, and a total despair, since it ignores those goods which are attainable, can express only a partial experience... The better a man evokes and realizes the ideal the more he leads the life that all others, in proportion to their worth, will seek to live after him, and the more he helps them to live in that nobler fashion. His presence in the society of immortals thus becomes, so to speak, more pervasive. He not only vanquishes time by his own rationality, living now in the eternal, but he continually lives again in all rational beings.

Since the ideal has this perpetual pertinence to mortal struggles, he who lives in the ideal and leaves it expressed in society or in art enjoys a double immortality. The eternal has absorbed him while he lived, and when he is dead his influence brings others to the same absorption, making them, through that ideal identity with the best in him, reincarnations and perennial seats of all in him which he could rationally hope to rescue from destruction. He can say, without any subterfuge or desire to delude himself, that he shall not wholly die; for he will have a better notion than the vulgar of what constitutes his being. By becoming the spectator and confessor of his own death and of universal mutation, he will have identified himself with what is spiritual in all spirits and masterful in all apprehension; and so conceiving himself, he may truly feel and know that he is eternal.

INDEX

References to a complete essay or extract are in bold type.
Italic type indicates other major references.

235

Iudex

Brunelleschi, Filippo, 27
Buddhism, 56, 181, 218
Buffalo (N.Y.), 67–8
business, world of, 10, 34, 49, 61, 63, 68, 71, 74, 77
Byzantine art, 120
Byzantium, 217

California, 85, 96, 105–6
Calvin, John, 19, 32, 87, 90
Calvinism, 32, 34, 46, 87–90, 92, 96, 104, 173
Cambridge (Mass.), 51
Carlyle, Thomas, 87
categorical imperative, 178, 186
Catholic Church, 50, 97, 173; and philosophy, 56
Catholicism, 46, 96, 183; in America, 49, 50
Channing, William Ellery, 36
Chateaubriand, François, Vicomte de, 28
Chinese art, 24
chivalry, 80, 171
Christendom, 3, 45
Christian Church, 16–17, 37, 45, 173, 211, 217 n.
Christian church architecture, 26–7
Christian epic, the, **212–19**
Christian philosophy, 17, 164 n., 215–17; and theology, 213, 218
Christianity, 5, 9, 17, 18, 26, 32, 34, 37, 46; and Calvinism, 87, 90; and Protestantism, 173–5; spirit of, 79; see also Christian epic
Christians, 26, 35, 37, 38, 39, 108, 114, 116, 215, 216, 217 n., 229; and martyrdom, 80
churches, 20, 26; American Protestant, 29, 35, 90; Christian, 230; national, 39, 181
civilization, 3, 113, 185, 194, 217; English, 72, 74
classic liberty, **15–18**
classic principles, 19; contrasted with Oriental, 214–15, and with romantic, 96, 98–9; see also classic liberty
classicism, romantic, 183
community, 211; American, 29, 47, 48, 50, 88, 97; English, 72
consciousness, 7, 109, 125, 131, 166, 192–5, 196, 198, 199, 219, 220,

221; and Bergson, 137–45 passim, 150, 154, 155, 158–9, 160; contrasted with instinct, 139, 189
conservative outlook, 48, 63, 66; and Greeks, 16; and traditionalism, 33, 60, 108
cosmology, 103
Constantinople, 26
Croce, Benedetto, 111
Cronos, 218
culture, 10, 21–3; American, 97; British, 41; New England, 28

Dante, Alighieri, 215
Darwin, Charles, 8, 56, 65, 100
  Origin of Species, 56
death, 11, 129, 177; and Bergson, 10, 125, 126, 154–6, 159; and William James, 102; survival after, **219–33**
Demeter, 214
democracy, 3, 19, 68, 75–6, 80; and American, 48–9, 60, 70–2; and early Christianity, 214; and England, 70; and Whitman, 97; underlying morality of, 68, 120
Dickens, Charles, 5
Dioscuri, the, 219
divine Intelligence, 216
doctrine, 14; and Harvard philosophers 48, 57; and transcendentalism, 92, 95; religious, 153, 215, 219, 222, 224, 230
dogmas, 141, 150, 153, 162, 228, 229; and dogmatism, 21, 112, 130, 146, 164 n., 223; and Protestantism, 175; and transcendentalism, 90, 93
Don Quixote (Cervantes), 68
Dover, straits of, 68, 69
dualism, 104, 114, 145, 174
Dürer, Albrecht, 174

Ecclesiastes, Book of, 102
education, 5, 19, 189; classic, 16; see also American education
Edwards, Jonathan, 32, 87, 89
egoism, 117, 168–70
egotism, 38, 59, 70, 79, 225; and transcendentalism, 91, 95–6; in Hegel, **179–86**; in western philosophy, 37, 106, 175; see idealism, philosophical, and romanticism

236

Index

Egypt, 26, 143, 144, 191
eighteenth century, 5
Emerson, Ralph Waldo, 32, 36, 46, 88, 89–90, 93–6, 98, 172
empirical outlook, 13; and the English, 70, 73; and the supernatural, 219, 222, 228
empirical philosophy, 146; and Bergson, 127, 128, 134; and William James, 31, 57, 102–3, 105; and Kant, 92; British, 40, 41–2
England, 40, 57, 58; and Englishmen, 24, 25, 41, 166; see also English liberty
England, Church of, 69, 73
English civilization, 72, 74
English liberty, **68–81**
English philosophy, 40–2, 73, 124
Epicureans, 116; and Epicureanism, 40
equality, 18, 205
eternity, 126, 199
ethics, 49, 165, 167, 191, 231; and Bergson, 153; and Hegel, 181; hypostatic, **161–71**; naturalistic, 109, 112, 120, 161–2, 167
Europe, 40, 60, 68, 93, 149; and Europeans, 66, 68–9; and European students, 51; and William James, 98; genteel tradition in, 106
evangelical churches in America, 35, 90
evil, 34, 66, 88, 93, 106, 185, 191, 200, 220, 231; and Plotinus, **108–21**; and Russell, 163, 166; false 'problem' of, 118–21; true explanation of, 113
evolution, 9, 10, 35, 46, 120, 132, 202; and Bergson, 123–4, 128, 129, 136, 141, 147, 152; and William James, 102–3; and Spencer, 146; and transcendental theory, 91
Ezekiel, 229

fanaticism, 80, 170, 184, 210
Fénelon, François de Salignac de la Mothe, 5
Fichte, Johann Gottlieb, 32, 39, 154, 173
final causes, 38
France, 5, 75
Francis of Assisi, St, 114, 123
Franklin, Benjamin, 88
freedom, 17, 29, 33, 51, 59, 62, 79–80, 125, 172, 174, 180, 193; and America, 76–7; and Harvard

school of philosophy, 55, 56, 58; in ancient Greece, 15; Bergsonian, 127, 137, 152, 153, 157, 158; modern, 16, 18, 19; see liberty
French language and literature, 122
French Revolution, 19, 81
Fuller, Benjamin Apthorp Gould, 108–21 *passim*, 168 n.
The Problem of Evil in Plotinus, 108 n.
German philosophy, 42, 57, 172–3; idealistic, 38, 123, 174–6; transcendental, 90–2, 227; see also Hegel
German religion, 174
Germany, 45, 46, 55, 79, 90, 175, 176; and Germans, 21, 38, 72, 91, 166, 174, 181
Gibbon, Edward, 40
God, 18, 109, 114, 115, 198, 209; and Americans, 34, 64, 89; and Jews, 37, 211; and Bergson, 145, 147, 151, 153; and Hegel, 123, 180, 184, 185, 186; and William James, 102–3; and Plotinus, 114, 118; and Protestant philosophy, 38, 172; Greek notion of, contrasted with Hebraic, 118–19, 213, 216
gods, 139, 219, 225–6; Greek, 11, 15, 118, 178, 226, 227; William James' attitude to, 31, 102
Goethe, Wolfgang, 3, 12, 127, 183
Faust, 8, 47
good, 7, 35, 47, 66, 88, 106, 124, 191, 200, 207, 212, 220, 224, 231, 232; and Fuller, 108–11; and Hegel, 123, 185; and Plotinus, 112–17, 119–21; and Russell, **161–71**; and Socrates, 37; relativity of, 37, 65, 110–11, 113, 118, 120, 163–71, 212
Gospel, 212–15
government, 15, 20, 45, 185–6, 206; divine, 216; parliamentary, 6, 73, 74, 76
Greece, 9, 123, 149
Greek philosophers, 15–16, 17, 37, 116, 134, 226; and philosophy, 119
Greek tragedy, 211, 215
Greeks, 15–16, 24, 27, 37, 178, 183; Christian, 26, 213–16; in Homeric times, 10–11

237

Index

Index

Index

240

Index

Index

Index